A Theology of Alterity

A Theology of

Theology

of

Levinas, von Balthasar,
and Trinitarian Praxis

Alterity

Glenn Morrison

**DUQUESNE
UNIVERSITY
PRESS**
Pittsburgh, Pennsylvania

Published in the United States of America by
DUQUESNE UNIVERSITY PRESS
600 Forbes Avenue
Pittsburgh, Pennsylvania 15282

Library of Congress Cataloging-in-Publication Data

Morrison, Glenn.
    A theology of alterity : Levinas, Von Balthasar, and Trinitarian praxis /
Glenn Morrison.
        p. cm
    Includes bibliographical references and index.
    Summary: "Strives to radically utilize Emmanuel Levinas's philosophical
framework, bringing it into conversation with the theology of Hans Urs von
Balthasar, to construct a post-ontotheological account of theology that unites
theory and praxis. By allowing Levinas's Judaism to challenge von Balthasar's
Catholicism, Glenn Morrison develops a perspective that is both theologically
rich and philosophically provocative"—Provided by publisher.
    ISBN 978-0-8207-0460-9 (pbk. : alk. paper)
1. Philosophical theology. 2. Other (Philosophy)—Religious aspects—
Christianity. 3. Lévinas, Emmanuel. 4. Balthasar, Hans Urs von, 1905–1988.
5. Trinity. I. Title.

 BT40.M696 2013
 230—dc23
                                                                2012050957

∞ Printed on acid-free paper.

For Kyo Te

The Lord is near to the broken-hearted,
and saves the crushed in spirit.

—Psalm 34:18

Because the Holy Ghost over the bent
    World broods with warm breast and with ah! bright wings.
        —Gerard Manley Hopkins, "God's Grandeur"

CONTENTS

ACKNOWLEDGMENTS

I am indebted to the encouragement, inspiration, and goodness of others. I am forever grateful to Fr. Gordon Jackson SSC who first instilled in me a love for philosophy and theology, spoke passionately of the writings of Saint Thomas Aquinas, and nimbly combined study with friendship. Fr. Gordon's passion and affectivity taught me to value the heart, mind, and spirit in the approach to the Bible and theology. I am also deeply thankful to Rev. Dr. John Begley SJ, who introduced me to the thought of Emmanuel Levinas and fostered my development in the areas of philosophy and theology. I remain indebted to his everpresent willingness to support and read my work. I am also forever grateful to Professor Emeritus Tony Kelly CSsR, whose wisdom and vision have always been a great source of light by which to explore the realm of the theological imagination. I acknowledge his generosity and the far-reaching contribution he has made to theology in Australia. In addition, I would like to express my thanks to Dr. Robyn Horner, whose expertise in phenomenology was a beacon of hope amid the complexities Husserl, Heidegger, Rosenzweig, and Levinas. Furthermore, I owe special thanks to Rev. Dr. Aloysius Rego OCD, who showed invaluable support of this book.

The collegiality and friendship of Professor Emeritus Roger Burggraeve led me to explore Levinas's writings in areas of pastoral and systematic theology. In many ways, this work represents the benefit of his support and inspiration. Particularly, the ideas of ethical melancholy and bodiliness were born out of conversations we had together on Levinas and Christian theology.

In a heartfelt way, I acknowledge the enduring and life-giving encouragement of my wife, Kyo Te, to whom this book is dedicated, and her family, who have taught me much about the sense and meaning of otherness. To my parents, John and Kathy, I am forever grateful, as they have imparted goodness and opportunities for my love for both philosophy and theology to emerge. Also to my colleagues and students at the University of Notre Dame Australia, I express my gratitude for their engaging conversations and generous spirits, which create a warm and friendly environment to share, teach, research, and study. Finally, I extend my deep appreciation and gratitude to Susan Wadsworth-Booth, Brock Bahler, and Kathleen Meyer at Duquesne University Press, who have guided me over the years with insightful direction, hope, and support.

Portions of the book have been taken or adapted from previously published journal articles, book chapters, or conference presentations, as listed below. These are reprinted with permission:

"The (Im)possibilities of Levinas for Christian Theology: The Search for a Language of Alterity." In *Festschrift Roger Burggraeve: Responsibility, God and Society, Theological Ethics in Dialogue,* edited by J. De Tavernier, J. A. Selling, J. Verstraeten, and P. Schotsmans, 103–22. Leuven: Peeters, 2008 (chapter 3).

"Building Jewish-Christian Friendship." Paper presented at the Council of Christian and Jews Western Australia. Claremont, Perth. September 20, 2011 (chapter 6).

"Children of a Lesser God: Truth as Bodiliness and Forgiveness." *Australian eJournal of Theology* (August 2011): 175–88 (chapter 5).

"Living at the Margins of Life: Encountering the Other and *Doing* Theology." *Australian eJournal of Theology* (February 2006): 1–7 (chapter 6).

"A Phenomenology of St. Paul's Encounter with the Risen Christ." Religious Studies and Theological Studies in a Globalised World: A Combined University Series. August 15, 2011. The University of Notre Dame Australia (chapter 3).

"Phenomenology, Theology, and Psychosis: Towards Compassion." *Heythrop Journal* (July 2007): 561–76 (excerpts appear in chapters 2 and 4).

"Renewing Christian Theology with Levinas: Towards a Trinitarian *Praxis.*" *The Awakening of Meaning: A Provocative Dialogue with Levinas,* edited by Roger Burggraeve, 137–60. Leuven: Peeters, 2008 (chapter 6).

"A Review of Michael Purcell's Theological Development of Levinas' Philosophy." *Heythrop Journal* 44 (April 2003): 147–66 (chapter 6).

"Understanding Levinas's Origins: Husserl, Heidegger and Rosenzweig." *Heythrop Journal* 46 (January 2005): 41–59 (excerpts appear in chapter 1).

ABBREVIATIONS

WORKS BY HANS URS VON BALTHASAR

GL	*The Glory of the Lord: A Theological Aesthetics,* vols. 1–7
LA	*Love Alone*
MP	*Mysterium Paschale*
TD	*Theo-Drama: Theological Dramatic Theory,* vols. 1–4
TL	*Theo-Logic: Theological Logical Theory,* vols. 1–3
VBR	*The von Balthasar Reader*

WORKS BY LEVINAS

AT	*Alterity and Transcendence*
BPW	*Basic Philosophical Writings*
BV	*Beyond the Verse: Talmudic Readings and Lectures*
CPP	*Collected Philosophical Papers*
DF	*Difficult Freedom: Essays on Judaism*
EE	*Existence and Existents*
EI	*Ethics and Infinity: Conversations with Philippe Nemo*
EN	*Entre Nous: Thinking of the Other*
GCM	*Of God Who Comes to Mind*
GDT	*God, Death, and Time*
IR	*Is It Righteous to Be?: Interviews with Emmanuel Levinas*
ITN	*In the Time of the Nations*
NT	*Nine Talmudic Readings*
OB	*Otherwise than Being or Beyond Essence*
TI	*Totality and Infinity: An Essay on Exteriority*

ONE

Toward a Levinasian Lens for Christian Theology

The theological imagination is an intriguing phenomenon, perhaps because it represents the challenge to bring together meaning about mystery, truth, and being. This intent not only creates some space for theological reflection but also centrally reveals a search and quest for Jesus the Christ. Providing an avenue by which to nurture and sustain meaning, a theological imagination thereby speaks of a journey of faith and a search for understanding. The progress toward such understanding and appreciation of the mystery of God remains an ongoing one. Although we never quite arrive at a final destination, a horizon of meaning signifies the possibility, creativity, and discovery of a Christian theological imagination. This process may begin inchoately, but as the horizons of faith, hope, and love instill the participation of both the heart and intellect into the mysteries and stories of the Christian narrative, the human spirit and imagination will want to explore and encounter the glory of God all the more.

Theology itself has long been influenced by philosophy. Given that each generation is called to revisit the relationship between those disciplines, there will most likely always be new perceptions in the making. A number of temptations arise in the desire and passion to make a contribution to tradition and contemporary analyses, particularly when theology encounters the totality of Being's essence. For instance, where the essence of self-interest, proofs, or facts takes theological form, reductive or totalizing tendencies may come into play to contaminate mystery and truth. It is not surprising, then, that new theological perspectives are not easily borne into the present; they necessarily must also face the maturation of time to test their relevance and substance. In a way, then, theology is a process of discernment and reflection; it is guided by purpose and a sense of mission, not for oneself, but for the good of humanity and the world. This is to say that theology is thinking "otherwise"—the duration of a moment in which the logos of reason unites with the search for God. Such a moment or revelation can last a lifetime. And for Christians, these moments point to the quest for Jesus the Christ: "Are you the one who is to come, or are we to wait for another?" (Matt. 11:3).

The quest for Jesus the Christ signifies the hope to encounter the tripersonal God of Christian faith. The nature of a quest evokes a sense of praxis. And by developing and pursuing—in the context of our study—a "Trinitarian" praxis, something ethical and metaphysical comes to mind: the language of alterity or otherness, wherein ethics unites with prayer. Otherness, specifically, is a way of being otherwise than the everyday desire of the self to be for-itself; it is to have a heart for the other person—namely, the neighbor, the poor one, the widow, the orphan, and the stranger (Exod. 22:22; Deut. 10:18–19). In theological terms, otherness speaks of the desire to encounter Christ in the face of the other person as he or she is in his or her needs, fears, hopes, personhood, and identity. Where the self seeks to attune to a sense of otherness, the possibility for a Trinitarian praxis unfolds as a radical gift of passivity. Passivity, then, is an essential component of otherness.

The state of passivity is a radical one. It not only opens the self up to God's will and work in the innermost part of the human spirit, but it also commands the ordinary senses of the self to see, hear, and touch the world of the other with greater intensity. To journey toward the world of the other in an utmost state of passivity unveils what we may term a Trinitarian praxis, gifted by the momentum of the Father's will, the Son's word, and the Spirit's command to be responsible. The Spirit's command resonating in the inner self provides the condition of possibility (the Father's will) for Christ's word of truth to be heard in the face of the other. Such a moment of grace unfolds as participation in the mission of Christ and represents the states of ethical transcendence, ethical melancholy, ethical vigilance/insomnia, eschatological existence, gifted passivity, and eucharistic living. We may use the term "Trinitarian praxis" to succinctly refer to all of these states together.

The meaning of a Trinitarian praxis depends upon developing a language of alterity for theology. To this end, this study employs the philosophy of Emmanuel Levinas to rethink and enhance the theology of Hans Urs von Balthasar. At the outset, this may not seem a natural match, given especially that Levinas is a Jewish philosopher and talmudic scholar and von Balthasar is a Christian theologian. Yet such difference offers much inspiration for the theological imagination. In many ways, Levinas's philosophy develops a new fundamental language of ethical metaphysics, in which ethics is primarily metaphysics rather than ontotheology.[1] Rather than setting out on a Heideggerian quest toward the ground of Being ("the essence of being in general"), Levinas diverges toward the interhuman. While Heidegger reduces "the God of metaphysics" to the "god of ontotheology" and takes on a search for the ground of Being or the "divine God of the early Christians and mystics," Levinas dismisses that approach as the contamination of ontology and theology. In effect, this suggests that Heidegger is less interested in God than he is in Being, which in the end takes a pagan, mystical turn toward the fourfold. It seems that Heideggerian Being is greater than God; given such a belief, one can speak of "gods" rather than God. We can see then how Levinas's approach takes on an anti-Heideggerian tone; it is radically otherwise than Heidegger's quest and notion of Being.

Christian theology in the twentieth century fell in love, as it were, with Heidegger's philosophy. We can see this in the writings of Rudolf Bultmann, Karl Rahner, Hans Urs von Balthasar, or even Henri Nouwen. Ontotheology takes up the language of ontology (and ontological phenomenology). In other words, so much of Christian theology relies on the categories of Being, objectivity, and presence to find a rational way to articulate the mystery of God. Theology in the twentieth century has achieved so much, particularly partaking of ontology, phenomenology, and existentialism to develop its insights and ideas. However, there are always temptations in doing theology. Levinas's critique of Heidegger and ontotheology demonstrates the danger of believing that there is an answer to the meaning of Being. Ontotheology parallels this with the temptation to reduce God to a set of propositions, personal experiences, or facts of knowledge.

The ontotheological problem is inherent in the infinitive "to be" when we state "God *is*." My intent is not to dismiss the joy of experiencing and knowing Christ, but to emphasize the need for a language of alterity to help to interpret our experiences, reflections, and knowledge. For example, if we want to say that God is love, we face the ontotheological danger of reducing God to our personal experience or knowledge of love.

We also face here the challenge of the meaning of Being. How can we journey to understand divine love through our being-in-the-world? Can we do this through reflecting on *Dasein,* time, anxiety, death, reality, existence, or care-for-one's possibilities in life? We can go far to reflect on the ontological categories of Being and discover much about the mystery of God, humanity, and the world. But the danger for Levinas is that ontology can contaminate theology with violence. In other words, when *theoria* dominates *praxis,* the face of the Other, or the interhuman relation, is given a secondary priority. For Levinas, ethics is first philosophy and even first theology. His language of alterity is an ethical metaphysics.

Both Levinas and Heidegger are in pursuit of developing phenomenology. Heidegger, focusing on the "thought of Being," takes a more ontological approach and hence develops an ontological phenomenology.[2] In contrast, Levinas seems step back toward prioritizing the ontic, that is, "beings" rather than Being. Yet, he does this ethically, hence producing an ethical metaphysics or a postphenomenology. And it is this development of phenomenology that gives a new horizon to encounter von Balthasar's theology. In a like manner, von Balthasar develops theology with a renewed phenomenology of the beautiful, the good, and the true. Levinas's focus on "the good" and von Balthasar's priority on "the beautiful" offer a dialectical opportunity not only toward dialogue but also "beyond dialogue" in the sense of developing new perspectives with and beyond both Levinas and von Balthasar.

At first sight, it may seem more natural to employ Levinas's philosophy to develop fundamental theology, particularly, for example, in the work of Karl Rahner. However, von Balthasar's systematic theological dramatizations of the paschal mystery and the Trinity offer a whole new set of possibilities for Levinasian engagement. Rather than just focusing on fundamental theological themes such as grace, the human person, God, sin, and revelation, von Balthasar's theology offers a fertile plain, as it were, to engage in the relational aspects or perichoresis of the Trinitarian drama of the paschal mystery.

Von Balthasar's theology offers not only a rational way to speak about God, but also a dramatic, vigilant one whereby the reader is called to enter into the drama of faith and become a person-in-Christ. In a similar manner, Levinas's philosophy engages the reader dramatically toward a life of responsibility for-the-other. Von Balthasar's theology finds a way to bring eros and agape together. This suggests that it is centered also by an implicit theological attitude of melancholy. Levinas speaks of agape without eros, yet his notions often have an underlying presence of eros. The way the self journeys to the world of the other expresses a profound bodiliness, vigilance, and purified eros. In essence, this produces not just a sense of melancholy, but what I call an "ethical melancholy" (and "ethical vigilance") in Levinas's thought. The element of melancholy in Levinas and von Balthasar offers alternative ways to engage their writings. For example, Levinas's Jewish "passion" of the Shoah together with von Balthasar's Christian passion of the paschal mystery evidence possibilities for fruitful engagement.

In a way, both Levinas's philosophy and von Balthasar's theology provide a context for ideas and emotions to each have a particular role. Therefore the challenge for a theology of alterity is to develop a sense of a Trinitarian praxis or ethical transcendence that is animated by such emotions or (bodiliness) of ethical melancholy and ethical vigilance (or insomnia). In a way then, we are setting out to develop metaphysics and theology. Juxtaposing Levinas with von Balthasar provides a way of showing that ethical metaphysical emotions such as melancholy and vigilance are a path of revelation to return to Being and doing theology; they animate a Trinitarian *praxis* of ethical transcendence. These emotions also provide an ethical development or readjustment through Levinas of Heidegger's insight into the phenomenology of emotions (*befindlichkeit*). As philosophers and theologians, we must also search for practical applications.

It is not uncommon to criticize both philosophy and theology for lacking the practical element; neither Levinas nor von Balthasar are beyond such criticism. However, when their development of ideas and thought are brought together, something emerges beyond both their writings—a hope to find a way to unite language and behavior or to nurture theory into praxis. Von Balthasar's theology is not afraid to enter into nonthematizable realms (or mysteries of the faith) or take risks to offer thematizations. Levinas, who criticizes the way in which theology falls into ontotheology, also takes risks to thematize or return to Being through the language of ethical metaphysics, namely, alterity. In a sense, then, both Levinas and von Balthasar set out to find a way to explain the unknowable through the transfiguration of God-in-the-finite and the transcendence of responsibility for the Other.

A theology of alterity includes phrases such as "liturgy of responsibility," "difficult freedom," and "difficult adoration." It speaks of the courage to encounter the face of the other, to put our conscience into question, and to take personal responsibility for those on the margins of society. Levinas's thought almost commands or even ordains the reader to develop a heart for the "widow, the orphan, and the stranger" (Deut. 10:18), in other words, those living on the margins. Levinas's complex writings define a prophetic process of finding an ethical, prayerful, and kenotic way to speak of God, the world, and humanity.

Developing von Balthasar's systematic theology with Levinas's philosophy provides a way by which to present intimately to Christians that not only the Jewish people are of value, but also Judaism itself.

Levinas himself was very much open to the possibility that his thought might find meaning in Christian theology. Christian theology that is more is mindful of and engaged with Judaism and Jewish thinking can have a deeper appreciation of its identity, mission, and understanding of the mystery of God.

Levinas and his student, Michaël de Saint Cheron, expressed this hope in a conversation of May 9, 1983. Saint Cheron posed a question on the value of Judaism for Christianity; in response, Levinas makes a key reference to Hans Urs von Balthasar:

> *Q.*: The Church, Christianity in general, has been teaching for two thousand years, until recently, that since Christ Judaism, the Synagogue, has contributed nothing new. Is this not contradicted by the evidence given by the whole of twentieth century history, with its nameless tragedy and its intellectual, philosophical, spiritual, and indeed political renewal?
>
> *E.L.*: But we can already say that the entire reading of the Torah is an incessant renewal, through the study and commentaries that arise from it. It's a *hidoush,* as we say in Hebrew. Your question is the old Judeo-Christian discussion whereby the Jews would have ceased before Christ. But what I remember, in an article on my work you gave me, and I thank you for doing so, are the words of the great German theologian Hans Urs von Balthasar, who wrote that the only viable interlocutor for Christians was "post-Christian Judaism," which he qualified as the "only partner worthy of being taken really seriously." The article quotes a Spanish theologian who wrote a book [Vázquez Moro, *El Discurso sobre Dios en la obra de Emmanuel Levinas*] on my last few works, and which employs the word "syntony." The use of this word insists on the common tonality between Jews and Christians. From our point of view, it's also the idea that Jews don't have anything less than what Christians have, but that we see the revelation in a different way."[3]

Levinas's remarks ground Hans Urs von Balthasar as a primary interlocutor. There is almost a specific invitation for Christian theologians to develop a sense of "syntony," or adjustment and openness to learn from and engage with Jewish thought. Perhaps here we are also talking about the prevenience of grace and the possibility to witness to it; Levinas refers to a "crooked line," which, ultimately, God's word must "write straight."[4] In this isolated reference to von Balthasar, Levinas unveils a Christian and Jewish horizon for doing theology. The challenge then is to nurture our "common tonality" beyond totalizing temptations.

The question of whether it is possible to renew theology with the inspiration of Emmanuel Levinas's philosophy faces both a possibility and impossibility. The possibility arises when we can learn the ability to take Levinas's prophetic thinking literally to heart[5] and renew theology with a language of alterity. The impossibility results in the fact that we need an eternity, the very consummation of the Reign of God, to discover a space and time of grace wherein language and ethical transcendence are one. Or perhaps, with the fission of God's word in us, the Reign of God may rupture through time into the heart and conscience. Granted such an (im)possibility, Levinas's ethical metaphysics resounds upon the minds of a growing number of Christian theologians today. His development of metaphysics beyond the thought of Husserl, Heidegger, and Rosenzweig has proved to be of special interest, especially in the domain of ethics.

From a Levinasian perspective, the deepest problem to be faced by theology is one of giving priority to the ethical over the ontological. To speak of God by way of ethical transcendence is literally to take to heart the biblical call to be like God, welcoming the stranger, the widow, and the orphan (Deut. 10:18–19). Such praxis demands sensitivity, openness, and enough desire to love one's neighbor. We can call this a language of alterity; to go further and attempt a theology of alterity will necessitate finding new ways of speaking of the Christian mysteries, such as Holy Saturday and the Resurrection, in a nonphenomenal manner and in new contexts, to come to a vision of a Trinitarian praxis. Consequently, by learning from Levinas, we can imagine ways to theologize beyond the traditional categories of objectivity, presence, and Being, and even learn to renew Levinas's pure philosophy into more practical perspectives.

Doing theology with Levinas is exciting in many ways. It fuels the theological imagination with an abundance of notions and ideas that uncover and penetrate human existence with the gravity of God's self-communication. Extending the dialogue between Emmanuel Levinas and Hans Urs von Balthasar leads in the direction of more practical and dramatic expressions: Paul's encounter with the risen Christ, the moods and difficulties of psychosis, bodiliness, forgiveness, film, building Jewish-Christian friendship, and living at the margins of society. These connections, guided by the desire to nurture the theological imagination, reveal that there are a variety of possible contexts in which Levinas's pure philosophical thought and von Balthasar's dramatic theology are related.

This approach toward a theology of alterity presents some challenges. Some, especially Christian theologians who remain indebted to the tradition of ontology and phenomenology, understandably resist Levinas's critique of metaphysics. Such resistance indicates the difficulty of accepting Levinas's development of phenomenology with ethics and the Bible. Approaching Levinas's thought demands not only reflecting on mystery, truth, and Being, but also witnessing to it otherwise through a radical otherness and love for one's neighbor. Ultimately, this is a conflict and challenge through which all Christian theologians must be tested, be tempted, and persevere.

Other theological attempts that appeal to Levinas for inspiration tend to partake of his thought with both the language of ethical metaphysics and of ontotheology. For example, with reference to Levinas's philosophy, Michael Purcell engages the theological writings of Karl Rahner; Graham Ward turns to those of Karl Barth; Michael Barnes refers to Paul Ricoeur's and to the life of Roberto de Nobili; David Ford's frame of reference includes Eberhard Jüngel, Paul Ricoeur, Saint Thérèse of Lisieux, and Dietrich Bonhoeffer; and Michele Saracino compares the thinking of Levinas and Bernard Lonergan. In short, there have been a number of attempts to enrich Christian theology, praxis, dialogue and spirituality from Levinasian resources.[6]

These theologians have begun the task to question why the logos, the very discourse of reason, should be confined to analogies and the categories of objectivity, presence, and Being. They have struggled with the language of ontology and used Levinas's ethical metaphysics to develop it. The ontological mediums such as analogies provide much of the language of theology with the aim to make the mystery of God comprehensible. However, the use of analogy, for instance, despite its enriching qualities, retains the risk of thematizing and limiting the divine to the realm of the human senses. In this regard, objective propositions might be a disclosure not necessarily of divine truth but of the language of totality, that is, the quest to uncover the meaning of Being. For Levinas, such a quest results in an anonymous experience or a depersonalizing presence. Any attempt of subjectivity is ultimately thwarted by the egocentrism of the self. In stark contrast, a language of alterity aims to think otherwise toward an ethical and Trinitarian existence of hearing and responding to the cries of the widow, orphan, and stranger.

For the most part, recent attempts to employ Levinas's philosophy for the benefit of Christian theology have hesitated to go beyond ontotheology. This study sets out to be different. In many ways, the challenge to imagine a theology of alterity has been nurtured by my conversations with Roger Burggraeve. Burggraeve would often meet with Levinas, and having such a connection is a testimony of otherness, that is, of the need to be generative and to pass on Levinas's personal spirit and legacy. And indeed, where doing theology becomes an encounter of openness and generosity of spirit, it speaks of a time of encountering the "true beauty" and "good truth" of God's glory taking shape in our lives and the world.

Theology can gain much by trying to conceive of the logos through alterity. This approach is not meant to ignore ontological analogies and categories, but ultimately to return to the language of Being while acknowledging ethical transcendence and Trinitarian praxis. It is not necessarily new to emphasize the need for the interhuman element to develop theology. But through establishing a Levinasian-inspired theology of alterity, theology (taking the form of a Trinitarian praxis) becomes inherently a transformative journey and a process of discovery leading to ethical transcendence deepened by ethical emotions like melancholy and vigilance. In a Levinasian sense, given that the disposition of otherness overwhelms the intentionality of consciousness and puts into question the self's egoistical ways, it is not surprising that the self can feel a great momentum of obligation swelling up to sacrifice for the Other, even to the point of obligation transforming into expiation. If this is combined with theological reflection, a whole new way of doing theology could very well be initiated and nurtured.

Yet, to make use of Levinas's philosophy will always remain a complex task. The process is demanding because it must not be read in accord with tendencies that could contaminate Christian theology into a totality of self-interest. Nonetheless, it is nearly impossible to omit ontological and phenomenological thematizations in theology, especially given the dominance of the verbal meaning of Being flowing over into the structure of language and even behaviors that foster self-interest. However, a language of alterity facilitates a return to the language of Being with a heightened sense of ethics, peace, and prayer. On the face of things, this is not a new tactic for theologians or philosophers. But the difference in Levinas's approach is that the return to Being is more ethical-metaphysical rather than ontological. In other words, a statement about ethics will have a diachronic element—the statement is not finished, as it were, until it coincides through time with peace and prayer. Statements about God are to be made, hopefully, in a spirit of faith, hope, and love rather than in ways that lead into obscurity, vanity, and violence. However, the attempt to develop a language of alterity is one of risk and ambiguity. To have an ethical metaphysical sense in Being, to theologize otherwise, denotes the risk of falling back into the objectivity and presence of self-interested Being. In short, there will remain a sense of ambiguity or confusion where perhaps the language of alterity or ethical transcendence could well be the totality of Being.

Levinas's language of alterity alerts us that we are not good at being responsible for others; we seem to be reticent to encounter the often hidden and painful world of the neighbor. But there is a momentum running through his philosophy to rupture our sense and sensibility and remind us of the world of ethics, prayer, and the grave responsibility of agape. Levinas's writings introduce a whole new lexicon of terms. The challenge is to allow their meaning to resound in a multitude of contexts. Our context is Christian theology. On the face of things, it would seem that Levinas himself would not invite our interest eagerly, lest we homogenize his sense of otherness into our personal experience. Yet he may be intrigued to see how we Christian theologians return to his writings with awe, respect, and a search for the word of God.

Using Levinas's thought for theology opens up a richness of pos-sibilities (and impossibilities). Even though this study will no doubt fall prey to the totality of Being, a Christian reading and application of Levinas's philosophy to Christian theology will result not only in a Levinasian recontextualization of von Balthasar's theology, but in a new attempt to contribute to theology by way of a language of alterity.

Levinas's language of alterity (particularly in his later writings) seems almost allergic to objectivity, Being, and presence. These cat-egories, for Levinas—who was mindful of Heidegger's rendering of Being and stance in life, particularly during the Nazi horror from 1933 to 1945—contaminate philosophy and theology with self-interest, grasping representations, and thematizations of God to forge a cold totality of knowledge. For example, when Levinas defines objectivity as "Being's essence revealed in truth" (*OB* 3, 131), he imparts it with a sense of knowledge,[7] verging on the hither side of a depersonalized life. The essence of Being speaks of a distorted consciousness and truth that subsumes others into its own idolizations. Because Being, in the Heideggerian sense of disclosed Being, depends on conscious-ness, Levinas argues that objectivity distorts truth.[8] Objectivity can-not be trusted given the ego-self's determination to be for-itself. So the distortion occurs when consciousness is reduced to the horror of self-interest, an anonymous state of depersonalization in which exis-tence loses its substantive nature. In other words, the subjectivity of the subject is absorbed and enclosed by the objectivity of Being. This suggests that subjectivity (as intelligibility) is subordinated to objective propositions of experience, that is, to the totality of ego-isms struggling with others (*BPW* 99; *OB* 3–4). This gives subjectiv-ity a transcendental status (for it is subordinated to Being's essence).[9]

Furthermore, such transcendental subjectivity signifies presence, "the fact-of-Being," in which the ego reduces its subjectivity with others to its own experience or re-presentations (lived experiences).[10] In this context, presence is that which encompasses, absorbs, and encloses things and consciousness.[11] In sum, for Levinas, these categories evoke a horror of a depersonalized life of egocentric behavior weighed down by the yoke of self-interest.

Levinas's philosophy is a testimony to the good in response to the excess of evil that aims, in all its horror and contamination, to seek us out. To do theology with Levinas is to face the possible and the impossible. It becomes possible to utilize Levinas's thought like a treasury of keys, so to speak, to unlock the mysteries of personhood, prayer, and ethics. Yet, we also face a sense of the impossible as the language of alterity beckons a whole eternity to be proclaimed.

It might seem harsh to assert that Levinas is making of ontology and, in particular, Heideggerian ontological phenomenology. However, even such eminent scholars as Purcell, Ward, Barnes, and Ford have not been able to resolve the problem of the nonontological basis of theology. This study takes up a different sounding by aiming to bring out a more radical or sustained reading of Levinas — particularly of his later work — to critique theology. In comparison, for example, Purcell has emphasized the need of "*being* otherwise than Levinas's comprehension of Being" to the point of speaking of "the Goodness of Being."[12] In a similar vein, Ward finds that Levinas's idea of otherwise than Being implicitly espouses the analogy of Being.[13] Barnes is perhaps more straightforward on Levinas's idea of alterity when he states, "it is impossible to speak of a relationship with what is other without dropping back into the language of totality."[14] In contrast to Purcell, Ward, and Barnes, Ford points to how Levinas's thought has been woven into his own thinking "in ways too pervasive to trace." Nevertheless, it is obvious enough that Ford has used Levinas's thought to construct analogies of Christian life, such as the analogy of joyful obligation.[15] In contrast, this study will strive to take Levinas's language toward a theological site of alterity rather than ontotheology.[16]

Drawing on Levinas's ideas to do theology, Purcell, Ward, Barnes, and Ford teach us that it is virtually impossible to sever ties with ontology (the search to understand the meaning of Being); intentionality (consciousness itself); and, hence, analogy (a method using the categories of Being and consciousness to make rational statements concerning God, humanity, and the world).[17] We have an ongoing challenge to face from Levinas: to question the way theologians develop conceptions that rely on transcendental consciousness, phenomenal experience, and analogical thinking. In Levinas's mind, there is a need to challenge the ontological quest for the meaning of Being and the primacy of lived experience. For Levinas, it is the person and not a theory that has priority.

Despite the difficulty to accept the full logic of Levinas's approach, we can ask why it is that the logos, the very discourse of reason, should be confined to ontotheology. Clearly, it will be my argument—following Levinas—that theology must conceive of the logos otherwise. If the word "God" is going to be pronounced, a difficult condition and language of alterity is demanded, which, in turn, will demand that theory and praxis must coincide. The basic question, then, for the development of this study is: How might Levinas's philosophy inspire a language of alterity for Christian theology? Or, more simply: Is a theology of alterity possible? Toward responding to this central question, this study will step into key terms and concepts in the Levinasian vocabulary of alterity, and then set out to enhance and renew the theology of Hans Urs von Balthasar in the light of a Levinasian language of alterity, finally working toward articulating a Trinitarian praxis and theology of alterity.

Levinas's Philosophical Origins

The writings of Husserl, Heidegger, and Rosenzweig together form the fertile ground in which Levinas's thinking took root and from which it grew. While Levinas incorporated many of their insights and developed many of their ideas in his distinctive fashion, there is always a recognizable and multifaceted dependence upon their influence.

For example, Levinas uses Heidegger's thought to free himself from Husserl's phenomenology, and employs Rosenzweig's thinking to go beyond Heidegger's.[18] In some cases, Levinas's thought is clearly different from that of any of these others, his insights sometimes owe their origins more to Plato, Descartes, Shakespeare, Blanchot, Lévy-Bruhl, Dostoyevsky, Vassily Grossman, and Hayyim of Volozhin.[19]

Husserl provides much of the phenomenological language of Levinas's ethical metaphysics and some of the analytical resources necessary to articulate such notions as consciousness, experience, being, truth, and the other. Husserl is fundamentally concerned with how and why phenomena, including the phenomenon of the other, are intuited or approached. Intentional experiences (*Erlebnisse*)—such as perception, judgment, imagination, and memory—are always consciousness of something.[20] In his transcendental phenomenology, these *Erlebnisse* of intentional experience are the foundation for determining the meaning of truth and being in an intersubjective world.

Levinas's philosophical discourse is a revolutionary development of Husserl's thought, especially in regard to the notion of experience as *Erlebnis*. In this regard, Levinas employs his distinctive notions such as encounter, approach, enigma, *illeity*, and passivity. Furthermore, in his postphenomenological expressions, he uses such terms as the face, the saying, diachrony, immemorial past, sacrifice, the Infinite, and otherwise than Being to mark his progress beyond Husserl. Here, a major contrast with Husserl is Levinas's emphasis on the ethical and alterity. For Levinas, consciousness—instead of being conscious of something—is primarily nonintentional in the sense that it is not a lived state of experience so much as a state of being overwhelmed by the other. The passive or receptive character of consciousness is thus privileged at the expense of intentional activity in the usual sense. Paradoxically, Levinas articulates the activity of consciousness as residing in an absolute passivity. Levinas does not speak in Husserlian terms about the lived experience (*vécu*) or experience (*expérience*) of the other, but rather in terms of encounter (*rencontre*).[21]

For Husserl, the *noesis* is the act of consciousness itself, while the *noema* gives visibility to Being.[22] But Levinas rejects this correlation.

He endeavors to isolate the positive value of nonintentionality, which, in turn, leads to his ideas of pure passivity and immemoriality. He understands that a prereflective consciousness may have bearing on an ethical metaphysical conception of consciousness. Here, his thought has parallels with Descartes's idea of the Infinite in which thought overwhelms consciousness, as Levinas conceives of a *noesis* without a *noema* (*EN* 175; *OB* 146–47). In other words, the act of consciousness itself (the *noesis*) is to be conceived as not simply correlative to an object in an objectifying act (the *noema*). It is more than mere representation. Levinas depicts the act of love as having a sense of that which overwhelms the self's consciousness.[23] To understand that the act of love is irreducible to representation is to grasp more clearly what Levinas means by an implicit consciousness preceding all (representable) intentions.

Levinas's postphenomenological inversion of Husserl's thought turns the act of being conscious of something inside out so that it becomes an absolute passivity. Ethically speaking, the approach of the other determines the meaning of truth in an intersubjective world. Yet, before we can speak more about Levinas's developments, we must offer a preliminary remark on the influence of Heidegger and Rosenzweig.

Heidegger's phenomenology, grounded in ontology, is an important bridge for Levinas to traverse and even to dismantle. Levinas first encountered Heidegger and his work, *Sein und Zeit,* while studying at the University of Freiburg. Immediately, the work began to influence Levinas's doctoral dissertation on "The Theory of Intuition in Husserl's Phenomenology."[24] Levinas admired Heidegger's philosophy until 1933, when Heidegger's "unthinkable" collaboration with the National Socialists, especially the infamous rectorial address in the same year, proved an intense shock for Levinas (*EI* 38). His rupture with Heidegger proved to be a turning point in Levinas's philosophical development. From then on, he was intent on refuting the philosophy of his former mentor. Although Levinas had once deeming *Sein und Zeit* among the five greatest works of Western philosophy,[25]

Levinas began to see how Heidegger was beginning to manipulate his philosophy for the cause of Germany's spiritual destiny.[26] Levinas increasingly found Heidegger's thinking "pagan," especially his "talk of 'poetic dwelling,' of the 'mystery,' of the fourfold of earth and sky, mortals and divinities."[27]

If Heidegger was concerned with the spiritual destiny of Germany, Levinas was concerned with the spiritual destiny of European civilization. The impact of the horrific events from 1933 to 1945 affected profoundly Levinas's judgment of Heidegger's whole project. Levinas began to think otherwise as far as Heidegger's notion of Being was concerned. For example, in the programmatic work, *Existence and Existents,* Levinas defines the meaning of Being in general ("the idea of the cause of existence")[28] as anonymous Being—the "there is" (*il y a*) or "existence without existents." As a result of Being's anonymity, and the strangeness with which it seeks us out like the night's "suffocating embrace," there is no future in the questioning of the meaning of Being in general. No response is possible. Being remains "alien" (*EE* 57, 23).

The fundamentally anti-Heideggerian factor in Levinas's philosophy is not merely a revision, but an attempt to dismantle the totality of Being contaminating ontology and to give priority to ethics as first philosophy. For Levinas, ontology reduces otherness "to comprehension or understanding."[29] Such a criticism makes Levinas's thought all the more intriguing for theology. Setting out to underline the nonthematizable relation to the other (*L'Autrui*) provides theology with a new perspective of alterity. The interhuman relation is something beyond the essence of menacing formulations that subdue the personhood of the other. Levinas's work strives therefore to name such a menace and unmask its reality. For example, *Dasein*'s being thrown into the "there," sucked into the turbulence of the "they-self,"[30] Levinas's formulation of the menacing *there is* sounds more like the shattering of such an analysis of inauthentic existence or the notion of Being as "gifting." The horrible eternity of the "there is" calls into question any attempt to derive meaning from Being

(*OB* 176). This is one aspect of Levinas's attempt to prioritize ethics over any fundamental ontology—or over any other theory of Being. Levinas reflects in "Is Ontology Fundamental?":

> To Heidegger, being-with-the-other-person—*Miteinandersein*—thus rests on the ontological relation. We reply: Is our relation with the other a *letting be*? Is not the independence of the other achieved through his or her role as one who is addressed? Is the person to whom we speak understood beforehand in his being? Not at all. The other is not first an object of understanding and then an interlocutor. The two relations are merged. In other words, addressing the other is inseparable from understanding the other. (*EN* 6)

The Other, then, for Levinas, is outside the horizon and comprehension of Being. In other words, the Other "does not affect us in terms of a theme . . . or a concept."[31] Giving an ethical priority to the Other, Levinas leashes ontology to seek out a language beyond essence and knowledge. In a few years before his 1951 essay, "Is Ontology Fundamental," he began an embryonic search for a language of alterity in *Existence and Existents* (1947). Here, Levinas attempts to revise Heidegger's distinction between Being (*Sein, Être*) and beings (*Seindes, étants*) by replacing such a distinction with the "there is" (*il y a*) and existents (*existants*). Edith Wyschogrod describes the existent (*l'étant*) as "Comparable to Heidegger's *Seiendes* but used by Levinas to designate the other person to whom one relates prior to an understanding of being, the other who is one's interlocutor."[32] Levinas considers the existent as a personal subject who has taken up a position toward the "there is." He describes *l'existant* as a hypostatic event whereby the consciousness of the I moves its position away from the "there is" (Being in general or the unnamable verb *to be*) toward a new subjectivity that points to a horizon of freedom, responsibility, and hope. In *Existence and Existents,* hypostasis is understood as a twofold passage, from an egotistical existence of indolence and fatigue to an ethical existence of responsibility for the Other and hope (*EE* 82–83, 92–93). Hence, Levinas uses the term, *l'existant,* to designate the self's hypostatic state of existence. Accordingly, in reaction to the anonymity and strangeness of Being, Levinas begins to move away from the ontological-phenomenological truth of Being, and into a horizon containing a Platonic notion of the good, namely, the good beyond Being. This idea is evident in his two major works, *Totality and Being* and *Otherwise than Being or Beyond Essence.*

In disassociating himself from Heidegger's vocabulary, already in *Existence and Existents* Levinas has begun to move away from ontology to ethical metaphysics. Later and throughout in his writings, more enigmatic developments of ethics and the notion of the "there is" emerge. In the essay, "God and Philosophy" (1975), Levinas speaks of the ambiguity between the notions of the "there is" and *illeity* (the way the Infinite or God is heard in the face of the Other) (*CPP* 165–66). These are attempts to develop phenomenology through the primacy of ethics. And not far from Levinas's philosophical imagination—we must always remember—is the very memory of the Shoah.

Levinas's time of captivity in a German stalag informed his familiarity with the anonymous experience of Being as well as his subsequent reaction to Heidegger's Nazi political stance: "We know what Heidegger was in 1933, even if he was so during a brief period, and even if his disciples—many of who are estimable—forget about it. For me, it is unforgettable. One could have been everything except Hitlerian, even if it was inadvertent."[33] Caputo, who uses Levinas's writings to demythologize Heidegger's thought, also points out: "What Heidegger regards as the inner truth of the spiritual relationship of Greek and German, which in 1933 is Heidegger's attempt both to elevate Nazi mythology to the level of metaphysics and to give a deeper, spiritual mooring to the revolution, is a "truth" that Heidegger never renounced."[34] In a way, Levinas's writings give testimony to how philosophy can be distorted by a grim and menacing self-interest of nationalism and hatred of the Other.

Indeed, from the background of being regarded as a nonexistent without a name while in captivity, Levinas laments: "In horror a subject is stripped of his subjectivity, of his power to have private existence. The subject is depersonalized. 'Nausea,' as a feeling for existence, is not yet a depersonalization; but horror turns the subjectivity of the subject, his particularity qua *entity,* inside out. It is a participation in the *there is* which returns in the heart of every nega-tion, in the *there is* that has 'no exits.' It is, if we may say so, the impossibility of death, the universality of existence even in its annihi-lation."[35] The subject, shorn of subjectivity, cannot even feel human enough to partake of nausea. The horror of the "there is" gives the existent nothing to remind it of its life and subjectivity, resulting in the negation and horror of nonfeeling. Levinas later rejected Heidegger's notion of time in his search for the meaning of Being. At the end of *Being and Time,* Heidegger asks, "Is there a way which leads from primordial *time* to the meaning of *Being?* Does *time* itself manifest itself as the horizon of *Being?*" Heidegger hopes, "Within the hori-zon of time the projection of a meaning of Being in general can be accomplished."[36] In contrast, Levinas rejects the search for the mean-ing of Being in general by "deformalizing" the notion of time. In "Diachrony and Representation," he writes, "But I have sought for time as the deformalization of the most formal form that is, the unity of the *I think.* Deformalization is that which Bergson, Rosenzweig, and Heidegger, each in his own way, have opened the problematic of modern thought, by starting from a concreteness 'older' that the pure form of time."[37] Levinas, attempting to think of time ethically beginning from the face of the Other, imagines a past distinguished from the presence of Being. Levinasian time nurtures the relation with the Other. With such a conception, Levinas transforms the ontological difference between Being and beings into a nonindiffer-ence between the self and the Other. In this way, Levinas rejects both the verbal form of Being and the thinking of time on the basis of "to be" or "toward-death." The Heideggerian projection of the Other as one among many (the "they") is therefore rejected.[38] Levinas's emphasis is on the idea of ethical transcendence, which is irreduc-ible to the immanence of the self's interests (essence) structured by time and death.[39] This entails also the rejection of the Husserlian idea of immanence—that is, arising out of—the lived experience of an object's essence.[40]

Yet, despite Levinas's determined break with the German philosopher, there are Heideggerian influences built into the fabric of
Levinas's ideas, informed by Heidegger's prominence in the phenomenological tradition and by the way Levinas engages his writings. It is
not always useful, then, to pit Levinas against Heidegger. A comparatively unexplored area in this context is Heidegger's conception of
encounter (*begegnen*) and his treatment of experience as *Erlebnis* and
erfahren.[41] In *Being and Time*, Heidegger developed the notion of
encounter (*begegnen*) by seeking to overcome the problems inherent
in the notions of *erfahren*/experience[42] and *Erlebnis*/experience. We
have, then, some indication of how Heidegger sought to find a way
into the question of the meaning of Being in general, firstly through
Dasein, and then through the nothing. *Erlebnisse*, the perceptions
of lived experiences, fail to provide *Dasein* with the opportunity to
encounter Being in its potentiality and as care (*Sorge*). *Erfahren*, the
active experience of environmental entities, results in the same failure,
since they are insignificant in themselves. However, *erfahren* is paradoxically necessary for it points to the nothing, namely, the world-
hood of the world. Where *Dasein* allows itself to be encountered
by the nothing in the form of anxiety, the possibility exists for it to
overcome its ontic character as the they-self. Ontologically, *Dasein*
is in a position of Being-free by means of encounter for its authentic
possibilities.

There are some similarities between these two approaches to
encounter, in that both seek to address the problem of lived experience and the oppressive experiences of the world.[43] But differences
remain. Whereas both Levinas and Heidegger reject lived experiences
as foundational, the latter highlights the oppressiveness of the nothing. For Levinas, however, the oppressiveness of the world is not to
be overcome through care for one's existential possibilities, but by
the path of responsibility for the Other. To what extent, then, has
the Heideggerian notion of encounter influenced Levinas's development of a similar category? This question is beyond the scope of this
study, but it seems safe to say that Levinas has developed the idea of

encounter in respect to alterity, an otherness that exceeds the *conatus* of Being in a Heideggerian sense.

Levinas's relation to Heidegger's philosophy is also evident in regard to each philosopher's critical stance toward Husserl: both are critical of Husserl's transcendental phenomenology, in which the meaning of truth and Being begins with lived experience.[44] For Levinas, truth does not depend on transcendental knowledge or on the unconcealment of Being. Rather than using Husserl's language of subject and object, Heidegger characterizes the object as related to the meaning of Being in general (the Being of entities), whereas the subject is related to *Dasein* (being there),[45] the locus of the existential analysis intent on disclosing and even clarifying the meaning of Being. In this way, his notion of *Dasein* moves beyond Husserl's *noesis-noema* structure of consciousness. But in contrast to Heidegger, Levinas aims at an ethical subjectivity beyond any form of philosophical objectivity. Truth does not depend on objectivity and the meaning of Being in general, since it is more a testimony of responsibility for the Other, transcending the *conatus* of philosophical intelligence (*BPW* 102–03).

Heidegger approached the idea of truth as the unconcealment of Being and transcendental knowledge as an ambiguous unconcealment of Being. The Being of entities remains hidden, revealing itself by disclosing or by covering up itself. Accordingly, a forgetfulness of Being and its meaning can arise. The problem for Heidegger is how to arrive at phenomenological truth. *Being and Time* is his attempt to probe this enigma through an existential-ontological analysis of *Dasein*—which bears the fundamental structure of Being-in-the-world and discovers its meaning in temporality (*Zeitlichkeit*). For the most part, *Dasein* is realized in an inauthentic, routinized form of consciousness, dependent on what is called the they-self. To give one example, Heidegger explains that the common sense of the they-self "knows only the satisfying of manipulable rules and the public norms and the failure to satisfy them."[46] Where Heidegger sees truth as the quest for the disclosure of the unknown in Being,[47] Levinas understands truth as the testimony of responsibility on "the hither side" of the self's freedom (*BPW* 101–03). Levinas's conception of truth resists any Heideggerian thematization; it is beyond all totalizing explanations.

In a way then, different from Heidegger, Levinas has developed Husserl's idea of intentionality by discovering the value of nonintentional consciousness and forging it in the final form of ethical transcendence. According to Levinas, consciousness, in the sense of representation, implies presence. In reference to Husserl's idea of intentionality, he distinguishes between two types of consciousness, namely, the nonintentional and the intentional. He describes intentional consciousness as reflection; it objectifies the I, lived experience, and mental acts. In other words, intentional consciousness is consciousness *of something*. In contrast, Levinas describes nonintentional consciousness as an unreflective form of consciousness. This unreflective quality lies in the fact that the sense data (*hyle*) in lived experience are nonexplicit and not necessarily objectified in consciousness.[48] A confusion in the act of reflection results. The reflection proper to intentional consciousness can forget its own limitations, bringing to light only a confused representation of data so that any explanation of the world occurs in a context marked with obscurity.

Levinas's discussion of consciousness, however, does not end simply with the recognition of confusion and obscurity. He comes to accept that nonintentional consciousness can have a positive value for reflection: "Does the 'knowledge' of the prereflective self-consciousness *know*, properly speaking? As a dim consciousness, an implicit consciousness preceding all intentions—or coming back from intentions—it is not an act, but rather pure passivity? It is a passivity not only by way of its being-without-having-chosen-to-be, or by its fall into a pell-mell of possibilities already realized before any assumption, as in the Heideggerian *Geworfenheit*. It is a 'consciousness' that, rather than signifying a self-knowledge, is effacement or discretion of presence" (*GCM* 173–74).

Levinas's understanding of prereflective consciousness clearly differs from Husserlian and Heideggerian accounts. Admittedly, Heidegger's analysis of 'the hammer' in *Being and Time* does have some similarity to Levinas's notion of a nontheoretical consciousness, especially where he emphasizes that the more one uses the hammer, the more primordial one's relationship becomes. But, unlike Levinas, Heidegger is searching to encounter the kind of unveiled Being that a thing (like a hammer) possesses.[49]

Levinas makes a reference to the Heideggerian idea of *Geworfenheit* ("thrownness"), one of the three major features of *Dasein* (along with "existence" and "falling").[50] Heidegger's analysis of *Dasein* contrasts with Levinas's philosophical discourse on a number of key points. First, Heidegger distinguishes two types of existence, inauthentic and authentic. Inauthentic existence is related to the everyday kind of Being-in-the-world of the they-self. Heidegger is highly critical of this routine mode of Being. The states of mind or emotions, modes of understanding, and types of discourse associated with it disclose the presence of entities in an inauthentic manner. Inauthentic existence is characterized phenomenally as idle talk, curiosity, and ambiguity; it results in what Heidegger names as the movement of falling. As a result of this "downward plunge" (*Absturz*), *Dasein* falls into the "turbulence" (*Wirbel*) of the they-self's inauthenticity. Heidegger names this phenomenal unveiling of facticity as "thrownness." While this seems to imply mostly inauthentic existence, when it takes the form of an authentic existence, it finds itself in an unfamiliar realm of conscience.[51]

Here, it is sufficient to point out that Heidegger develops his unique vocabulary to give an existential-ontological interpretation of the corruption of human nature, which can lead to *Dasein*'s discovery of authentic existence. Levinas, in contrast, unconvinced of Husserl's emphasis on the objectivity of lived experience, also questions the ontological foundation of Heidegger's phenomenology.[52] Because the idea of thrownness, for example, evokes "a pell-mell of possibilities" (*GCM* 174), Levinas devises another vocabulary. He does not focus on the corruption of human nature and its possibilities for human existence, but speaks of ethical transcendence. In other words, Levinas's critique of Heidegger leads him to speak of "limit-experiences like insomnia, fatigue and nausea," thereby renewing

Heidegger's phenomenology of the emotions.[53] Similarly, the bodiliness of "ethical melancholy" and "ethical vigilance," are states of mind that can animate "knowledge of the unknown,"[54] such as loneliness and the fear of death on the Other's face.

Outside the tradition of phenomenology, we find another major influence, namely, the life and writings of Franz Rosenzweig, a German-Jewish thinker. His major work, *The Star of Redemption,* is a complex interweaving of epistemological, ontological, and theological concerns. It explores the realms of politics, aesthetics, and religion from pagan and Jewish-Christian perspectives. The book interrelates the three primordial elements — God, the world, and humanity — and connects these with the three "dimensions of temporality,"[55] namely, creation, revelation, and redemption. Each of these topics represents a point on the "Star of Redemption."

Rosenzweig's *The Star of Redemption* played an important role for Levinas and inspired him to shape his departure from Heidegger's way of thinking. Levinas was impressed by Rosenzweig's rejection of the idealistic, pagan world of thought and the consequent totality of Being for the sake of a messianic and eschatological idealism based on Judaism and Christianity. Rosenzweig's work moves away from the totality of God, Man, and the World (where "God appears to be concealed, man secluded, the world enchanted"[56]) to their reciprocal interrelationships signified by the theological notions of creation, revelation, and redemption. In a "shattering of Being,"[57] the primordial elements (God, the world, and humanity) are set free from their Western cultural milieu and liberated from the consequent temptations of paganism, politics, and aesthetics.

Levinas strove to rework many of the elements in Rosenzweig's new system of Idealism and totality, recognizing Rosenzweig had replaced one system of totality, that is to say, created a new messianic theory of Redemption.[58] Levinas's writings took on both a Jewish and Christian perspective in the Rosenzweigian sense. By advocating an eschatological and messianic vision that encompasses all humanity, he overcame Rosenzweig's dualism between the "eternal life" of Judaism and the "eternal way" of Christianity. Though for Levinas, the Jewish people are still the eternal people and those who, without equal, live out the life of alterity, all peoples bear an irrefragable and preoriginal responsibility.[59] Like Rosenzweig, Levinas cast himself as a biblical prophet, trying to awaken and challenge the consciousness of the West to that pagan and totalizing behavior that too often conceals God with thinking, secludes humanity in the darkness of violence and war, and enchants the world through the temptations of politics and aesthetics.

Levinas acknowledged his debt to Rosenzweig as the preface to *Totality and Infinity* attests, "We were impressed by the opposition to the idea of totality in Franz Rosenzweig's *Stern der Erlösung,* a work too often present in this book to be cited."[60] In fact, the influence of Rosenzweig's work resonates throughout the Levinasian oeuvre. For example, Rosenzweig's criticism of art and its aesthetical categories is taken over and deepened in Levinas's emphasis on alterity over eros (*EN* 113). Similarly, we see Levinas's postphenomenological development of Rosenzweig's notion of the face. The term, postphenomenology, describes Levinas's desire to go beyond both Husserl's phenomenology and Heidegger's ontological phenomenology. For Levinas, the face cannot be seen, thought, or re-presented. Accordingly, its nonphenomenality is beyond the range of both Being and experience. In contrast, Levinas describes phenomenality as, "the exhibition of being's essence in truth." This amounts to a game of obscuring and veiling Being's essence in consciousness (*OB* 132).

Furthermore, Rosenzweig's concept of time helped Levinas's postphenomenological and messianic development of alterity and passivity. Levinas's notion of time also draws from Heidegger and Bergson (*EN* 176). In the wake of Bergson, Levinas considers that time is the articulation of what is meaningful (*IR* 269), which he interprets as responsibility for the Other. Instead of establishing a connection between primordial time and the meaning of Being in a Heideggerian fashion,[61] Levinas seeks to unburden himself from ontological phenomenology. In this respect, he seems to have been influenced by Rosenzweig's three "dimensions of temporality," namely, creation, revelation, and redemption.[62] Admittedly, Rosenzweig was unfamiliar with Husserlian phenomenology. Yet if we take Rosenzweig's and

Husserl's influences together, we can detect a messianic development of phenomenology in Levinas's approach.

Toward the end of *The Star of Redemption*, Rosenzweig discusses the idea of "God's time" for the Jewish people (the eternal people). He writes of an inversion of time in which the life of the eternal people precedes being for the world. As a result, redemption creates the possibility for the creature's consciousness to be first revealed in its proper state. This would suggest a diachronic conception of time: through the time of redemption, history awakens to a consciousness of the eternal way. For Rosenzweig, this eternal way is characterized by passivity and alterity, for "it is God who experiences while man merely watches." The implication is that human existence participates in the truth of God passively, even if it is always on the way to truth. To walk in the light of God's countenance is to do justice, love mercy, and walk humbly with God (Mic. 6:8).[63] In Rosenzweig's analysis of God's time, diachrony, passivity, and alterity are inextricably interwoven.

Under the influence of Rosenzweig, Levinas develops an idea of time along messianic lines. He distances himself from Husserlian and Heideggerian influences. His idea of time moves more in the direction of passivity, alterity, and diachrony in response to divine revelation. His analysis of time is further elaborated by a number of elusive postphenomenological notions, namely, *to-God,* diachrony, and the trace of an immemorial past. The idea of *to-God* refers to the infinity of time. It implies a moral order irreducible to objectivity, thematization, and the presence of Being (*IR* 176; *GDT* 96; *EN* 177). It is "diachronic" reality (*EN* 176). The idea of diachrony speaks of transcendence in the sense of disinterestedness, a state in which the ego-self (the Same) turns toward the Other. In this context, Levinas will often write "disinterestedness" in French as "*dés-inter-esse-ment,*" as a complex verbal wordplay to indicate the break with Being (which in Latin is "*Esse*"). Levinas writes: "A dis-interestedness that, in my phenomenology, is explained as a responsibility for the other, as a holiness in which the self is constituted as the uniqueness of an irreducible I, in the impossibility—ethical or holy—of seeking a replacement for oneself" (*IR* 233). In this condition of diachrony, a responsibility comes to the self as an imperative and an accusation beyond consciousness and presence (*OB* 9–10; *EN* 176).

Diachrony also speaks of a trace of an immemorial past, which is a vestige of a past more ancient than sin in that it has never been present. This trace lies awakens the self to a unique responsibility (*OB* 89).[64] In itself, this Levinasian idea is enigmatic in its signification. It evokes both the nonphenomenality of the face and the way in which God or the Infinite come to mind. Levinas writes: "The trace of a past in a face is not the absence of a yet non-revealed, but the anarchy of what has never been present, of an infinite which commands in the face of the other, and which, like an excluded middle, could not be aimed at" (97). In a sense, the trace signifies transcendence to the point of absence, a confusing ambiguity that accuses, traumatizes, and commands.

The Levinasian conception of time points to an ethical relation beyond knowledge, experience (*Erlebnis*), and the synchrony of presence. Time is an encounter with the Other in which the trace of an immemorial past accuses the self of having delayed. This understanding of time points to the collapse of phenomenality at a point where the face of the Other arouses the obligation and responsibility (*OB* 88–89).

Rosenzweig's philosophy is original and far-reaching for Levinas. It represents a prototype of Jewish thought and Christian theology in a situation of mutual enrichment. While Levinas's philosophical discourse never seeks to replicate Rosenzweig's attempt to construct a twofold Jewish and Christian path toward redemption and eternal truth, he does seem to acknowledge Rosenzweig's understanding of Christianity's missionary dimension.[65] Levinas's ethical metaphysics and talmudic writings concentrate more on transcending consciousness through an emphasis on a life of alterity as the difficult freedom characterizing the practice of Judaism. Furthermore, Rosenzweig's openness toward Christianity—while remaining Jewish—figures in Levinas's thought as a moment of joyful hope. Levinas continues in a path of reconciliation between Jews and Christians, especially in the aftermath of the *Shoah*—the very moment at which all was lost.[66]

Two

A Step into Levinas's Philosophy

Levinas's thought and style are of unusual difficulty. Adriaan Peperzak, to give just one example, implies that it is impossible to arrive at a complete overall grasp of Levinas's thought.[1] But Richard Cohen argues against trying to simplify or systemize it, or even relate it too quickly to other disciplines, lest it be reduced to the ordinary level of moral imperatives.[2] It seems clear that Levinas does not leave us with a body of thought or system in any recognizable sense; it is more a deeply person-centered philosophy of moral conscience, developed in a context made up of a certain range of interlocutors. There is indeed something biblical and prophetic about stepping into the nature of Levinas's philosophy, because it challenges and puts into question the very fabric of the conscience. Levinas places the conscience beyond the realm of consciousness, giving it a home in the gravity of face-to-face relations.[3] There seems to be something almost melancholy about Levinas's notion of the conscience. Fueled by a vigilant sense of justice, the conscience acts in a way to transform suffering into compassion and responsibility for the Other. Behind the conscience's reality to take up responsibility in society, its essence takes on an expiating and messianic form. Levinas reflects:

> I am in reality responsible for the other even when he or she commits crimes, even when others commit crimes. This is for me the essence of the Jewish conscience. But I also think that it is the essence of the human conscience: All men are responsible for one another, and "I more than anyone else." One of the most important things for me is that asymmetry and that formula: All men are responsible for one another and I more than anyone else. It is Dostoyevsky's formula, which, as you see, I quote again. (*EN* 107)

29

The tone of Levinas's conscience looks toward a messianic time. This is where ethical responsibility heralds the promise of peace to the far and the near (Isa. 57:19). The meaning of the "essence of the Jewish conscience" unveils a disturbing expiation; it perceives responsibility even for the crimes of the perpetrator. In practical terms, this invites us to translate God's justice and mercy in the face-to-face relation. The Levinasian conscience signifies further an eschatological attitude to safeguard essence from self-interest. For example, essence must learn to savor something from the world beyond or world to come (*Olam Ha-Ba*) so that it can be transformed and find a place in consciousness as mercy and forgiveness. This is key to having a sense in Being. The Levinasian conscience requires, as it were, humility and holiness on a journey toward hope beyond Being and back to Being. The trouble with such a transformed conscience is that it may be quite difficult to recognize; it has been ethically transfigured and transformed. But we may be able to unveil its presence by noticing its quality of ethical melancholy and ethical vigilance. These two states of being and affectivity are at the core of Levinas's philosophy.

Levinas's sense of the conscience aims to shock and rupture our consciousness. Invoking a sense of infinite responsibility, Levinas unveils our human condition as guilty. Having a conscience is therefore having a "bad conscience" (*EN* 175). Yet this should not discourage us. The approach to the conscience needs to embrace humility so that it breaks through the totality of the ego (and sterility of the superego). Departing from a self-interested and sterile world of Being, the Levinasian conscience sets out to be transfigured by an encounter with face of the Other. Where the conscience responds to the word of God in the face of the Other, the difference between ethical responsibility and prayer dissolves. The Levinasian conscience is the very hope by which to bear forth mercy and peace. In this way, the conscience is not a cold act of the intellect's power, but an embodied opening to God's law, particularly mediated by the word of the God in the face of the Other. Part of this embodied nature of the conscience (bodiliness) is dependent upon the ethical intimacy with the Other. The intimacy is overwhelming, particularly in situations in which

Levinas describes the relation as a "hostage" or "expiation of me for the Other" (60). Not only is the conscience shaped by a developing habit of otherness and passivity, but also by emotions that animate such habits. Levinas's writings are clothed, so to speak, in ethical melancholy and ethical vigilance.

In comparison, the Catholic position on the conscience has also taken up an existential position and vigilance for the world. *Gaudium et Spes* provides a "famous definition of the conscience."[4] This definition, while deeply concerned with humanity, does not seem to possess the voice of an angry prophet as Levinas does. The Catholic tone is more propositional and didactic, and its strength resides in the depths of the way it carries the conscience in spiritual and ethical terms. *Gaudium et Spes* para 16 states:

> In the depths of his conscience, man detects a law which he does not impose upon himself, but which holds him to obedience. Always summoning him to love good and avoid evil, the voice of conscience when necessary speaks to his heart: do this, shun that. For man has in his heart a law written by God; to obey it is the very dignity of man; according to it he will be judged. Conscience is the most secret core and sanctuary of a man. There he is alone with God, Whose voice echoes in his depths. In a wonderful manner conscience reveals that law which is fulfilled by love of God and neighbor. In fidelity to conscience, Christians are joined with the rest of men in the search for truth, and for the genuine solution to the numerous problems which arise in the life of individuals from social relationships. Hence the more right conscience holds sway, the more persons and groups turn aside from blind choice and strive to be guided by the objective norms of morality. Conscience frequently errs from invincible ignorance without losing its dignity. The same cannot be said for a man who cares but little for truth and goodness, or for a conscience which by degrees grows practically sightless as a result of habitual sin.[5]

The definition of the conscience in *Gaudium et Spes,* which centers on the experience of the conscience inasmuch as it can seek to become self-responsible, begs a phenomenological or ethical metaphysical perspective or development. Karol Wojtyla (Pope John Paul II) takes up the development of the conscience phenomenologically. For Wojtyla, the conscience is in relation to the experience of the ego-self and the self must be in a position to govern and possess itself to the point of "self-determination"; the "voice of the conscience" gives authority to the ego/self to make judgments over oneself. Wojtyla applies the conscience specifically to the experience of responsibility. Moreover, he implies a movement of the conscience, like Levinas, from trans-descendence/passivity ("from within" or "something happening to him") to transascendence/activity ("man's acting"). In other words, where God's voice echoes in the depths of the self, it may search for truth and goodness through responsibility for others: "The structure of responsibility is also intimately connected with man's acting, with the person's action, but not with what only happens in man, unless what only happens is a consequence of and thus depends on his act-ing or nonacting. Moreover, it is first appropriate to the person from within; and only because of the primordial intersubjective nexus of moral and social participation, coexistence, and collaboration within the human world does it become a responsibility *to* somebody."[6]

Levinas's philosophy offers a dramatic and stirring perspective to the development of the conscience as the self is ordered to be respon-sible *for* others. In contrast, Wojtyla's nuanced approach is in "acting *with* others."[7] The advantage for Wojtyla and Levinas in employing a more phenomenological understanding of the conscience is that they both wrestle with the fundamental ethical and moral founda-tions of the self. The definition of the conscience in *Gaudium et Spes* is a proclamation and witness of faith for the world. The difference of both Jewish (Levinas) and Catholic (Wojtyla) phenomenological perspectives is that they bring to the world of the conscience a more structural horizon of the acting person. The identity of the acting person is uncovered as an image of God. Phenomenology represents a key movement in the development of the moral conscience with the theological and philosophical tradition.

Husserl should not be forgotten as playing a mediating role for philosophy and theology. Before Levinas and Wojtyla, Husserl's phe-nomenology sought to discover how the mind might take responsi-bility for itself and for its own freedom by deepening its knowledge of things. According to Levinas, Husserl believes that phenomenology was the realization of the ideal of first philosophy. This is to say that phenomenology, as first philosophy, is independent from any scientific theory, and further acts as a critique and foundation for all other forms of science.[8] For Levinas, on the other hand, ethics is first philosophy: "The ethical, beyond vision and certitude, delineates the structure of exteriority as such. Morality is not a branch of philosophy, but first philosophy" (*TI* 304). As he reflects on how Heidegger's fundamental ontology has revolutionized Husserl's intention of deepening our knowledge of the Being and truth of things, Levinas questions the foundational status of ontology as well (*EN* 11). It is the ethical encounter with the Other that is primary. Levinas will go so far as describing the discourse between the self and the Other as prayer. This suggests that prayer and ethics are interwoven in Levinas's distinctive style of analysis of human existence. For example, he writes, "the essence of discourse is ethical" (*TI* 216), but also states, "the essence of discourse is prayer" (*EN* 7).

As Levinas develops the phenomenological tradition, he is also subject to biblical influences. Indeed, Derrida argues that messianic and eschatological thinking inspired Levinas's thought. Yet Derrida is careful to point out that Levinas's messianic-eschatology should not be reduced to philosophical truisms, theology, Jewish mysticism, dogmatics, a religion, or a morality. Derrida clearly understands Levinas's thought not as a specific theory but as a discourse focused on the encounter with the Other. This eschatological encounter is therefore described as a "naked experience," for it is not reducible to lived experience.[9] There is a strong sense of being beholden to the Other and of the connection between God and justice (*OB* 160–62). Furthermore, Levinas will at times refer to Isaiah or, when speaking to Christians, to Matthew 25.[10] The general context of his thought assumes a messianic-eschatology and an ethical metaphysics centered on the encounter with the Other. Levinas's thought, it seems, is never far from prayer.

In a number of countries, especially Holland, Belgium, France, the United States, Italy, and South America, Levinas's work has found its greatest readership among Christian philosophers and theologians.[11] Despite this intense interest, there is a tendency for Christian theologians to interpret Levinas's philosophy with an ontological, and hence analogical, approach that is foreign to it.[12] Levinas, guided by the sense of the weight of responsibility before the Other, discovers something deeper and more primordial than providing everyday meaningful thematizations such as metaphors and analogies. Levinas places a priority on literally hearing the word of God in the face of the Other. This encounter unveils a drama of ethical transcendence. Ontotheology, or our ability to give our own word of interpretation and explanation, can let us down so easily. Levinas is not rejecting the category of Being; ultimately he develops a way to transcend the totalizing ways of Being—such as competitive self-interest—to return to Being (existence and reality) with a sense akin to love. We can call this the grave reality of agape or ethical transcendence; a transformation has taken place in which ethics or the interhuman is given a priority. There is something quite messianic and even ideal about Levinas's approach as he hopes for a future world of infinite and mutual responsibility. This hope is further animated by an inward movement of ethical emotionality of melancholy and vigilance or insomnia.

Ward and Purcell bring out a sense of Levinas's writings between ontological phenomenology and ethical metaphysics. For example, influenced by Derrida's critique of Levinas, Ward pursues the reduction of Levinas's ideas on the Other to analogy. He writes, "What is distinctive about Levinas's position is his castigation of binary oppositions—Same and Other, presence and absence. He wishes to construct analogies through a presence-by-absence." In another instance, Ward says, "Despite, then, espousing Husserl's analogy of appresentation, Levinas cannot articulate such an appresentation without implicitly espousing the analogy of being."[13] Purcell also notes this paradox in Levinas's writings. He states, "Levinas refuses an ontological understanding of subjectivity and refuses Being as the appropriate or adequate category for articulating the relation between the same and the Other. Yet, the ethical relationship of the same to the

Other must also in some sense be taken as analogical and for a number of reasons. . . . To speak meaningfully about responsibility and its
demands, there must be some analogical sense in which the terms can
be used."[14]

Both Ward and Purcell are convinced that Levinas employs analogy indicating the difficulty of refusing the category of Being. In fact,
Purcell appeals to Ward for evidence.[15] Similarly, in the approaches
of Ford and Barnes, Levinas's ideas are still not sufficiently removed
from the language of ontology.[16] While Ford is aware of Levinas's
argument against the language of ontology, he uses such a process
to do theology. He speaks of feasting as an analogy and as a personal
experience of aesthetics to explain how the reality of God transcends
all categories: "For this metaphysics the danger to which Levinas
alerts us is that of a new totality. Feasting, however, allows for his
ethical pluralism of being; it can enact the union of substitutionary
joy in the joy of others with substitutionary responsibility."[17]

Without doubt, Ford levels a challenge to Levinas's grave sense of
metaphysics. Whereas Levinas would perhaps be more open to the
emotion of melancholy, the pensive sadness that could ignite prayer
and ethics, Ford shows affinity for the joy of being immersed in a
feast and excited by its reality. Rather than feasting, Levinas's thought
takes us to another world of unveiling the Other's hunger and the
need to share a piece of bread with a stranger. Ford notes the lack
of joy in Levinas's thought and endeavors to think otherwise. In this
regard, Ford seems to have challenged the ethical-metaphysical significance of Levinas's writings.[18]

In another example, following Derrida's argument against
Levinas, Barnes states, "Levinas's overcoming of ontology is dependent on the totalizing ontology it seeks to overcome. . . . Derrida's
critique supports my basic contention that Levinas is locked into
the terms of a phenomenology which risks a certain dualism. The
problem for Levinas is that the one thing that the phenomenological
method leads Husserl to assume — namely the possibility of an intentional consciousness by which the ego intuits the other through the
means of analogical perception is the one thing that Levinas will not

permit." Like Ward, Barnes finds Derrida's argument appealing. Levinas remains within analogical perception; he cannot extricate himself from ontological phenomenology. So Barnes uses terms that Levinas himself would most likely seek to avoid. He describes Levinas's thought as "the presence of the other," "the experience of alterity" and "Levinas's project." In another example, Barnes, with the help of Raimon Pannikar, demonstrates that the "face to face encounter, dialogue...is transcendence," indicating the experience of dialogue and of transcendence.[19]

Barnes's position in relation to Levinas represents a sense of disbelief that ontotheology can be abandoned. The difference between Levinas and Barnes is perhaps that Levinas believes that ontotheology can and must be abandoned for some time; there needs to be a hiatus to venture beyond Being so that we can return to Being with a sense of ethical transcendence. Ontotheology therefore undergoes a conversion into the language of alterity, but there will always be traces of ontotheology and times of falling back into it even to the point of ambiguity—of not knowing whether it is the language of totality or the language of alterity. Levinas remains radical and confronting in his use of the language of alterity; his response places more emphasis on what remains beyond dialogue, experience, and analogies, namely, the absolute passivity of God's work in the innermost part of the self and of in the face of the Other. This suggests, for example, redefining dialogue as taking responsibility for the persecution and humiliation of the Other to the point of expiation—the giving-of-oneself-for-another. This is not just transcendence, but ethical transcendence animated and guided by ethical melancholy and ethical vigilance.

Ward, Purcell, Ford, and Barnes have wrestled with Levinas's understanding of Being and set out to deconstruct it by showing its ontological and analogical relevance. The criticism of these eminent scholars is not intended to dismiss or undermine their approaches, but to create a space in which to reflect upon how theology can be done with Levinas's intentions of going beyond Being. Levinas's complex lexicon brims with new and suggestive terms to help us test out this possibility. Many of the Levinasian terms such as the "there is," trace, diachrony, ambiguity, immemorial past, the face, the Other, otherness, *illeity,* the Saying, testimony, incarnation, God, encounter, passivity, substitution, expiation, sacrifice, gift, conscience, death, prayer, truth, transcendence, and humiliation beg to be employed into discovering a theology of alterity. Altogether, these terms signify two key states of Being and affectivity, which I refer to as ethical melancholy and ethical insomnia or vigilance.

In the body of Levinas's writings, the sense of the horror of existence is always present. Purcell, Ward, Barnes, and Ford do not forget this. Nonetheless, in their attempt to safeguard ontology and analogy in theology, there seems to be something forgotten about the essence or Being of Levinas's thought. This something is affectivity or the emotions underlying Levinas's philosophy. While Levinas does not name melancholy as a key concept, his philosophy oozes such an emotion not just as an infected wound, as it were, but also as a lament of hope in God. Added to this is his notion of insomnia or vigilance. All of Levinas's major terms are animated by the emotions of ethical melancholy and ethical vigilance. With this in mind, how can we ever try to explain away great suffering, trauma, or the murder of loved ones? Levinas's experience of the Shoah and the Nazi horror has more than given impetus to his writings. Facing the raw reality of the cruelties of war and totality, he sets out to wait for the good. And for Levinas, the good remains beyond Being. But in order to understand what Levinas means by "beyond," it is important to step back toward the beginning of his thought and development to the notion of the "there is."

The "there is" remains one of the most enigmatic notions in the whole of Levinas's writings. In *Existence and Existents,* this notion occurs as Levinas contests Heidegger's analysis of Being and nothingness. He reflects: "Is not anxiety over Being—the horror of Being—just as primal as anxiety over death? Is not the fear of Being just as originary as the fear for Being? It is perhaps even more so, for the former may account for the latter. Are not Being and nothingness, which, in Heidegger's philosophy, are equivalent or coordinated, not rather phases of a more general state of existence, which is nowise constituted by nothingness? We shall call it the fact that *there is*" (*EE* 20). Where Heidegger associates anxiety with death, Levinas interprets anxiety as the horror of Being.[20] For him, Being is both a grim and menacing notion. Being-in-the-world is an experience of horror, fear, and anxiety—a frightful occurrence of violent inhumanity. In a fascinating passage, the American psychiatrist, Willard Gaylin, reflecting on the state of nonfeeling in the experience of schizophrenia, seems to come to close to touching upon the unbearable horror of the "there is." He writes:

> Feeling good and feel bad are not necessarily opposites. Both, at least, involve feeling. Any feeling is a reminder of life. The worst "feeling" evidently is non-feeling. This phenomenon is described by schizophrenics and is commonly known as anhedonia. It is a concept I have struggled with and something that I understand only suggestively and faintly. The pain of anhedonia—non-feeling—is so unbearable that schizophrenics are prepared to endure physical pain rather the feeling of deadness. It explains, beyond some psychological meanings of self-punishment, why schizophrenics often burn themselves with cigarettes and lacerate themselves with razors. It is the need to have some feeling! And while pain is as painful to them as it is to us, it is one stage above the death that is anhedonia.[21]

Gaylin's description could give some insight into how Levinas's own vulnerability as a prisoner in a German stalag during World War II made him more sensitive of the horror of the "there is." But for Levinas, his encounter signifies an alterity or otherness to counter the feeling of deadness or more poignantly, "the impossibility of death." Alterity, therefore, marks the polar opposite of the "there is." In this latter state of "existence without existents" (*EE* 57),[22] where even death is impossible, the existent has been subsumed by fear, idolization, and confusion with the good. For Levinas, the "there is" underlines a terrible aspect of Being: an anonymous and depersonalized state of existence.

The experience of Being without existents is literally horrible. In this light, Levinas employs the phrase "there is" to underline Being's impersonal and anonymous (verbal) form, "like in 'it rains or it is warm'" (*EE* 58). The "there is" strips consciousness of its subjectivity and depicts the frightening inability to ascertain the presence or absence of anything. Levinas writes, "a presence of absence, the *there is* is beyond contradiction; it embraces and dominates its contradictory. In this sense being has no outlets" (64). In a metaphorical mode, he aptly depicts the experience of "there is" as the horror of the night (62).

Levinas is particularly indebted to Maurice Blanchot's description of "the neuter," particularly in the novel *Thomas l'Obscure,* where "the night" is markedly similar to Levinas's conception of the "there is":

> I discover my being in the vertiginous abyss where it is not, an absence, an absence where it sets itself like a god, I am not and I endure. An inexorable future stretches forth infinitely for this suppressed being.... Here is the night. The darkness hides nothing. My first perception is that this night is not a provisional absence of light. For from being a possible locus of images, it is composed of all that which is not seen and is not heard, and listening to it, even for a man would know that, if he were not a man, he would hear nothing. In true night, then, the unheard, the invisible are lacking, all those things that make the night habitable. It does not allow anything other than itself to be attributed to it; it is impenetrable.[23]

Appreciating and almost learning from Blanchot, Levinas writes, "*Thomas l'Obscure,* by Maurice Blanchot, opens with the description of the *there is.*... The presence of absence, the night, the dissolution of the subject in the night, the horror of being, the return of being to the heart of every negative movement, the reality of irreality are there admirably expressed" (*EE* 63n1).[24]

In another conversation with Philippe Nemo on the "there is," Levinas states, "It is a theme I have found on Maurice Blanchot, even though he does not speak of the 'there is,' but of the 'neutral' or the 'outside.' He has a number of suggestive formulas: he speaks of the 'hustle-bustle' of being, of its 'clamour,' its 'murmur.' A night in a hotel room where, behind the partition, 'it does not stop stirring'; 'one does not know what they are doing next door.' This is something very close to the 'there is'" (*EI* 50–51).

Levinas's philosophical imagination is no doubt fueled in conversation with Blanchot and with others. He does not just remain stuck in the trauma of his experience in the stalag, but in the midst of his life and reflections, he is able to incorporate meaning in suffering. To a lesser extent, Levinas's notion of the "there is" draws from Lucien Lévy-Bruhl's sense of "participation" (*EE* 60). There is a further aspect to the "there is" in relation to the sacred. Levinas suggests that the experience of the sacred tempts one to cover up one's guilt before the Other.[25] The elemental power of the "there is" can nourish a pretension to a divine perspective, at least to the extent that ambiguity drives our basic fears toward idolization and ethical escapism. John Caruana posits: "Lévinas suspects that the sacred entails a *confusion* of the absolute or divine with the elementary powers of the *il y a*." Later, Caruana reflects: "Rather than having to face up to the consequences of the profound ambiguity of existence—indeterminate being provides us with no signposts that might help to lead a purposeful life—our fears, Lévinas contends, can drive us to establish idols that we imagine can arrest the incessant ambiguity of being."[26]

The act of participating in sacred transcendence—such as experiencing awe, enthusiasm, mystery, rapture, and mystical ecstasy—is an illusional state that results in the depersonalization of the self. For Levinas, these sacred feelings result from the horror of being possessed by the experience of them. For example, Levinas writes, "Horror is somehow a movement which will strip consciousness of its very 'subjectivity.' Not in lulling it into unconsciousness, but in throwing it into an *impersonal vigilance,* a *participation,* in the sense that Lévy-Bruhl gives to the term. What is new in the idea of participation which Lévy-Bruhl introduced to describe an existence where horror is the dominant emotion, is the destruction of categories which had hitherto been used to describe the feelings evoked by 'the sacred.'" The destruction of categories signifies that the subject is depersonalized; there is no private existence. Hence, the horror of participating in the "there is" strips subjectivity inside out. It is not surprising that Levinas describes this state as the "impossibility of death" (*EE* 60, 61). In this terrifying and enthralling state, God is idolized as a direct experience of the sacred. As Caruana succinctly describes it, "the self merges with the exhilarating power of the *il y a*."²⁷ In this context, Levinas's critique of the sacred seems like a scathing attack upon private mystical experience. For example, Caruana points to David Tracy's remark: "I am unpersuaded by Levinas's consistent polemic against the religious phenomena he variously names mysticism, the violence of the sacred, and paganism."²⁸ Properly understood, however, Levinas's critique calls into question any emotional or mystical understanding that would veer toward totalization and evasion of ethical responsibility.

Levinas's critique of the sacred could become a feasible entry point for drawing connections between his writings and those of Saint John of the cross, who also is quite vigilant against the temptations of developing bad habits such as pride and vanity in the journey toward union with God.²⁹ Specifically, Levinas, like Saint John of the Cross, is opposed to mysticism as drunkenness. Despite his mitnaged background, mysticism (or rather spirituality) should not be easily dismissed from a discussion of Levinas, particularly since it often has, as in the case of many works by fathers of the church, a philosophical background. Moreover, Levinas's writings have a hidden mark of affectivity, deepened by ethical metaphysics. Mysticism is not a spiritual gluttony in relation to God, but a deeply spiritual, biblical, theological, and philosophical openness to the world of God in the innermost self. In this view, Levinas's writings on how the word of God in the face of the Other puts the conscience into question and orders responsibility should not be judged as incompatible with the mystical writings of the church fathers and their emphasis on the relational and moral aspects of faith and conduct.³⁰

THE LONELINESS OF THE OTHER'S FACE

Through a variety of experiences, certain moments impact the self so deeply that they stay within the heart and mind for many years, and perhaps always. Whether these moments are terrible or wonderful or even just mundane, there is something about the quality of otherness that makes them so memorable and defining. Such a moment "sticks" to consciousness because somehow it relates to the Other's face. Moments underpinned by broken relationships seem especially long. Moreover, moments that ultimately end in forsaking others sap a lot of energy from the heart, leaving it frozen in fury and resentment. A moment of betrayal can turn into a life turned toward revenge and hatred; that excess of revenge and hatred can, in turn, lead to a moment of waiting for the good. It is here, in the "little good," where we may come to appreciate Levinas's emphasis on the face of the Other.

Consider, for example, the pain of loneliness on the face of the Other. The fall into loneliness creates a deep and painful wound within the heart. Where the fear of being alone grows, despite relating to others during the day, new feelings emerge. If emotions are intense and overwhelming, then being alone may translate into feelings of loneliness. The experience of loneliness defines how clearly each person needs intimate relationships with others in order to find meaning in life. A bold response to loneliness could unfold as the very hunger to relate with the word of God in the hope of fulfillment and well-being. The challenge for the Levinasian self is to reflect: Who then is the Other?

For Levinas, "the Other" (*l'Autrui*) refers to the personal other. It is often characterized in biblical language as the poor one, neighbor, stranger, widow, or orphan. In contrast, "the other" (*l'autre*) refers to all personal others or every neighbor in a more general sense (*OB* 11, 86). Levinas also connects the idea of the Other with that of the face in an enigmatic manner, revealing an important movement of transdescendence, that is to say, the hidden world of God's relation to the self through the face of the Other. Adding more complexity, the face of the Other is signified as a nonphenomenal trace. Further, it can be an effaced trace commanding an approach to the Other. This suggests that a direct encounter with God is rare; as humans we tend to be late to recognize God's voice in our life. Moreover, being preoccupied with our own lives, we face the guilt and tragedy of being late to recognize the Other's face of suffering. Admittedly, it can be quite difficult to discover the extent of the Other's pain and loneliness.

Often, ambiguity shrouds the relation because our perspectives may readily misinterpret the Other's suffering. Levinas writes, "A face as a trace, trace of itself, trace expelled in a trace, does not signify an inde-terminate phenomenon; its ambiguity is not an indetermination of a noema, but an invitation to the fine risk of approach qua approach, to the exposure of one to the other, to the exposure of this exposed-ness, the expression of exposure, saying" (*OB* 94). For Levinas, the face can ambiguously be a trace and be effaced at the same time. This is because the face signifies itself as an absence to indicate that the self has not been present enough in its responsibilities. In other words, the face of the Other is a nonphenomenal phenomenon. It is the locus in which God or the Infinite might be heard. On this matter, Levinas writes, "The Other is not the incarnation of God, but precisely by his face, in which he is disincarnate, is the manifestation of the height in which God is revealed" (*TI* 79).[31] The idea of the face of the Other signifies an extreme state of passivity, which overwhelms theoretical consciousness and evokes the biblical themes of the love of neighbor and being made in the image of God (*GCM* 148–49, 172–73).

In the epiphany of the face of the Other, Levinas discerns three aspects, namely, destitution, facing, and demand. He brings them together in the following condensed statement: "The first thing which is evident in the face of the other is this rectitude of exposure and defenselessness. In his face, the human being is most naked, des-titution itself. And at the same time, he faces. It is a manner in which he is completely alone in his facing us that we measure the violence perpetrated in death. Third moment of the epiphany of the face: it makes a demand on me. The face looks at me and calls me. It lays claim to me" (*IR* 127).

The first aspect of the moment of the face is the poverty of the Other. The face reveals the nakedness and neediness of the human being. Paradoxically, the face is also nonphenomenal. This is strange because it is the naked phenomenon. To understand this ambigu-ity, Levinas points out in the second moment that in the face is the command to be responsible, which can never be represented in consciousness. This suggests that the self encounters a messianic and immemorial dimension of time in which the Other's destitution is exposed. In a third aspect of the epiphany of the face, the self is confronted with a demand to be responsible to and for this Other, in a particularity that transcends the abstractions of Being and the more routine experience of the Other. These three aspects of the face of the Other define a sense of love for our neighbor, with the fear for the Other's death and solitude.

These aspects also illustrate Levinas's attempt to conceive of an inexpressible particularity beyond Hegel's dialectical and speculative reason, Husserl's view of intentionality, and Heidegger's existential and ontological construction of *Dasein*'s facticity.[32] Levinas goes beyond Husserl and Heidegger by appropriating Rosenzweig's criticism of Hegelian totality. His philosophical strategy is, however, markedly different. Instead of following Rosenzweig's graphic and symbolic description of a face that goes beyond Hegelian logic, he utilizes it to develop a nonphenomenality of the face. Hence, the encounter with the face of the Other signifies ethical responsibility that cuts through any attempt to re-present the Other through synchrony and abstract thought. The face of the neighbor enigmatically escapes representation by having a nonform: it is a trace of a past that has never been present (*OB* 97). Such a nonform speaks of the Other's alterity as having a claim on the self even before the encounter occurs. Levinas's idea of alterity is intriguing because it imagines the world otherwise as a place where ethics and prayer unite; his prophetic language resonates as a grave responsibility for the Other.

Alterity, or otherness, refers to the disturbing proximity of the neighbor (*BPW* 80–81). Levinas states, "Proximity is a disturbance of the rememberable time. One can call that apocalyptically the breakup of time. But it is a matter of an effaced but untameable diachrony of nonhistorical, nonsaid time, which cannot be synchronized in a present by memory and historiography, where the present is but the trace of an immemorial past. The obligation aroused by the proximity of the neighbor is not to the measure of the images he gives me;

it concerns me before or otherwise. Such is the sense of the non-phenomenality of the face" (*OB* 89).

The proximity in question has a disturbing effect because it imposes on the self an unheard-of responsibility; the self's consciousness is overwhelmed by the demands placed on it. Levinas describes this overwhelming effect in such dramatic terms as trauma, persecution, and being held hostage (*OB* 112, 117–18, 148–49). The character of the Other, its alterity, is declared in "the Saying". The Saying is an extreme passivity of substituting oneself for another. Such kenotic-like responsibility witnesses to the glory of the Infinite. For what is expressed in such Saying is the ambiguous unheard-of obligation that gives rise to the possibility of ethics (*BPW* 74, 103–05; *OB* 48). As Levinas describes it: "The Saying as testimony precedes all saying. The Saying, before stating a Said—and even the Saying of a Said—is the approach of the other and already testimony" (*BPW* 103). The Saying suggests that the self's relation to the Other constitutes a form of extreme passivity that activity inherent in the *noema* necessarily obscures. On the other hand, because of this passivity, the Other so occupies the self that it is turned inside out and prevented from being self-enclosed as an untroubled being-for-oneself. Accordingly, the saying expresses for the self that radical disinterestedness that is being demanded in its becoming an other-directed subjectivity—being for-the-other (*OB* 49–51).

In another range of reference, alterity is described as the trace of *illeity*. The word *illeity* is a neologism derived from the French third person singular (*il*) and Latin (*ille*), meaning "that one." Levinas describes it as "the *he* [that one] in the depth of the you" (*CPP* 165). This is one of Levinas's more complex and, indeed, complicated, notions because of its large and shifting range of connotations. The referential scope of *illeity* extends on occasion to God, the Infinite, or "the Third" (*le Tiers*), or even to what might be confused with the stirrings of the "there is." In regard to the notion of the Third, Levinas also refers to it as justice, the other Other, the absent Other, and the neighbor (*OB* 148). Eschewing precise definitions, Levinas is not always consistent; he is occupied, for the most part, with the dyad of the self and the Other. His elaboration of the interrelationship within the triad of the self, the Other, and *illeity* receives less attention, which does not make for any simple clarification in this area.

As Levinas's thought progresses, his exposition becomes more idiosyncratic and exponentially more difficult to unravel. His idea of *illeity* might be best interpreted by comparing it with the unnameable Tetragrammaton (YHWH). Just as the Hebrew words *Adonai* (the Lord) or *Ha Shem* (the Name) are spoken in place of the Tetragrammaton, the Saying functions as the encounter with divine alterity. Just as the Tetragrammaton is unpronounceable, so the *illeity* in the face of the Other is nonphenomenal; both remain an enigma that can never be re-presented by thought and thematized as an object (*OB* 12, 147). Perhaps, the word of God is like a vapor, obscuring meaning, understanding, and experience.

Some words turn into open wounds. Words that terrorize, threaten, accuse unjustly, or embody indifference ulcerate time into long moments of pain and hurt. While the body and spirit might endure such wounds for many years, there are also words that can offer hope and healing. These are words of grace that may take the form of a smile, a thank you, or more acutely, the bearing of the Other's pain and heartache. And it is in this latter giving of self that Levinas's notion of God comes to mind. The human person benefits deeply by the love and goodness of others. Taking another self literally to heart, a new word may emerge every day to be testified in the story of the Other. The self, who takes on a calling or the giving of a word of hope and healing, responds to an unthematizable realm of God's kingdom. Given then that the realm is unthematizable, we may suggest that Levinas—in the spirit of Ecclesiastes—portrays God's vapor or obscurity through his ethical metaphysics and talmudic writings.[33] Levinas often speaks of the word of God in the Other's face. Such a word represents the bodiliness of suffering through the suffering of the Other. God's word, lying in the vapor, unveils itself in a way otherwise than our everyday intentions.

Safeguarding the realm or vapor of God's presence from self-interested Being, Levinas reflects on the notion of God through his opposition to Heideggerian philosophy and ontotheology, as well as to theodicy. In *Otherwise than Being,* Levinas begins by pointing to the need of rationally speaking of God without the contamination of Heideggerian ontology and ontotheology. As translator Alphonso Lingis notes, "But to hear a God not contaminated by Being is a human possibility no less important and no less precarious than to bring Being out of the oblivion in which it is said to have fallen in metaphysics and onto-theology" (*OB* xlviii). In another instance, Levinas reflects: "But a question arises: did onto-theo-logy's mistake consist in taking being for God, or rather in taking God for being? ... To contrast [*opposer*] God with onto-theo-logy is to conceive a new mode, a new mode of meaning. And it is from a certain ethical relationship that one may start out on this search" (*GDT* 124–25). For Levinas, God is not reducible to the presence of personal experience and historical thematizations. The temptation would be to fall into a theodicy and employ ontological reasoning to justify and explain belief in God in a world of suffering and evil.[34] Regarding the end of theodicy in "Useless Suffering," Levinas remarks: "The disproportion between suffering and every theodicy was shown at Auschwitz with a glaring, obvious clarity" (*EN* 97). In contrast, one must *hear* God's word in the Other's face through the momentum of ethical subjectivity. The meaning of God is found in the search for God. The searching includes three movements: desire for the Other, perseverance of waiting for God, and substituting for the Other (*GCM* 95). It is motivated by the ideal of holiness. The subject approaches the realm of the holy by thinking "otherwise than Being," which entails giving the Other priority over the self (*EN* 109, 114).

Levinas's talmudic writings place an emphasis on responding to God's obscurity and suffering through prayer, kenosis, justice, mercy, and faithfulness. For example, he writes, "The power of God subordinated to responsibility becomes a moral force.... Man's deeds count before God because they engage others. The fear of God is the fear for others."[35] His philosophical writings show a different emphasis: God is articulated as breaking into thematic, objectifying consciousness through the notion of the Infinite (*BPW* 136). This notion implies an unequaled passivity and trauma when confronted with the impossibility of conceiving of God as an object, a presence, or as Being itself. Ultimately, God is unnamable and beyond conscious thematization (*OB* 162).

For Levinas, the nonintentionality of consciousness gives rise to the transcendence in which the word of God resonates. Consciousness signifies a moral conscience marked by passivity and receptivity to the hunger and fear that is being suffered by the Other (*GCM* 172–73). Such consciousness, in fulfilling responsibility in the face of the Other, demands devotion, passion, and expiation. The word "God" can be pronounced only in a condition of radical alterity. Especially in his later works, Levinas speaks of God as beyond presence, objectivity, and any attempt to explain or prove the divinity. As a result, Levinasian discourse extends into further complexity and ambiguity. For example, Levinas locates God between transcendence and visibility or invisibility. God is transcendent to the point of absence—beyond Being, presence, and immanence; and beyond any distinction between Being and beings (*BPW* 62–63; *OB* 158). Levinas's philosophical writings refer to God in a vocabulary inspired by the biblical themes of justice, mercy, and love for the neighbor; Levinas describes mercy as a word of God inspiring the endurance of the Other's sufferings and persecution. In another context, he will speak of mercy as maternity, that is, the gestation of the Other in the Same (*OB* 75). But basic to his language of alterity is the constant effort to relate the self, the Other, and God in what he terms an encounter.

ENCOUNTER: TURNING ONSELF INSIDE OUT

The pursuit of peace is a journey of healing. Peace and healing come together in a long awaited, heartfelt encounter, which triggers a desire to be responsible for the Other's welfare and life. And where a genuine encounter makes the presence of life's problems and concerns more bearable, an inversion of gifted passivity begins turning the self inside out. The giftedness of human presence begins to emerge as the self becomes an Other in the passivity of the encounter.

This can occur in a variety of situations, even when encountering or meeting a stranger. The stranger may ask a few questions, and this could set off a string of connections to inspire trust and a desire to share a personal story. If the peace of the encounter has the possibility to touch everywhere, then it may not feel so strange to invite a conversation of the heart. This is not only empathy, understanding the Other's experience, but also the substitution and compassion of being in the Other's skin.

The encounter leads us beyond *my* experience and thus into depersonalization. This suggests that Levinas is suspicious of the word "experience" (*expérience*) because of its totalizing connotations and tends not to use it when treating the relation of alterity;[36] his use of the term *expérience* tends to reflect the terrifying aspect of *Erlebnis*. He notes that *expérience* "expresses always a knowledge of which the I is master," and concedes, "I am very cautious with this word. Experience is knowledge" (*IR* 97, 136). In *Existence and Existents*, Levinas speaks about insomnia as manifesting a quality of the "there is" because it pertains to the "experience of being an object" and as an "experience of depersonalization" (*EE* 66). In this sense, insomnia is almost prior to experience, for it is being gripped by the nothing or "of being" exposed by the very eternity of Being. Later, Levinas develops this concept ethically in terms of disinterestedness, indicating hypostasis, the realm in which subjectivity coincides with ethics (*BPW* 133).

Another way Levinas places limits on the notion of experience is in regard to the unthematizable and Infinite realm of God. He writes, "My responsibility for the other is precisely this relation with an unthematizable Infinity. It is neither the experience of Infinity nor proof of it: it *testifies* to Infinity. This *testimony* is not appended to a subjective experience in order to proclaim the ontological conjuncture disclosed to the subject. This testimony belongs to the very glory of the Infinite" (*BPW* 103). Levinas suggests that there can be no experience or knowledge of Infinity, but only the testimony of answering to the Infinite's prophetic call within: "Witness is humility and admission; it is made before all theology; it is kerygma and prayer, glorification and recognition" (*OB* 149). The sense of Infinity, unlike experience, speaks of the desire for the good and the overflowing of the Other in one's consciousness. It is manifest in the desire to hear the word of God in the Other's face. Hence, experience is the mode of Being that reduces the Other to the Same.

The notion of encounter is further illuminated when placed in a larger context of terms that includes approach, enigma, signification, proximity and nonindifference. Levinas tends to use these terms in apposition. While this enriches the meaning of encounter, it does not make for an easy thematization of their respective meanings (*OB* 139).

The term "approach" signifies being obsessed with responsibility for the Other. It connotes a situation in which one is inspired by the Infinite to sacrifice for the Other in a way that does not reduce the Other to lived experience. Levinas states, "I approach the infinite insofar as I forget myself from my neighbor who looks at me; I forget myself only in breaking the undephasable simultaneity of representation, in existing beyond my death. I approach the infinite by sacrificing myself. Sacrifice is the norm and the criterion of the approach" (*BPW* 76).[37]

The sense of "enigma" is perhaps more specific in that it denotes moral responsibility beyond all cognition. It identifies the effaced trace of God as the nonphenomenal way in which the Other makes the self responsible: "The enigma, the intervention of meaning which disturbs phenomena but is quite ready to withdraw like an undesirable stranger, unless one harkens to those footsteps that depart, is transcendence itself, the proximity of the Other as Other" (*BPW* 74). Similarly, the Levinasian term "signification" evidences the quality of nonphenomenality, bespeaking the relation to the Other. But the meaning of this term is further complicated because of its association with ideas such as anarchy (nonbeginning) and infinity. In short, the meaning of signification can be condensed as a sense of our being ordained from a time without beginning to an endless responsibility. For example, Levinas reflects: "Signification is the contradictory trope of the-one-for-the-other. The-one-for-the-other is not a lack of intuition, but the surplus of responsibility. My responsibility for the other is the *for* of the relationship, the very signifying of signification, which signifies in saying before showing itself in the said" (*OB* 100). The "said" [*le dit*] here refers to the experience of synchrony, onto- logical language, or the manifestation of Being. Levinas also speaks of the "unsaid" [*dédit*] in the sense of denying all that should be said about saying.[38]

At the risk of straining further an already overstretched rhetoric, we could suggest that "proximity" is the signifyingness of significa- tion, inherent in the very *for* of the relationship with the Other (*OB* 83, 100). More simply, proximity signifies that there is never enough responsibility. For example, in the relationship with the Other, prox- imity signifies that there is not just one Other involved in the relation, but a multitude of Others. It connotes the presence of "the Third Party" in the relation with the Other in a world of intersubjectiv- ity, as Levinas implies: "Proximity is quite distinct from every other relationship, and has to be conceived as a responsibility for the other; it might be called humanity, or subjectivity, or self" (46). Related to this indeterminate intersubjective range of others is the term "non- indifference," which indicates that the self's responsibility is unique and undeclineable: "The non-indifference to the other as other and as neighbor in which I exist is something beyond any commitment in the voluntary sense of the term, for it extends into my very bearing as an entity, to the point of substitution" (138).

Stepping into Levinas's notion of encounter, there are still fur- ther group of terms that require comment. Encounter signifies being exposed to "the death of the Other," which produces the imperative of responsibility over an indifferent state of personal freedom. It calls for the priority of being-*for*-the-Other in the form of nonindiffer- ence and love. In his lecture, "Bloch: Toward a Conclusion," Levinas states, "We encounter death on the face of the other." Several years later he reflects, "I sometimes ask myself whether the idea of the straight line — the shortest distance between two points — is not orig- inally the line according to which the face that I encounter is exposed to death" (*GDT* 105; *IR* 65, 127).

Through "inversion of the self," encounter requires that the egoistic self be turned inside out to become an authentically ethical self. In what amounts to a moral conversion, the encounter with the Other's face entails a "radical turnabout." Levinas suggests: "This human inversion of the in-itself and the for-itself (of 'every man for himself') into an ethical self, into a priority of the for-the-other—this replacement of the for-itself of ontological persistence by an *I* henceforth unique certainly, but unique because of its chosenness for a responsibility for the other man—inescapable and non-transferable, this radical turnabout would take place in what I call an encounter with the face of the other" (*EN* 202).[39] The inversion is certainly dramatic. In responsibility, the I cannot escape as it radically develops an acute sensitivity for the Other.

With regard to the relation with God, Levinas writes, "The direct encounter with God, *this* is a Christian concept. As Jews, we are always a threesome: I and you and the Third who is in our midst. And only as a Third does He reveal Himself."[40] While Christian theology can question Levinas's statement in this context, it is clear that he considers divine revelation to occur only in a consciousness that is turned inside out in responsibility for all others in love and justice. Finally, encounter is associated with "mercy." One must take responsibility for the Other's suffering. Levinas describes this mercy as "a word of God," "an eschatology without hope for oneself," or "a theology without theodicy" (*IR* 133, 193–94, 146). By taking all these diverse senses together, we can understand encounter as the self's state of passivity and alterity before the Other.

To appreciate Levinas's notion of encounter invites a learning process not only of these various associated terms, but specifically of our everyday habits (being) so that we might transform them into a habitus or praxis of being-for-the-Other. Typically, the self may settle into the enjoyment of patterns along the journey of life, and when a path of alterity comes to mind, a struggle may emerge as to whether to take the risk or not. The attitudes of melancholy and vigilance may persuade the self to be thrown into the new phase of life, particularly if there is something of God's word resonating. In effect, there is a whole momentum occurring. The new path toward alterity will give a number of new burdens and challenges; it will become a difficult freedom demanding a difficult devotion for the Other. In messianic terms, this is the enigmatic process of rehabituating to God's will flowing into one's life. And where rehabituation becomes transfiguration and transformation, this does not mean that the old ways have been conquered or forgotten. Rather, a new maturity has settled within the self, flowing naturally out of the heart and mind toward creative possibilities, in the hope of encountering God in the exposure to the Other's face of loneliness and suffering.

Levinas's philosophy testifies to the ever-present exposure of God to human suffering: God is near to the broken hearted (Ps. 34:18). To accept this reality involves the deepening of pain and bearing forth of compassion. The difficult freedom and adoration of encountering the Other's broken heart and spirit crushed by the weight of adversity and suffering invites the exposure or bodiliness of being wounded by the wounds of the Other. This opens an affective state of melancholy and vigilance for the Other. The sense of exposure to the Other's poverty and destitution unveils the need for vulnerability. The encounter with another's tragedy is defining for the human condition because it indicates that the self is not all powerful and in control but affected by the weakness of the Other's condition and emotional state. To have the courage to accept the fragility of the human condition allows one to question the ambitions of the self-interested ego. And it is here, in the exposure to the Other's hemorrhaging and brokenness, that the weight of a crushed spirit awakes consciousness.

Levinas's phenomenology of exposure depicts a state of consciousness profoundly affected by the wounds, outrage, and insult suffered by the Other. In this sense, it implies a hyperbolic passivity or vulnerability to the Other. As Levinas explains it, "Here exposure has a sense radically different from thematization. The one is exposed to the other as a skin is exposed to what wounds it, as a cheek is offered to the smiter." Such exposure is the cause and result of an acute responsibility. Levinas graphically describes it as a hemorrhaging for the Other (*OB* 49, 74). This kind of exposure also has erotic overtones.

Though Levinas disassociates love from eros, he nonetheless employs a number of erotic ideas and images in his elaboration of the meaning of exposure (*EN* 113).

Levinas's ethically modulated idea of exposure to the Other is not above using a wide range of images. For example, Levinas makes a linguistic and theological connection of his notion of maternity to the Hebrew terms mercy (*rakhamim*) and uterus (*rekhem*), respectively. He recognizes that *rekhem* is the origin of the word *rakhamim*. It is therefore not surprising that he suggests, "*Rakhamim* is the relation of the uterus to the *other,* whose gestation takes place within it. *Rakhamim* is maternity itself. God as merciful is God defined by maternity."[41] Here, displaying a talmudic influence, Levinas brings together the ideas and images of mercy and maternity, but paradoxically in a context that stresses love as distinct from eros. He clarifies this by observing, "For the encounter with the face I still reserve another word: *miséricorde,* mercy, when one assumes responsibility for the suffering of the other. This appears naturally as the phenomenon of love" (*IR* 145–46). The encounter with the Other remains a painful and difficult condition. When love is related to such all-exacting alterity, there is little room for imaging love as an experience of joy.

When eros is made to surrender so completely to ethical intersubjectivity, an outer limit of self-renunciation is presumed: the personal experiences of joy, desire, and personal taste or disposition cannot be primary in the face of the gravity of the suffering, hunger, and loneliness of the Other (*CPP* 136). Such an exposure to the Other's destitution and the necessity of bearing of the Other's faults results in a divine comedy, a grave drama whereby "the laughter sticks to one's throat when the neighbor approaches—that is, when his face, or his forsakenness, draws near." In this ironic, role-reversing plot of ethical existence, God's transcendence is shown in the self's responsibility for the Other. The ethical self can no longer refer to God through objectivity, presence, and Being, but through the self's passivity toward the Other (166).

Passivity is not a concept to be taken lightly. It is a grave reality that cannot ultimately be understood by ideas or even personal experience. Passivity toward the Other speaks of the exposure of the innermost self to the personal and demanding word of God. Passivity is perhaps better understood as moments of exposure to God's word in the face of the Other. And even a present moment is not enough to contain God's word. Encountering the face of the Other unveils the diachrony of time; the deeper the facing, the more any concept of the Other will fail to capture and thematize its meaning. Perhaps this helps to explain why Levinas employs and interconnects many notions to explain the enigma of passivity. We will attempt a brief remark, then, on such notions as the hither side, recurrence, the individuation of the ego, openness, and the good beyond Being.

The notion of the hither side suggests the contraction of the uncaring ego as it is affected by the new demands it encounters. The recurrence of the self signifies the change that occurs as one moves from a violent sense of the Other to an expiatory stance. Through individuation, the self in this expiatory relationship signifies a certain fusion of identity between the self and the suffering reality of the Other. Levinas cryptically states, "I am an Other." This new identity is described as openness. In its receptivity or passivity to the Other, the imperialistic, self-enclosed identity of the ego is broken open (*OB* 195, 11, 118, 119). Openness and compassionate receptivity are in the thrall of the good beyond Being. The good brings out a dislocated passivity in the ego formerly habituated to its command of objects in time and space. The good is beyond Being, coming out of an immemorial past that can be invoked as God (*CPP* 136). Any uncritical technique associated with an ontological style of analogical thought is called into question. The analogy of Being can represent neither God nor humanity where it does not, for example, have the analogy of faith at its foundation. God's Being cannot be reduced to anonymous experience as the place and time of the logos, the discourse of reason. If the word "God" is to be pronounced, then it is to be risked in substitution for the Other to the point of expiation

(*OB* 156, 162). It is along these lines that von Balthasar makes a good dialogue partner with Levinas

Von Balthasar situates Christ, the analogy of Being, in disinterestedness. Von Balthasar's *analogia entis* christology dramatically portrays the Trinitarian otherness and passivity of Christ in the paschal mystery. We can see then that the notions of alterity and passivity become instrumental to develop the dialogue. Both these terms lead us toward a number of other key Levinasian terms: fear, fission, trauma, diachrony, anarchy, and persecution (*GCM* 78, 175; *OB* 111–12, 147–49, 154). Each of these and all of them together refer to the overwhelming passivity in which the self bears witness to God. They intensify the meaning of the *illeity* of God's passing and provide a fertile horizon to study the paschal mystery (*OB* 158).

Specifically, Levinas speaks of a fear before the face of the Other (*GCM* 175). In this regard, fear is not a lived experience, for it exceeds consciousness by way of the nonphenomenality of the Other's face. Levinas considers that fear is accompanied by responsibility for the Other. He goes as far as saying that fear is a responsibility for the Other's death. Hence, fearing for the Other signifies that the self's personal experience and intentions are not the primary concern: fear is not simply the objectification of *my* feeling frightened or sad.

Through fear in the Levinasian sense, the face of the Other provokes a radical turnabout. The subject is turned inside out, moving from the self-enclosure of being in-oneself and for-oneself into a relational state of being for-the-other (*EN* 202). This site of ethical transcendence discloses a surplus of meaning in the way that it overwhelms and overflows consciousness. Here, Levinas refers to Descartes's third meditation, which speaks of glory overflowing the present in the thought of God (*OB* 146). In this fear for another in the face of the Other, a fear that touches on reverence and awe, the word God takes on a relational meaning. Levinas can say that this is the fear in which we have the birth of the logos, the very discourse that effaces presence and signifies consciousness as passivity and moral conscience (*GCM* 175–76).

Even though Levinasian "fission" and "trauma" tend to receive less attention than "fear," they are richly suggestive. In one instance,

Levinas combines both, speaking of "the trauma of a fission of one-self [that has] come to pass in a venture risked with God or through God" (*GCM* 78). Elsewhere, he identifies fission as an inward secrecy, related to the description of *illeity,* or the ways in which God commands the self to testify to the divine glory. Fission also enables the possibility for the *noesis* to be articulated without attachment to the *noema,* and so gives rise to ethical subjectivity that looks to the Other beyond the scope of experience. This fission of the self leads to trauma. The self is taken by surprise by the face of the Other. It begins to feel the force of an "unheard-of obligation," "ambivalence," and the "possibility of inspiration" (*OB* 146–48).

Levinas describes the trauma of encountering the trace of *illeity* as "a diachronic ambivalence." The diachrony at work here is related to the awakening to responsibility in a time beyond experience (*OB* 149, 155). The ambivalence resides in being ordered to a responsibility for the Other in a way that can never be represented. The ambivalence is intensified in Levinasian usage since he describes the time of diachrony as a past that is not present, and also as a past without origin. Furthermore, Levinas occasionally connects diachrony, or the past without origin, with "anarchy," literally, the "unoriginated." In perhaps more manageable language, Levinas describes diachrony as the self's responsibility for others and as transcendence (*BPW* 119). In contrast, the idea of anarchy emphasizes the preoriginality of diachrony. Levinas explains that anarchy implies the bond between the subject and the good, identifying the good beyond Being and constituting ethical transcendence (*CPP* 136–37). Levinas thus uses the idea of anarchy to emphasize that transcendence cannot be reduced to the event of Being and intentional consciousness but is signified through an immemorial past.

A further complexity arises when Levinas describes anarchy as persecution or obsession. An inversion of consciousness from intentionality to passivity occurs in this anarchy and produces an ethical state of persecution: it is "being called into question prior to questioning, responsibility over and beyond the logos of response. It is as though persecution by another were at the bottom of solidarity with another." To be called into question beyond the logos of response is to find that the self is stretched to the limits of responsibility. Levinas considers persecution as obsessive in that, through an infinite passion of responsibility, the passivity of the self turns into expiation. In all this extreme language, Levinas is attempting to find a language adequate to an ethics responsive to the good beyond Being. In short, persecution is the passivity of the self. Because the self is liberated from any project of mastery on the part of itself or others, it has an openness to what is otherwise than Being, namely, the possibility of sacrificing for the Other (*OB* 101, 102, 112–15).

Taken together, these modalities of passivity signify an ethical transformation overwhelming consciousness and turning it inside out. There is a point of particular reference to Christian theology in this depiction of passivity. Levinas speaks of the self as a gift to the Other, writing: "Hospitality, the one-for-the-other in the ego, delivers it more passively than any passivity from links in a causal chain. Being torn from oneself for another in giving to the other the bread from one's mouth is being able to give up one's soul for another." The self-gift is marked with an unthematizable sign of God's trace (*illeity*) (*OB* 79, 147, 151). The very possibility of giving (transascendence) signifies an unheard of command that overwhelms and traumatizes consciousness (transdescendence). Here, by way of a double movement of alterity — "the forward, rising transascendence" of responsibility for the Other and the "backward, descending transdescendence"[42] of encountering the trace of God in the innermost depths of the self—the word "God" is heard. In the same way, hearing the word of God depends on the extent that the self witnesses to it as an incarnate in otherness. To give up one's soul for another must coincide with sacrifice for another. And in such ethical transcendence and double movement of alterity, the self reduces the tendency of consciousness to betray the divine word.

Interestingly, in conversation with Roger Burggraeve, Levinas revealed that most Christian theologians in their use of his sense of radical alterity tend to favor focusing on the sense of ethical transcendence as transascendence while not giving due attention to the importance of the downward movement or interior ethical effect of transdescendence, whereby the face of other awakens the innermost depths of the self to hear the word of God. Does this then suggest that theologians favor alterity over passivity? The effect of transdescendence emphasizes Levinas's articulation of passivity. For instance, transdescendence is very much at play in the Levinasian idea of incarnation, identifying the extent to which the self is exposed to the sufferings and failures of the Other. It expresses the impossibility of escaping responsibility for the Other in the concrete (*BPW* 89) and deals with the flesh and blood reality of the Other and oneself or, as Levinas would say, it is "being-in-one's-skin, having-the-other-in-one's skin" (*OB* 115). To this degree, incarnation is a mode of that substitution by which the self inverts its identity and moves from being for-itself to being for-others. Incarnation, then, is one among the many terms that feed into Levinasian understanding of passivity.

Another example of transdescendence in Levinas relates to the way he speaks of the need to have a "bad conscience" (*GCM* 174–75). For Heidegger, the voice of conscience stirs to pronounce, "Guilty!" It overwhelms *Dasein* with the fact of its bad conscience, of its "Being-evil." This voice of conscience is associated with the experience of primordial truth. Because authentic *Dasein* desires to have a conscience, this suggests its desire to discover itself in the truth of its Being-in-the-world.[43] In contrast, Levinas conceives of conscience by way of ethics. For him, a bad conscience is not the condition or result of the quest for the meaning of Being in general; nor does it imply any exposure to truth. He argues that a bad conscience lies at the heart of sociality, for it is a responsibility preceding all intentionality (174–75). Facing the limits of the self-interest, the Levinasian self can unmask its terrible eternity to create a paradise out of totality. So where the self acknowledges and confesses its lack of the good, the hunger for the good arises. Facing the truth of the Other in humility marks what Christian theology would characterize as transfiguration and transformation, or in Levinasian terms, transdescendence. In this light, we can recognize that the conscience is not too far from a sense of ethics as prayer.

Prayer: Assuaging the Suffering of God

Emotive states, like lament and melancholy, offer opportunities to awaken prayer. Where melancholy and pain come together, a new space in consciousness is forged. Repressed issues about family, work, relationships, dreams, failures, and hopes could well use this new space as a home. Being in touch thoughtfully with pain and sadness is also a way to begin exploring the realm of prayer. Levinas does this ethically with a touch of melancholy. The feeling of melancholy, because of terrible pains of meaninglessness, nausea, anxiety, or even depression, could feel like a crisis. And here, in the painful and dark reaches of the self's encounter with absurdity and fear, the melancholy that falls into crisis is also a starting point and opportunity for prayer to emerge. When the self is left bereft of hope and vision for the future, the time for lament has come to reshape the self into conversation with the spirit.

The human spirit, bedeviled by curses and enriched by blessings, is helped by the compass of intimacy with God. Beyond a literal interpretation of the Bible, there are a multitude of theologies or ways to find a rational way to speak of and be with God. And it is such openness to the biblical and theological imagination that Levinas develops a compass to lead us to the face of the Other and the word of God. Blessing may very well be born from the experience of suffering and excess of evil seeking us out. However, given the ambiguity and difficulty of trying to discern the difference between a blessing and a curse, the relation with God becomes absolutely personal in the desire to assuage the suffering of God and others.

Levinas acknowledges, "Prayer is one of the most difficult subjects for a philosopher, as it is for a believer" (*DF* 269). He does not disappoint when he suggests in his philosophical writings that prayer in the form of testimony, kerygma, confession, and humility might well represent the very limit of recurrence.[44] Also, in an audacious talmudic reflection, Levinas wonders whether intentionality, distinguished from a thematizing and objectivizing type of intentionality, could be derived from prayer. He reflects on this prayerful intentionality as the search for an inchoate reference to an unnamable God (*BV* 215–16). This discourse has some similarity to the state of being affected by the trace of *illeity*. In a reflection on prayer found in both his philosophical and talmudic writings,[45] Levinas implies that the trace of *illeity* affects the self. He writes:

> When you are truly in distress, you can mention it in prayer. But are you going to eliminate in this manner a suffering that wipes away sins in expiating them. If you want to escape your own suffering, how will you expiate your own wrongdoings? The question is more complex. In our suffering God suffers with us. Doesn't the Psalmist say (Ps. 91:15): "I am with him in distress"? It is God who suffers most in human suffering. The *I* who suffers prays for the suffering of God, who suffers by the sin of man and the painful expiation for sin. A kenosis of God! Prayer, altogether, is not for oneself. (*AT* 182)

Levinas speaks of prayer together with God's suffering to stress that prayer is not for oneself. Levinas admits that he is doing theology. Following the above-cited passage, he claims, "I have presented you with the most rigorous of theological conceptions" (*AT* 182). Given his theological aside in this instance, perhaps the talmudic understanding of the relation between God and the world is only a step removed from his philosophical concerns. If "it is God who suffers most in human suffering," how God might communicate such meaning? The answer, it seems, is that the suffering of God is to be found in discovering the meaning of suffering by way of radical passivity of the self in the face of the Other, that is, in personal relation.

The self is thus ordered (and ordained) into a kenotic, if not prayerful, life. In French, the term "ordered" [*ordonné*] implies a double meaning of being ordered and ordained by the Other's otherness to be responsible, as Levinas relates: "The word *ordonné* in French means both having received orders and having been consecrated. It is in this sense that I can say that consciousness, subjectivity, no longer have first place in their relationship to the other" (*EN* 111). So when the suffering of the Other so intimately involves the self, the

"I" is living witness to being-for-the-Other (*BPW* 146). This kenotic aspect of prayer suggests a kind of conformity to the God who atones and suffers. But basically prayer is understood as related to a liturgy of responsibility. It is one aspect of the spiritually disciplined praxis through which the sufferings of the Other are acknowledged as sacred (*DF* xiv). Levinas points in this direction when he writes:

> At the same time there is, in this being closed up within oneself of suffering, the sigh or the cry which is already a search for alterity: I would even say, but many precautions would be necessary here, that it is the first prayer. It is this first prayer that the spiritual really begins. And by saying prayer, evidently I anticipate the word *God*. But I think this exteriority of which I speak, this intending of the face...is always at once the approach of the face and a hearkening to the voice of God. (*IR* 57)

This passage comes from a reflection titled, "Useless Suffering." Though suffering is likened to the lived experience of color, sound, and contact, it transcends any ordinary mode of consciousness. Suffering results from the radical passivity that receptivity to the Other demands. Levinas occasionally suggests that suffering is the originating condition or locus in which passivity is realized. In this condition of suffering, the self is held accountable; it feels the painful question as to whether suffering is for nothing. "Useless suffering" becomes productive precisely as suffering for the Other's pointless suffering. This kind of comprehensive compassion "opens suffering to the ethical perspective of the inter-human." From this perspective, the passivity of consciousness ceases to be purely subjective and becomes truly intersubjective and interpersonal. It is not the result of an imposed ontological theodicy or a generalized notion of suffering, but is entirely governed by the relationship of the self in its openness to the approach of the actual suffering Other. The ethical relation goes beyond calculation and expectation of reciprocity (*EN* 91–101). In this regard, the value of prayer and liturgy can never be reduced to the spiritual cultivation of oneself alone (*AT* 181). This suggests that the center of the interhuman relation is meant to have a sense (or spirituality) of peace, justice, and mercy.

HAVING A SENSE: BLOWING EMBERS UPON THE HEART

The tragedy of meaning is to stumble upon it too late. In moving toward the meaning of being human, the death of another may come to mind. The implication is that the Other's death has an infinite amount of meaning; any attempt to thematize it will fall short. To reflect upon death is perhaps like stumbling upon something valuable and enduring. There is no illusion to death; its meaning is frank and compelling. The attempt to draw meaning from the death of another becomes a stumbling block, as it were, because the experience of death itself cannot be contained by consciousness. Death leaves the self in a debt of responsibility, owing at least prayer and concern for the Other. In a paradoxical sense, when meaning fades into death, a radical turnabout of the way the self approaches meaning could eventuate. Where the self has relied on its habitual thinking and imaginative processes for meaning, and faced the dead end of its own plans, possibilities and desires, a thinking otherwise might emerge: having a sense.

Blowing embers upon the heart, so to speak, Levinas seeks to overcome the difficulty of describing experience that defies objectivity and thematic consciousness. Accordingly, he refers to the example of love by elaborating on the notion of "having a sense."[46] This has some similarities to a broader philosophical and theological tradition on "affective" or "connatural knowledge," which gives primacy to love over conceptual or rational cognition.[47] Levinas does not, of course, rely on the metaphysical or psychological framework that this tradition assumes. He writes, "But 'to have a sense' does not mean the same as 'to represent.' The act of love has a sense, but this does not mean that it includes a representation of the object loved together with a purely *subjective* feeling which has no sense and which accompanies the representation. The characteristic of the loved object is precisely to be given in a love intention, an intention which is irreducible to a purely theoretical representation."[48]

This passage, coming from Levinas's earliest writings, is remarkable not only for his understanding of the affectivity involved in our knowledge of the Other, but also in its notable similarity to those strands of sapiential or mystical affectivity that are found in the scholastic tradition and in its current developments. For Levinas, however, this affectivity enters precisely into his descriptions of ethical consciousness, as it relates to the Other beyond any abstract form of representation. Experiences such as love cannot be contained in egoistic or inner subjective consciousness. In love, consciousness transcends itself beyond the range of intellectual, moral, or culturally conditioned objectification. In short, by distinguishing representation from "having a sense," Levinas indicates his concrete ethical concern to transcend purely theoretical analysis. He subsequently moves more consistently beyond both Husserlian phenomenology and Heideggerian fundamental ontology into the realm of alterity. His "having a sense" is set in contrast to any presumption of apprehending Being or, indeed, infantile emotionalism. The following dense passage illustrates this point:

> But the face, wholly open, can at the same time be in itself because it is in the trace of illeity. Illeity is the origin of the alterity of being in which the *in itself* of objectivity participates while also betraying it.
>
> The God who passed is not the model of which the face would be an image. To be in the image of God does not mean to be an icon of God but to find oneself in his trace. The revealed God of our Judeo-Christian spirituality maintains all the infinity of his absence, which is the personal "order" itself. He shows himself only by his trace, as is said in Exodus 33. To go toward Him is not to follow this trace, which is not a sign; it is through this illeity, situated beyond the calculations and reciprocities of economy and of the world, that being has a sense. A sense which is not a finality. (*BPW* 64)

These words illustrate, first of all, Levinas's postphenomenological inversion of Husserl's thought. Consciousness of something is inverted into an absolute passivity in the face of the Other. The passage also illustrates his departure from Heidegger; the subject is not defined by care for itself and its finite thinking no longer simply refers to the infinite. In Levinas's ethical emphasis, the Other's approach inverts the ego. The finitude of being for-oneself is turned inside out toward the infinity of being for-the-other. Levinas further posits that face can be in itself, in a fragile objectivity, because of the trace of *illeity*. However, the "in itself" of objectivity betrays alterity by arresting the movement of openness to the Other, due to the tendency to abstract and thematize. There is a recurrent tension within the self between ethical and self-referential behavior.

Later, in *Otherwise than Being*, Levinas develops the idea of "in itself" by employing the German terms, *an sich* and *in sich*, in reference to the self-recurrent character of the self, which authentically desires to remain on the hither side of the moral responsibility, exceeding all calculation (*OB* 108). For Levinas, the "in itself" of the self can be fully realized only in the life of disinterestedness. Levinas allows, "the face, wholly open, can at the same time be in itself because it is in the trace of illeity" (*BPW* 64). The trace helps to clarify: the trace of *illeity* in the Other's face disturbs the self's consciousness to the point where the self becomes aware of the truth that it is more fully itself when it is for-the-other. This is a more ethical and metaphysical reconstruction of the "in itself" as "being 'turned' to another" or "being turned inside out" (*OB* 49).

Levinas's later writings confirm that the trace of *illeity* is both unrepresentable and nonthematizable. The idea of *illeity* provides Levinas with a way to search for the meaning of Being by "having a sense" (a nonthematizable consciousness). The trace of *illeity* awakens a sense of God in Being, but without permitting God's divinity to be reduced to an objectification or any representable image. Levinas states later in *Otherwise than Being* that the trace of *illeity* is not a sign. He means that the self itself becomes a sign, testifying to having been provoked into responsibility by *illeity* (*OB* 150, 162, 49, 144–51).

According to Levinas, *illeity* is "situated beyond the calculations and reciprocities of economy and of the world" (*BPW* 64). This indicates a nonphenomenal link between the ethical self, the Other, and *illeity:* the ethical self signals responsibility for the Other without disclosing and proving anything about the trace of *illeity* (God's trace). The self can do this because it has a sense in Being that implies no finality. The nonfinality is necessary because the trace of *illeity* has imposed on the self a life of bearing testimony, but in a way that is absolutely detached from comprehending the meaning and invoking—or controlling—it as an ongoing, conscious presence. In an indirect (beyond essence) manner, God directs the self to be responsible, and to be a sign of alliance with the Other.[49]

In the resulting disinterestedness, the synchrony of Being and peace takes form (*BPW* 123). As consciousness goes toward something other there occurs a proximity with the Third in a pacific relationship of justice with others:

> It is on the basis of proximity that being takes on its just meaning. In the indirect ways of illeity, in the anarchical provocation which ordains me to the other, is imposed the way which leads to thematization and becoming conscious. Becoming conscious is motivated by the presence of the third alongside the neighbor approached. The third is also approached; and the relationship between the neighbor and the third cannot be indifferent to me when I approach. There must be justice among incomparable ones.... In this disinterestedness—when, as a responsibility for the other, it is also a responsibility for the third—the justice that compares, assembles, and conceives, the synchrony of being and peace, takes form. (*OB* 16; cf. *BPW* 122–23)

It seems that Levinas has found a way for Being to take on a just meaning without implying that alterity is a function of Being. It is only through the indirect ways of *illeity* that Being must be understood. In other words, although the "otherwise than Being" (alterity) is outside the ontological order, it is understood, nonetheless, as in Being (*OB* 16). The ideas of 'in Being' and 'beyond Being' are not separable, even if ambiguity is an inevitable outcome. If justice is to come to expression, some thematization and intentional forms of consciousness are required.

In *Otherwise than Being*, Levinas states that proximity, the very refusal of presence, converts "into my presence as present, that is, as a hostage delivered over as a gift to the other." This would seem to suggest that the gift has to be betrayed by presence in order to be given. However, despite the betrayal or the inevitability of thematization and consciousness, the gift contains within it the trace of the passing of God (*illeity*). But there is a further complication. What delivers the gift over to presence and thematization is the interruption of the third party or the absent other (who is also a neighbor of the Other) (*OB* 150–51, 157).

The Third, as Levinas understands it, signifies three key phenomenological moments of ethical transcendence. The Third is concretely manifested in suffering and the cry for justice (*CPP* 39; *OB* 158). The Third also imposes limits upon the extent to which self is responsible. Although responsibility is never mitigated, the self cannot ever fulfill its responsibilities. Moreover, the Third is the very fact of consciousness, for it demands that the self measure and know its cry for justice (*OB* 158). As a result, the Third gives rise to a dialectical relationship between justice and totality, even if the totality must be finally transcended.[50]

Responsibility for the Third or ethical transcendence initiates the possibility for the synchrony of Being and peace to take form. In other words, the presence of the Third enters consciousness to inspire the rationality of peace. So the self's recognition of the Third, inspired by *illeity* in the face of the Other, produces the work of justice. Such work of justice signifies the foundation of consciousness, the help of God, and the interruption of Being. To have a sense in Being signifies an ambiguous state of otherwise than Being (disinterestedness). This suggests that the knowledge of Being is not found in Being but through being otherwise, responsibly establishing justice and peace for others. To have a sense in Being acknowledges "the very possibility of gift...the subversion of essence into substitution" (*OB* 160, 162). Levinas dramatizes the ambiguity of life; his philosophy is a way to respond to find a rational meaning in ambiguity. On the hither side of ambiguity, the penetrating arrows of ethical metaphysical truth aim to seek out the self like a thief in the night.

Phenomenological and existential truth can be born out of deep reflection and the discovery of meaning and can be uncovered further by goodness or even by way of the tragic experiences of persecution and humiliation. At some level, truth demands the bodiliness of suffering for or with others, even to the point of forgiveness and expiation. Truth may well begin practically through rehabituation or individuation. Reflecting on change and transformation is no doubt easier than living it out. But having a strategy for change and an openness to the mystery of God could produce enough good will and grace to persevere toward truth in the practice of giving up some certain habits and desires to make space for the Other, the world, and God. One never knows, but in the depths of such a new space of relationality, the word of God might unveil a moment of truth.

In both Levinas's talmudic and philosophical writings, truth is articulated in connection with the ideas of persecution and humiliation, goodness, and transcendence. Significantly for the conversation between Levinas and von Balthasar, truth is never related to the "borrowed light" of beauty (*TI* 74; *BPW* 8, 100). For Levinas, the reason for this is clear: beauty results in idolization, and philosophy certainly does not begin in aesthetics. By way of contrast, Levinas asks, "But isn't what we really call the truth determined by the 'for-the-other,' which means goodness?" (*IR* 263). The way of truth is found in humiliation and persecution, within God's covenantal relation with those on the margins of society. He speaks of a "persecuted truth" in a manner far from the idea of truth as unconcealedness or as a presence in consciousness. The transcendent impact of truth is felt by being exposed to the destitution of the Other. It is found in the trace or proximity of God in the Other's face. In his every move, Levinas wishes to protect God's transcendence from ontotheological conceptions.

For Levinas, truth is neither a discovery nor a transcendental quality of Being (*BPW* 100). It is located in the transcendence of ethics. This is to say that ethical transcendence cannot be explained in consciousness, but has already effaced or withdrawn from it. It is found rather in persecution and humiliation. Levinas's notion of a persecuted truth overcomes the problem of reductive immanence and refuses to play "the game of unveiling." Rather, truth is found only by dwelling with the contrite and humble (Isa. 57:15) (*EN* 56–57). It signifies an eschatological-messianic existence.

Levinas connects messianism with the self's condition as a hostage: "Messianism is that apogee in Being—a reversal of being 'persevering in his being'—which begins in me" (*EN* 60). His philosophical discourse is redolent of biblical and eschatological themes. In this regard, the transcendence of exposing oneself to the Other's outrage and suffering is not just an ethical stance, but also messianic. Truth is not only otherwise than Being; it also belongs to the unthematizable realm of a biblical God. In such a context, truth is not a discovery or an experience, but is found in the testimony of suffering and expiating for the Other. This leads us to a perspective underlying Levinas's philosophy: truth as humility, humiliation, and persecution gives rise to another realm of truth as bodiliness and forgiveness.

Levinasian truth essentially reminds the self of its humanity and calling to be a likeness of God. Along the journey toward truth, the self will find forgiveness difficult as it must mean something miraculous like changing anger, so to speak, into the wine of love rather than the horror of wrath. Disarming the possibility of wrath (an eye for an eye) is perhaps something beyond seeing and hearing (1 Cor. 2:9; Isa. 64:4) putting the self in touch of a greater pain and suffering in the world (bodiliness). If, for example, the state of ethical melancholy can lead to the (im)possibility of forgiveness, does this not represent a journey and quest to uncover truth as both gift and passivity (gifted passivity)? In the radical uncovering of passivity deepened by ethical melancholy (and ethical vigilance), the self may encounter new possibilities and new ways of seeing and hearing the truth of the Other. This is what Levinas's philosophy wants to convey.

Levinas's notion of truth speaks essentially of ethical transcendence, that is, to be touchable by God's word. Such bodiliness also evokes a sense of ambiguity. By persevering through the night of anonymous Being and Being-for-the-Other, by trying to discern the difference between God's word and self-interest, ethical transcendence finds a place to exist. Its existence must seek out passivity and alterity as it shines a beacon along the dark road of Being. A certain humility is required to despise oneself and to put the conscience into question, but this is necessary so that the self may learn to pass through the ambiguity of Being.

Levinas's sense of ethical transcendence unveils a transfiguration of bodiliness—we are exposed and therefore touchable by God's word in the Other's face. Just as the self can suffer through the suffering of the Other and can be hurt by the hurt it provokes in the Other, it can also savor the word of God it encounters in the relation with the Other. This is a life otherwise; it is a journey toward a radical passivity of donning the yoke of super-individuation—ethical metaphysical intentionality—of being-for-the-Other. Exemplifying such intentionality, Levinas begins by probing the passivity that precedes all representational, axiological, and practical forms of consciousness. For him, consciousness is not thematic; it precedes both cognition and commitment: "Consciousness in all its forms—representational, axiological, practical—has already lost this close presence. The fact that the neighbor does not enter into a theme, that in a certain sense he precedes cognition and commitment, is neither a blinding nor an indifference; it is a rectitude of relationship more tense than intentionality: the neighbor summons me" (*CPP* 120).

As a result of ethical transcendence, consciousness reverts into what Levinas terms an "obsession," that is, "a responsibility without choice" (*CPP* 120). Such obsession, it seems, must also relate to the emotions, including fear. Levinas goes further than Heidegger's "brilliant analysis" of *Befindlichkeit* (phenomenology of the emotions) by developing the emotions ethically. He states, "Fear for the other doesn't enter into the Heideggerian analysis" (*EN* 117). Hence, there is not just the ethical metaphysical emotion of fear in Levinas's thought, but also ethical melancholy and ethical vigilance. These emotions specifically set out to animate and deepen the effect of ethical transcendence. In many ways, Levinas has much to be melancholy about. But his sadness does not remain only in a pensive state; it has been fine-tuned by the language of alterity. For example, reflecting on the phenomenology of suffering and the interhuman response of ethical transcendence, in "Useless Suffering" Levinas writes, "A high-mindedness that is the honor of a still uncertain, still vacillating modernity, emerging at the end of a century of unutterable suffering, but in which suffering, the suffering for the useless suffering of the other, the just suffering in me for the unjustifiable suffering of the other, opens suffering to the ethical perspective of the inter-human" (94). Essentially, Levinas's sense of ethical transcendence is affected by emotions like ethical melancholy and ethical vigilance, and ethical transcendence helps to transfigure and transform emotions into the realm of alterity and the tactility of God's word.[51]

LEVINAS AND CHRISTIAN THEOLOGY

Even though Levinas is Jewish, a number of Christian and theological notions appear in his writings, along with references to the New Testament, especially in areas of common concern to both Christianity and Judaism.[52] This fact alone provides a helpful context, even though Levinas, to the degree that he engaged Christian theology, exhibits a highly critical approach. It remains, however, that Levinas summons theology to find its starting point in the face of the suffering neighbor, and this is hardly a position foreign to the New Testament. The Levinasian lexicon abounds with possibilities for the development of new thought forms and linguistic usages that can only enrich theological discourse, especially when grappling with the rich content and refined methodology of a writer such as von Balthasar. Levinas—like Simone Weil—is not quite capable of expressing this in practical terms. Gillian Rose remarks: "Their inhibition with respect to law means that neither Weil nor Levinas is able to bring the sublime into the pedestrian, to suspend and resume the ethical with its features of modern state and society."[53] But, perhaps paradoxically, such a limitation is its strength, in that Levinas's creative and deeply concerned style of thought can never be reduced to any one interpretation in the challenge of introducing the language of alterity into theological thinking.

Still, in order to develop a preliminary theology of alterity, we must take Levinas's pure postphenomenological language and develop it in a way that guides the Christian theological imagination toward new insights and perspectives. Levinas's language is grave, dramatic, and confronting—even prophetic. By learning from Levinas and sharing a prophet's insight into God, humanity, and the world, we may come closer to directing our hearts and minds toward the good truth of Jesus the Christ, his Trinitarian praxis, and his radical gift-of-self-for-others.

THREE

Von Balthasar's Theological Aesthetics

What might it mean to imagine the world otherwise? Although our world is bent on making a fortune and then consuming it at great speed on projects of vanity and machinations of pride, there exists a way beyond the material gluttonies of the self. Thinking about God and the Other creates hope for a new vision of humanity. To do this, one must take up courage and confidence to reflect on difficult themes such as suffering, death, truth and the excess of evil. Often this work is motivated by personal experiences that shake and rupture the human soul out of its being. Levinas's philosophy grew out of his response to the passion of the Shoah.[1] Christians also have a dominant memory of a passion—the triune drama of the paschal mystery—which enabled God's word and Being to take hold upon the world.[2] The paschal mystery portrays the powerlessness of God the Father giving over the Incarnate Word for the world and "for us" (1 John 3:16). Like the Incarnation, this cannot be done without the activity of Spirit. In contrast, the Father's absolute passivity does not emphasize weakness, but the birth of the divine gift of love as word and flesh for us.

Central to the Christian narrative of faith is Christ's life, passion, death, and rising. The paschal mystery itself defines the way for each Christian to be incorporated into the drama of Christ's person and mission and to discover an identity as a person-in-Christ. For all eternity, the Spirit has set out to both veil and unveil Christ's being-for-us. However, given that the Gospels share the narrative of faith clearly and simply, how might we try proclaim, explain, or prove our faith in the world as meaningful and reasonable? It remains a temptation to manipulate the story of Jesus the Christ using political, social, economic and cultural motives or in self-interested and totalizing ways. The Gospels are not a hermeneutics of suspicion; they reflect the good news of encountering Christ through the otherness of mercy, forgiveness, love, sacrifice, healing, and even expiation for others. Levinas, when speaking to Christians, would often refer to Matthew 25:40 to point to the grave responsibility of ethics and agape. This suggests that the task to share and proclaim the paschal mystery represents literally a difficult freedom to partake of a liturgy of responsibility for others. And this becomes even more demanding when engaging the theology of Hans Urs von Balthasar with the Levinasian grammar of ethical transcendence.

It may seem peculiar to introduce Hans Urs von Balthasar by way of a comparison with *Life of Moses* by Saint Gregory of Nyssa (c. 330–95), especially given Levinas's approach to mysticism. In his 1957 talk, "A Religion for Adults," Levinas remarks: "Moses and the Prophets preoccupied themselves not with the immortality of the soul but with the poor, the widow, the orphan and the stranger. The relationship with man in which contact with the Divine is established is not a kind of *spiritual friendship* but the sort that is manifested, tested and accomplished in a just economy and for which each man is fully responsible" (*DF* 19–20).

Does Levinas deny spiritual friendship? He certainly does not deny intimacy with God, but underlines that prayer is first ethics: "Prayer, altogether, is not for oneself" (*AT* 182). The difference between Levinas and Gregory of Nyssa is more one of degree. Gregory's concept of friendship with God is dependent upon the virtuous life of doing good rather than a mystical relation with God.[3] While Levinas accentuates ethics as prayer and as a liturgy of devotion for the Other, Gregory of Nyssa equates them in a highly personal manner. Moreover, Gregory relates: "What then are we taught through what has been said? To have but one purpose in life: to be called servants of God by virtue of the lives we live."[4]

Levinas's cautionary approach to mysticism goes back to his roots. Levinas, a follower of Rabbi Hayyim of Volozhin (1749–1821), is naturally suspicious of sentimental mysticism. Hayyim's text, *Nefesh ha'Hayyim* (*The Soul of Life*), played an instrumental role upon the development of Levinas' thought; it seems analogous to Gregory of Nyssa's *Life of Moses* upon von Balthasar's writings. Levinas relates that *Nefesh ha'Hayyim* is "quite a remarkable work in which the glorification of the Torah, to which in particular the fourth and last part ('Gate 4') is devoted, is presented as an essential moment of a vast synthesis of Jewish spirituality, and as its crowning achievement" (*BV* 153). Levinas is not necessarily averse to spirituality. For Christian commentators on Gregory, *Life of Moses* "is a particularly important formulation of his Christian spirituality."[5] Moreover, they state, "In view of the lack of precision with which the word 'mysticism' is frequently used and of Gregory's close ties with the philosophical development, we have preferred to speak of his 'spirituality.'"[6] This suggests that Gregory's work, like Hayyim's, is perhaps better defined as spirituality rather than mysticism.

A comparison of Gregory of Nyssa and von Balthasar, by way of introduction, does not problematize the dialogue between Levinas and von Balthasar, but exemplifies the underlying presence of spirituality in both men's writings. In *Life of Moses*, Gregory's spiritual reflections engage with a world of biblical and spiritual encounters between God and humanity. A programmatic element converges toward von Balthasar's life and writings: an "eternal progress" to "see the glory of the Lord" emerges.[7] It is almost as if von Balthasar's theology journeys side by side with Gregory of Nyssa's allegorical exposition of the *Life of Moses*.

Reflecting on Moses giving the tablets of stone to God, Gregory writes, "For perhaps it is possible, as we are led by these events, to come to some perception of the divine concern for us." He comments further, "Having made the tables out of earthly matter, Moses submitted them to the power of the One who would engrave his Law upon them. In this way, while he carried the Law in letters of stone, he restored grace inasmuch as God himself had impressed the

words on the stone." In regard to Moses's early life, Gregory comments: "Whenever life demands that the sober and provident rational
thoughts which are the parents of the male child launch their good
child on the billows of this life, they make him safe in an ark so that
when he is given to the stream he will not be drowned. The ark, con-
structed out of various boards, would be education in the different
disciplines, which holds what it carries about the waves of life."[8]

Analogously, the momentum of von Balthasar's life can be seen
an encounter with the glory of God. His "tablets of stone"—the
15 volumes of the trilogy of aesthetics, dramatics and logic—are a
witness of Christian theological experience. Extending the analogy,
von Balthasar tries to "restore grace" to Catholic theology and to
return it to the spirit of the church fathers as a means to see and to
savor the glory of the Lord.

Like Moses, too, von Balthasar's early years show how he was
made "safe in an ark" of "education in the different disciplines." He
enjoyed the excitement of study as it came together with a sense of
vocation. Von Balthasar was born in Lucerne, Switzerland, on August
12, 1905, not long before Levinas (January 12, 1906). During his
childhood and youth, von Balthasar developed talents in music and
literature.[9] Educated with the Benedictines and later the Jesuits, he
finally matriculated at the University of Zürich in German literature
and philosophy. From there, and later in Berlin and Vienna, he pur-
sued doctoral studies on the subject of apocalyptic German literature. After submitting his dissertation in 1929, he joined the Bavarian
Province of the Society of Jesus to study for the priesthood.[10]

Gregory of Nyssa presents an allegorical interpretation of Moses'
return to his natural mother to discern the Christian life as a time
to be nourished by "the Church's milk." In a similar tone, von
Balthasar's journey into theological education represented a "return
to his natural mother." Although, like Moses, von Balthasar involved
himself with "profane teachings," he acknowledges of clerical studies: "By these the soul is nourished and matured, this being given the
means of ascending the height."[11] There was a time also when "the
Church's milk" may not have been so palatable. When von Balthasar

did his novitiate and philosophical studies in Pullach (near Munich, Germany), he had a rather negative experience of neoscholastic manuals.[12] However, during his theological formation in Fourvière (near Lyons, France), he encountered the means "to ascend the height" through his Jesuit mentor, Henri de Lubac. De Lubac introduced von Balthasar to the movement of *la nouvelle théologie*, which set out to overcome the manual tradition of scholasticism and to return theology to its rich patristic heritage. As a result, von Balthasar undertook significant studies in patristics. This led to his early writings on Gregory of Nyssa and Maximus the Confessor (c. 580–662).[13] In his free time, he read and translated contemporary French authors such as Paul Claudel, Charles Péguy, George Bernanos, and Paul Valery.[14]

After priestly ordination on July 26, 1936, he worked for the Jesuit journal *Stimmen der Zeit* in Munich. During this time, a second crucial influence upon von Balthasar was the Jesuit Erich Przywara, whom he met at Pullach. Von Balthasar once remarked that Przywara was the greatest mind he ever had encountered. Przywara not only shaped von Balthasar's philosophical inquiry, especially in regard to the analogy of Being,[15] he also led him to appreciate the true depth of the Spiritual Exercises of Saint Ignatius. Nichols remarks, "Indeed, it might not be too misleading to say that what Przywara, and Balthasar after him, hoped to do was combine the mind of St. Thomas with the heart of St. Augustine, all in the spirit of St. Ignatius Loyola, that burning obedience—at once interior and missionary—to the Word of God."[16]

In many ways, von Balthasar is like a twentieth century Church Father or even a Moses to liberate theology out of slavery to a realm of glory. Even Graham Ward invites us to imagine his theology as a pathway to the "the age of angels," to "teach us how to bear witness to what is other and glorious, how to worship, how to live ecstatically."[17] Ward describes, "Balthasar is a maker of myths. He is a Dante composing a *divina commedia* for the late twentieth century."[18] Continuing the analogy to *Life of Moses,* von Balthasar is a Moses who invites the Christian believer to the mountain to see the beautiful form of God's glory as an epiphany of "God's true being."

Gregory of Nyssa reflects on Moses' face-to-face encounter with God (Exod. 33:11): "Such an experience seems to me to belong to the soul which loves what is beautiful. Hope always draws the soul from the beauty which is seen to what is beyond, always kindles the desire for the hidden through what is constantly perceived. Therefore, the ardent love of beauty, although receiving what is always visible as an image of what he desires, yet longs to be filled with the very stamp of the archetype."[19]

For von Balthasar, that archetype is the analogy of Being par excellence — Jesus the Christ. Von Balthasar's theological aesthetics seem to transpose Gregory of Nyssa's reflection on beauty to attest to "seeing the unseen."[20] For example, von Balthasar writes, "We can, therefore, say that theological aesthetics culminates in the christological form (taking the word seriously) of salvation-history, in so far as here, upon the medium of man's historical existence, God inscribes his authentic sign with his own hand." The good truth of theology is to "be filled with the stamp of the archetype" and see the beautiful form of Christ in the paschal mystery. Therefore, the experience of an epiphany of the unseen represents a relation to the meaning of Being. Through encountering the glory of the Lord, we experience what God means for us and the world. And it is "God's living Spirit" that takes us to a space and time of "ardent love" and longing for God's glory (*GL* 1:646). Informed by Saint Gregory of Nyssa, von Balthasar's theology suggests a fivefold testament: savoring the glory of the Lord, seeing the unseen, receiving the Holy Spirit, possessing peace and love, and participating in the unity of the Father and Son.[21]

Part of von Balthasar's desire to articulate a theology of Christian experience indicates a prophetic stance to theology. He does not hesitate to change the way theology is done. He takes the reader on a journey beyond the wilderness of neoscholasticism into the promised land of *nouvelle theologie*. Breaking from the Augustinian-Thomistic tradition of substance-based metaphysics (essentialist ontology), he takes up the postmodern concern to rethink the logos of reason and Being. Rather than absolutizing rational articulations of divine Being, he places an emphasis on aesthetic, relational, and personalist categories. The aim is to rediscover and enhance the scholastic ontological understanding of Being and its transcendental qualities of the beautiful, the good, and true. Christ, as the analogy of Being *par excellence,* is the very access to the mystery of the Trinity.[22] Christ's glory in the paschal mystery is indivisible from the beauty, goodness, and truth of God (*GL* 7:242–43). For von Balthasar, the essence or nature of Being is not conceived as a substance in the abstract Augustinian-Thomistic sense, but more as relational: an indissoluble perichoresis between the philosophical and theological transcendental qualities of Being. The beauty, goodness, and truth of Christ's obedience to the Father's will in the Spirit manifest God's glory as "the unique ray of the divine majesty of love" (7:243). To return again to Gregory of Nyssa's mystical vision of Moses' face-to-face encounter with God: "He shone with glory. And although lifted up through such lofty experiences, he is still unsatisfied in his desire for more. He still thirsts for that with which he constantly filled himself to capacity, and he asks to attain as if he had never partaken, beseeching God to appear to him, not according to his capacity to partake, but according to God's true being."[23] Von Balthasar's theology may very well also be described as a beseeching theology; the "unsatisfied desire" evokes a response to the "initiative of divine love" to encounter "the immense movement of love inside of God: Being is a Super-Becoming."[24] This relational emphasis in von Balthasar's theology represents the desire to risk doing theology, like Saint Gregory of Nyssa, with spirituality. The risk, in von Balthasar's mind, was perhaps not just a risk, but more an act of faith in the quest to understand God's Being and to see God's glory.

Von Balthasar's attempts to bring faith, mystical vision, and reason together also bring into focus his relations with Karl Barth and Adrienne von Speyr. With war looming, von Balthasar opted to return to Switzerland to take up the role of student chaplain at the University of Basel. It was here that he met Adrienne von Speyr and the systematic theologian, Karl Barth, two decisive influences upon the further direction of his work.

Von Balthasar's admiration of Barth can be measured by his book *The Theology of Karl Barth.*[25] He was attracted to Barth's theology, especially by his conception of what theology should be, namely, a revelation-centered theology. In this regard, Barth held that the only true principle of theology was the analogy of faith, meaning, all knowledge of God is derived from Christ. Despite Barth's adamant rejection of the analogy of Being, von Balthasar sought to implement Barth's christocentric analogy of faith with the analogy of Being. Without the foundation of the analogy of Being, von Balthasar argued, Barth's analogy of faith would end up as a self-enclosed divine monologue.[26] Aware of the value of Barth's theology for Catholic theology, von Balthasar openly sought to convert his Swiss colleague to the Catholic view of things. His endeavors in conversion at Basel found more success in the case of Adrienne von Speyr.

Von Speyr, a medical doctor and Protestant, converted to Catholicism through von Balthasar's influence. Almost immediately, von Speyr began to share with him her mystical and theologically creative insights. Von Balthasar acknowledged that their work was inseparable: "It was Adrienne von Speyr who pointed out the fulfilling way from Ignatius to John, and thus laid the foundation for the most of what has been published by me since 1940. Her work and mine is neither psychologically nor philosophically separable, two halves of a whole which, as centre, has but one foundation."[27] John O'Donnell lists a number of theological themes that von Balthasar inherited from von Speyr: "Christ's descent into hell as his solidarity with the abandoned, Jesus' Sonship as obedience to the point of powerless identification with the Godforsaken, faith as Marian womb-like receptivity, virginity as spiritual fruitfulness for the word, personhood as unique sending from God, the vicarious representative character of prayer and suffering in the Church, the bodiliness of Christian existence, the naked standing before God and the Church in the sacramental act of confession as expressing the fundamental Christian attitude."[28]

With von Speyr's encouragement and support, von Balthasar made the decision to found, in 1945, a secular institute called the Community of St. John.[29] Eventually, von Balthasar was forced to make the heartbreaking decision to leave the Jesuits.[30] After several years of isolation, he was incardinated in 1956 in the Swiss diocese of Chur. But his struggle for recognition continued. Though he failed to be nominated as a *peritus* (expert theologian) for the Second Vatican Council, his work continued in the wake of the Council with his foundation of the journal, *Communio*—founded in opposition to the more liberal international journal, *Concilium*.[31] Despite ecclesiastical disfavor, von Balthasar was able to push ahead with his major writings, publishing works on literary figures and the first volumes of his trilogy.[32] After von Speyr's death in 1967 and with the post-conciliar crisis in Catholic theology, he received recognition from the Roman See, and was appointed to the International Theological Commission. His patristic-inspired, antiliberal, yet reformist theology began to be adopted by Rome.[33] Over the next 25 years, von Balthasar completed his theological trilogy of the Aesthetic, Dramatic and Logic. He died on June 26, 1988, at Basel, three days before his investiture as a cardinal.[34]

One of the enduring legacies of von Balthasar's theology is his theological aesthetics. For this venture, he takes on much of the spirit of Gregory of Nyssa's spiritual theology. Just as St. Gregory of Nyssa traced a "pattern of beauty" in the life of Moses, so Balthasar traces a pattern of beauty in the paschal mystery and in the way the believer can participate in its truth, goodness, and glory. Gregory of Nyssa's *Life of Moses* demonstrates an allegorical path to gain the hidden meaning of "the perfection of the virtuous life."[35] In contrast, von Balthasar's writings exemplify how ontotheology can be at its best, not preventing the theological imagination to be contaminated by the self-interest of Being. But this does not mean that everything should end with von Balthasar's theology. Both von Balthasar and Saint Gregory of Nyssa (and even Moses) would most likely have advocated that theology—the search to find a rational way of speaking of God—is an eternal progress.

ANALOGIA ENTIS METAPHYSICS AND THOMAS AQUINAS

Inherent in von Balthasar's theology is a rejection of a metaphysics of presence.[36] In the Derridean sense, this notion considers "that thinking is able to grasp the enduring reality of a thing—its essential meaning—by penetrating its appearance in fluid time and space."[37] Being, for von Balthasar, is thought analogically, particularly in terms of Christ's triune experience of the paschal mystery. Underlying Balthasar's theology, therefore, is the analogy of Being,[38] which in turn underlies his analogy of the transcendental qualities of God's Being.[39] To this end, in the desire to safeguard the transcendence of God from the "being of things," he takes up Aquinas's understanding of "esse as the non-subsistent fullness and perfection of all reality and as the supreme 'likeness of divine goodness'" (*GL* 4:393). Distinguishing the "fullness and perfection" of the "being of things" from God betrays the "radical way God is placed over and above cosmic being." Notice here how von Balthasar describes Being as cosmic. The implication is that God is its "efficient, exemplary and final cause" (4:393). Like Heidegger, von Balthasar does not want to equate God with Being as such, that is to say, as ontology without theology.[40] Like Heidegger again, von Balthasar looks toward "the absolute ground of all being" (*GL* 4:396) (or "the ground of beings as a whole") as a means to renew Thomas's ontology and theological ontology. But unlike Heidegger, von Balthasar does not focus exclusively on the search for the meaning of Being in general ("the thought of Being").[41] In effect, like Aquinas, von Balthasar is a "kairos" to think of philosophy and theology together (4:396): "By its very nature, theological insight into God's glory, goodness and truth presupposes an *ontological,* and not merely formal or gnoseological, infrastructure of worldly being. Without philosophy, there can be no theology."[42] The point here is that von Balthasar will not go as far as Heidegger to presume that Being must be thought outside theology. For Heidegger, God does not lie in the world of Being, but rather in the sacred (the realm of faith); hence, like Barth, he rejects the *analogia entis.*[43]

Although von Balthasar's theology is marked by the influence of Heidegger, his stance toward Being and God is an inherent challenge to Heidegger's thought. Renewing Aquinas's philosophy, von Balthasar takes up a different lens for the distinction between Being (the ground) and beings (the grounded) in "the history of metaphysics, as onto-theology."[44] Von Balthasar does not confuse the two or reduce it to a mere distinction of the intellect. Drawing from Aquinas, he sees how the structure of the relation between Being and beings point to the freedom and power of God to offer the creature the possibility to participate and share in divine Being.[45] To this end, von Balthasar develops "the how" by taking up Aquinas's philosophical analysis of the *analogia entis* into a theological context especially in terms of aesthetics, christology, and Trinitarian theology. Here, he was guided by Erich Pryzywara's philosophy of the *analogia entis*.[46] So like Pryzywara, von Balthasar unfolds his development of the *analogia entis* "in the Spirit of Aquinas."[47] However, von Balthasar's approach is flavored, as it were, by a "'German' interpretation of Thomas." Showing affinity to Thomistic, Christian philosophers like Josef Pieper and Gustav Siewerth, he opens to a "romantic and idealistic sensibility" to give life to the dry rationalism of the scholastics. This is further deepened by the "moderate" fashion he makes use of Hegel, Schelling, the later Heidegger, and Buber, for example.[48] Yet, in saying this, it must be remembered, "it is impossible to summarize the theological thought of Balthasar. It can neither be termed old or new; and it derives from no school."[49]

Aquinas's influence upon von Balthasar is certainly far more penetrating than Heidegger's. Moreover, von Balthasar regarded Aquinas "with perhaps more esteem than any other theologian in history."[50] Importantly, the input of Aquinas's philosophical writings on the *analogia entis* is far-reaching in the corpus of von Balthasar's theology. In fact, it becomes the basis for philosophy and theology: "I have accordingly attempted," von Balthasar writes at the end of his life, "to erect a philosophy and a theology on the basis of an analogy...of being [*Sein*] as it presents itself concretely in its (transcendental, and not categorial) properties."[51] The analogy of Being presents Christ as the glory and unity of beauty, goodness, and truth for all cosmic being. In other words, following Przywara, the analogy of Being is the "fundamental principle"[52] to clarify that intimacy with God demands a distinction between God and Being (*esse*). In the spirit of Aquinas, then, Balthasar is free to safeguard "a certain proportion between the creature and God." However, this does not deny the creature intimacy with God. For in God's "infinite transcendence," there is no distance between them (*GL* 4:403, 4:394). And this infinite transcendence is played out dramatically for von Balthasar in the Trinitarian drama of the paschal mystery. Christ is revealed as the analogy of Being par excellence.

At stake is von Balthasar's desire to develop the analogy of Being more profoundly in the light of the event of revelation. Von Balthasar asks, "How, ontologically speaking, can God become man, or, to phrase the question differently: Does creaturely *logos* have the carrying capacity to harbour the divine Logos in itself?" (*TL* 1:8). Hence, analogy is not just dependent on the ontological structure of worldly Being, but is also anchored in God.[53] This brings us to the connection between the analogy of Being and the analogy of the transcendentals.[54] This connection signifies the most difficult question of von Balthasar's trilogy, namely, how the circumincessive relation of the transcendentals might reveal the creature as an image and likeness of God's Being. The question can be answered only within a theological and Trinitarian horizon (1:9–10). The fundamental significance of this question bears on the ontological unveiling of God's revelation to the creature, on one hand, and on the ontological unveiling of the creature before God, on the other. It touches, therefore, on the objective and subjective experience of God. And because von Balthasar's prioritizes the beautiful, the relation between God and the creature favors an aesthetic starting point.

PROBING VON BALTHASAR'S THEOLOGICAL AESTHETICS

Von Balthasar names the beautiful as the starting point for the trilogy: "Beauty is the word that shall be our first" (*GL* 1:18). For him, the determination of God's Being must begin with aesthetics. Primarily, revelation radiates triune love in the form of true beauty, which he equates with disinterestedness.[55] For the believer, the experience of the beautiful is conveyed by receiving the Holy Spirit, responding to the divine vocation, and acknowledging the Son as a member of the

Trinity. To believe is to participate in the revelation of Trinitarian love. As a result, the creature is moved and possessed by the beautiful. Furthermore, such an epiphany of the beauty of Being produces a Spirit-inspired consciousness. The creature is enabled to grasp that Being unveils itself to the world as Trinitarian love. In the light of Being, the creature can perceive the divine light and experience the ecstatic overture of faith. Describing Spirit-inspired consciousness, von Balthasar writes, "Here we simply speak of the participation of man's entire sensitivity in the manner in which God experiences the divine" (*GL* 1:158–59, 246–49). Furthermore, to describe the experience of faith in the theological aesthetics, von Balthasar employs the German words, *erfahren, Erfahrung,* and *Einfahren.*[56]

Commentators such as Nichols and O'Donnell maintain that *erfahren* is the prevalent form.[57] In one example, von Balthasar writes:

> As an attitude, faith is the surrender of one's own experience to the experience of Christ, and Christ's experience is one of kenotic humiliation and self-renunciation, a reality which, as we have seen, rests on the foundation of Christ's hypostatic consciousness as Redeemer. For this reason, in "mysticism" every deeper experience (*Erfahrung*) of God will be a deeper entering into (*Einfahren*) the "non-experience" of faith, into the loving renunciation of experience, all the way into the depths of the "Dark Nights" of John of the Cross, which constitute the real mystical training for the ultimate renunciations. But these "nights" are precisely an "*experience* of non-experience," or an experience of the negative, private mode of experience, as a participation in the total archetypal experience of the Old and New Testaments. (*GL* 1:412–13)

Von Balthasar conceives of experience as a loving renunciation of experience. With this apophatic emphasis, faith is more a self-emptying experience, as it makes space and gives time to participating in the event of God's revelation. From this point of view, faith is an attitude of surrendering oneself to Christ's experience of kenosis and renunciation, that is, to "Christ's hypostatic consciousness as redeemer" (1:412). Though von Balthasar articulates the experience of faith as a journey of self-renunciation in order to participate in Christ's consciousness, there is an implication of another type of experience, namely, lived experience, signified in the word, *Erlebnis*. Von Balthasar's awareness of this *Erlebnis* is present in his description of G. Koch's theology of the resurrection:[58] the relationship between God's gift in Christ and the creature is "an originating relationship (like the *noēma* and *noēsis* of Husserl), existing only as personally actualized, which means to say in mutual encounter."[59]

To what extent, then, is this originating relationship of mutual encounter dependent upon the Husserlian idea of the unity between the *noesis* and *noema*? From a Husserlian perspective, it might appear that von Balthasar is referring to a thought, a *noesis,* explicitly, humanity's participation in God. From the divine perspective, this *noesis* is actualized as revelation; and from the human perspective it is actualized as faith (*GL* 1:125). In regard to the human perspective, faith involves knowledge and hence a partial understanding of God. This would entail a sense of a relationship between the *noesis* and the *noema*. There is an indissoluble reciprocal relationship between humanity's participation in God (*noesis*) on one hand, and, on the other, a partial conception of it (*noema*). But this is not a strict lived experience in the Husserlian sense. It would be more accurate to say that it is an experience of divine revelation in which the consciousness of the believer freely surrenders itself to the divine consciousness.

Moreover, in von Balthasar's theological aesthetics, faith and revelation speak of "*ekstasis*—God's 'venturing forth' to man and man's to God" (*GL* 1:126). This could aptly be described as a phenomenology of *ekstasis*.[60] In other words, within the horizon of the primal phenomenon of the beautiful, theology catches a glimpse of faith and revelation in the mutual encounter between God and the human self. Even though there is a lived experience with God at some level, the relation with God transforms it into an *ekstasis*. The relation of lived experience to mystery suggests a movement from everyday consciousness to an encounter with divine being: "God is known as mystery in the form of self-consciousness. In the small mystery of its self-apprehension in its inner light, in its personality and freedom, self-consciousness catches a glimmer of what the infinite identity of and freedom of the divine truth might be" (*TL* 1:272). This implies that there is at least some level of *Erlebnis* before the creature has an experience of faith as *erfahren* in the sense of the self's journey of participating in Christ.

In contrast to implicit acceptance of Husserlian terminology, however, von Balthasar shows a more explicit interest in Heidegger's ontological phenomenology. This is not surprising given that Przywara, who shaped von Balthasar's "philosophical inquiry,"[61] shared a "personal friendship with Heidegger which dates from their early association together as pupils as a Jesuit school in Austria."[62] Despite the different paths von Balthasar and Heidegger took toward Being and the Sacred, von Balthasar borrows some key Heideggerian notions such as wonder, the giftedness of Being, truth as unconcealment, and human thinking as thanking and doxological outpouring.[63] In the end, however, Heidegger's ontological phenomenology fails to impress von Balthasar: "In the work of Heidegger, the true wonder at the fact that something exists rather than nothing does not run its full course, for it points to a freedom which he does not wish to perceive."[64]

Von Balthasar's relation to Heidegger's thought bears some parallel to Levinas's approach. Both tend to leash Heidegger's notions in their own way, resulting in a form of critical deconstruction. Interestingly, Heidegger, Levinas, and von Balthasar all set out to renew philosophy and/or theology in unique and distinctive ways. In von Balthasar's thought, for example, a dramatic stage unfolds for his theological aesthetics: he leads us to a theory of vision, the fundamental theology that studies the subjective experience of the form of God's self-revelation in Christ. Von Balthasar then develops a theory of rapture, the dogmatic theology concerning the objective evidence of the incarnation and paschal mystery and the believer's participation in the divine glory. For von Balthasar, the form of God's revelation in Christ when seen through the eyes of faith reveals the Trinity. Through perceiving the beautiful form and splendor of Jesus Christ in the paschal mystery, the believer might realize what he or she needs to know and to be. Hence, the Triune God who in Christ becomes human is known and believed (*GL* 1:125–26).

INTRODUCING THE NONPHENOMENAL OTHER INTO VON BALTHASAR'S THOUGHT

How, then, to open von Balthasar's theological aesthetics with Levinas's language of alterity? Reflecting on Christ's Otherness provides the opportunity to extend the range of possibilities in von Balthasar's statement, "What God's glory in its good truth is, was to be revealed in Jesus Christ, and ultimately in his absolute obedience of Cross and Hell" (*GL* 7:243). Attempting to develop von Balthasar's thought with the aid of philosophy is not new. In their book *Balthasar at the End of Modernity*, Lucy Gardner, David Moss, Ben Quash, and Graham Ward contend, "Balthasar's work can be continued in directions only by engaging with current projects in philosophy."[65]

The journey toward a theology of alterity begins with what amounts to a nonphenomenality of Christ's face, and the resurrection reveals the drama of the nonphenomenality of Holy Saturday. For the disciples, it may seem that the postresurrection encounter occurs in a phenomenal way. But there is a significant dimension of the encounter that they clearly could not sense, for how could they ever comprehend the glory of Christ's suffering in his descent into hell? Here lies the tension between Christ and the world. Whereas the world seeks to explain God's revelation by way of consciousness and the event of Being, the face of Christ signifies a place and time of ethical transcendence beyond objectivity, presence, and Being. But when the risen Christ appears to the disciples, his face awakens in them an overwhelming desire for justice and love that cannot be reduced to consciousness.

The effect of the risen Christ's Otherness upon the disciples must be set within the previous event of Holy Saturday. The character of this event, where Christ is dead among the dead, leads to a consideration of the diastasis existing between the Father and the Son and how the Spirit bridges such a separation. Von Balthasar explains that the diastasis refers to "the infinite difference within God which is the presupposition of eternal love."[66] The diastasis is correlative to the *analogia entis* grounding the conciliar statement, "however great the similarity between creator and creature may be, the dissimilarity always nevertheless remains greater."[67] Such a statement is drawn from the difference within God and between God and humanity as an essential condition for the opening out of eternal love. The difference bespeaks kenosis or otherness.[68] In the context of Holy Saturday, von Balthasar likens Christ's experience of Otherness to an experience of the horror of anonymous existence: "At this moment, the Word cannot hear itself. It collapses into its scream for the lost God."[69] Von Balthasar is suggesting that the experience of the Father's abandonment enables Christ to encounter the sinner who wants to be without God. Consequently, Christ is right for any sermon to the damned because he is abandoned by God like one of the dead.

Christ's descent to the dead, like his death on the cross, in suffering the Father's abandonment, is beyond any phenomenal and ontological conception. It is not an experience; nor is it an ontological unveiling. It is an enigmatic and nonphenomenal encounter with the dead. Christ's encounter with the dead, then, is a response of extreme passivity toward their state of God-forsakenness. For example, Christ responds by substituting for their hatred of God and their state of anonymous existence. The dead are given the possibility of being overwhelmed by the impossibility of triune love piercing the depths of hell. But Christ's descent to hell is not only a partaking of the depths of utter loneliness and despair, but also an offering of triune love for the damned. Christ's going to the dead shatters the totality of loneliness and despair, for hell is now a place and time of Christ's alterity. This is to say that, for the dead, their relation with Christ can be interpreted as a traumatic encounter with his otherness in a way that opens the possibility for them to be redeemed from their anonymous and depersonalized state.

The nonphenomenal idea of otherness contrasts with von Balthasar's use of the Thomistic categories of form and splendor as constituent factors of the beautiful in his theological aesthetics. For von Balthasar, the phenomenality of form and splendor are the basis for an ontological unconcealment of God's glory. In contrast, by emphasizing the nonphenomenal sense of encounter and otherness, we can begin to deepen von Balthasar's theology of Christian experience; as such, seeing the glory (form and splendor) of the Lord in the paschal mystery signifies an encounter of Christ's Otherness or nonphenomenality. The following four questions and corresponding discussions as to the nonphenomenality of the diastasis on Holy Saturday help to shed light upon this interpretation.

> *Question 1:* How might the damned distinguish between their state of God-forsakenness and Christ himself who is now, like them, "debased to mere matter…incapable of any active act of solidarity"?[70]

The difficulty here exists in identifying the depth of God in the God-forsakenness of the damned. Von Balthasar explains that Christ's descent to the dead is an absolute passivity, an expiating substitution that "outlasts all the force of the pounding sin" (*VBR* 153). This parallels in some ways with Levinas' notions of passivity, *illeity,* and openness.

Levinas's idea of passivity refers to the extreme exposure to the Other's destitution, that is, exposure to the activity of the "hither side" (*OB* 114). The phrase signifies the site outside of Being and history where the self's identity contracts to a point that makes it nakedly exposed to God's will. At this point, the self transcends its consciousness to such a degree that the only response is expiation in a dimension of nonphenomenality. The dimension can also be defined as the trace of *illeity* or the proximity of God in the face. In the transcendence of the face, the trace produces an alterity that disturbs and overwhelms consciousness (*CPP* 68, 106–07, 136; *EN* 57). In this regard, the proximity of God is neither a presence nor an ontological unveiling. In a Christian theological sense, one could conceive *illeity* as a trace of the Holy Spirit communicated through the face of Christ. In the context of Holy Saturday, the trace would signify that even if the dead are God-forsaken, a sense of the Father's love is still possible, not only for Christ, but also for the dead. The Holy Spirit inspires the possibility for redemption. In a complementary fashion, we could conceive that the Holy Spirit communicates the Father's will through Christ's face. The Spirit indwelling in Christ instills a testimony of faith, hope, and love before the dead and God-forsaken ones. Even though Christ and the dead are abandoned by the Father, a sense of God's transcendence is possible through the trace of the Holy Spirit. Hence, such an encounter signifies that despite the diastasis between the Father and Son, there is still an opening for God's eternal love to penetrate the absolute loneliness of the damned.

The diastasis provides the conditions of possibility for Christ going to the dead, even to offer a sense of the Father's love. Moreover, it makes it possible for the damned to distinguish between Christ's gift of self as a forsaken one on one hand, and his love on the other. Christ expiates for their state of lostness and God-forsakenness through the trace of the Holy Spirit in him. The perichoretic indwelling of the Holy Spirit in Christ thus creates space for Christ's kenotic Otherness to respond to the Father's will to testify to the dead, disturb their hatred of God, and shatter their absolute loneliness.

> *Question 2:* How possible is it for Christ, now "debased to mere matter," to "possess" hell through an absolute passivity of solidarity with the damned (*GL* 7:233)?

Von Balthasar approaches this question of hell this way: "In various ways, it [hell] is a christological concept; first, inasmuch as only the dead redeemer, by virtue of his kenosis, has experienced the full seriousness of what Sheol must be; second, inasmuch—again by virtue of his kenosis—as his abandonment to death by the Father was a unique abandonment that was determined within the Trinity; third, inasmuch as in this *visio (secundae) mortis* the whole fruit of the redeeming Cross was seen together" (7:233). The experience linking the events of the cross, the Son's descent to the dead, and the Father's will, amounts to the kenosis of Christ. Von Balthasar speaks of hell as a second death in which "the whole fruit of the redeeming Cross was seen together." The emphasis on seeing is significant: Christ has seen the chaotic reality of sin, which is also to have seen the dead who wish to remain God-forsaken. That would imply that Christ was then in a position objectively to judge their eschatological fate. In other words, Christ's possession of hell rests upon his objective experience of hell's lostness in obedience to the Father's will. Christ's experience of seeing becomes the basis for determining the meaning of his eschatological Being on Holy Saturday. The priority given to seeing throws further light to von Balthasar's theological aesthetics.

Von Balthasar considers that, in regard to the senses, sight is privileged over hearing, particularly in the biblical perception of God. He assigns hearing to the imitative, earthly faith of the Old Testament, while seeing is related to the realized, archetypal faith of the New Testament. Despite this dichotomy between hearing and seeing, von Balthasar cautions, "assignations have something precarious and inexact about them, and very often are made on the basis of theological prejudices," and further, "even if sight is the chief sense and expresses man's innermost longing, nevertheless a living person is known primarily by his word." Accordingly, von Balthasar refers "to the senses without distinction" where "the accent, naturally, falls on sight" (*GL* 1:310). Hearing, therefore, complements seeing as a way of communicating humanity's innermost longing.

In regard to his examples of the objective events of God's will in the paschal mystery and the visions of the Old Testament and of Revelation, von Balthasar goes on to state, "the accent always falls on what is being shown" (*GL* 1:313). He recognizes also that seeing, as the ability to interpret God's absolute love, depends on an absolutely passive experience of being incorporated into the good truth of God's glory (7:291). In contrast, Levinas's writings place priority on hearing the word of God in the Other's face, rather than seeing through the radiance of God's Being (*EN* 110). Levinas's idea of the Other's face signifies the nonphenomenal phenomenon in which the word of God (the trace of *illeity*) might be heard. Might is important here, as Levinas cautions that *illeity* can be confused with the stirrings of the "there is" (*CPP* 166). Given this ambiguity, we cannot prove whether God's discourse has or has not been heard. Again, Levinas warns of the dangers of trying to thematize God's divinity as a presence in consciousness (*OB* 162).

Levinas places a great amount of emphasis on the face as the locus in which God withdraws transcendence and leaves traces (*CPP* 107).

He describes the face as possessing the quality of an ambiguous unheard-of obligation that gives rise to the possibility of ethics. In another sense, the nonphenomenality of the face signifies the saying, that is, the self's involvement with the Other. The saying transcends the *noema* of intentionality. As a result, a *noesis* or an act of consciousness is without an object, or *noema*. In the saying, there occurs an exposure to an Other. The nonphenomenality of the Other's face is uncovered. Hence, the saying provides the subject with a sense of transcendence or disinterestedness. It awakens in the subject the imperative to give, to suffer, and to live beyond the realm of ego-consciousness. Testimony and the saying coincide (*OB* 149).

Levinas's ideas of hearing the word of God in the Other's face, the signification of the saying, and the idea of testimony provide an alternative perspective to von Balthasar's understanding of hell as a christological concept. Where von Balthasar emphasizes Christ experiencing and seeing the full seriousness of hell (or Sheol), a Levinasian perspective would place an accent on Christ hearing the Father's word of salvation through the Spirit by exposing himself to the outrage, insults, and wounds of the damned. Such hearing would entail an extreme or hyperbolic passivity. For, in solidarity with the damned, Christ makes himself utterly available to them in their state of perdition. His existence is sacrificial. Exposed to the pain of suffering and trauma beyond any possibility of representation, Christ offers the grace of salvation to the dead.

Moreover, Christ's kenotic obedience to the Father's will is the radical explanation of the manner in which Christ encounters the pure state of sin. After hearing the Father's word of salvation, Christ is the Word that penetrates all hatred and lostness in the damned. He thereby goes down to hell in such a way that he can truly testify to the Father's reconciling love through his experience of God-forsakenness. The Son's testimony occurs beyond any representation, perception, or phenomenon. Christ's witness follows from the unique mission he has received from the Father to enter what is further from him, namely, to be one—through the excess of love—with the lost and damned.

Question 3: Can Christ's descent to hell be understood not only sote-riologically and eschatologically, but also equally in terms of God's act of creation (cf. Rom. 8:22; 2 Cor. 5:17; Gal. 6:15)?

The possibility of salvation for the dead suggests an unfinished aspect of the mystery of Creation. Von Balthasar reflects on this resistance and incompleteness when he writes: "Sin in its 'pure state' separated from man, 'sin in itself' in the whole formless, chaotic momentum of its reality, was seen by Jesus; and with it, the 'remain-der' that could not be absorbed into the Father's work of creation, because he had left man freedom to decide for or against God—the unfinished part of the creation, that it was left to the incarnate Son to finish; and the Son, obedient to his mission, is led by the Father now into the state of existence of this sin that 'remains'" (*GL* 7:233). The ontological foundation that sustains von Balthasar's theology of cre-ation and of sin is the analogy of Being. It is employed to safeguard the divine transcendence over the finite world. Christ, who is for von Balthasar the archetype of the analogy of Being, is the channel par excellence to God's gift of salvation. Analogy is the ontological form of reason that aims to elucidate the likeness and image of God in the creature and the creature's relationship to God.[71] However, Levinas presents different routes to analogical and theological thematizations of God, such as the notions of individuation, otherwise than Being, and passivity.

For Levinas, as noted previously, individuation refers to the iden-tity of the self as it is torn inside out to the point of expiation for an Other. An extreme form of substitution, expiation super-individuates the self by confronting it with alterity. Levinas also describes expiation as the overemphasis of openness. Individuation signifies that the force of alterity has broken the limits of one's identity and transformed it into an obsessive relationship of existing through and for the Other. Hence, the self's identity is inverted from Being to otherwise than Being, a radical turnabout from being for oneself to substituting for others (*OB* 117–18). In this understanding of individuation, the self's ethical transformation surpasses any attempt of ontological or ana-logical thematization. In this regard, the self is now located beyond the limits of identity. Extreme passivity exists as a state that cannot be contained by phenomenal consciousness, and in this site of transcendence, the self cannot compare or reduce the Other or God to a presence within consciousness through analogical logic. Where the self is freed from being in-itself and for-itself, it exists as responsible for others.

In the context of Creation and Holy Saturday from a Levinasian perspective, the process of Christ's individuation is one in which he goes beyond the limits of his identity by expiating for the damned. As a result, we see the possibility of Christ completing what could not be absorbed into the Father's work of creation. In a state of passivity (and super-individuation by the Spirit) Christ is led by the Father to take on the state of anonymous and depersonalized existence, "the deepest silence of death" (*GL* 7:234).

The idea of individuation is not entirely foreign for von Balthasar. Making reference to it in the context of Holy Saturday, he writes, "And yet this extremity of 'weakness' certainly can and must be one with the object of his vision: the second death which, itself, is one with sheer sin as such, no longer sin as attaching to a particular human being, sin incarnate in living existences, but abstracted from that individuation, contemplated in its bare reality as such (for sin *is* a reality!)." Von Balthasar addresses the possibility that Christ contemplates the sheer reality of sin. This possibility abstracts the experience of sin as such from the human person's individuation in a sinful state of life. The abstraction is "the product" of Christ's active and subjective experience of suffering on the cross, but not of Christ's own individuation in hell (*MP* 173). Although von Balthasar speaks of Christ's contemplation of sin as such as a second death, it would seem that he fails to speak of Christ's own individuation and leaves the Spirit's role in it to his theo-logic. The idea of a second death, namely, the experience of God-forsakenness in hell, bears some similarity with the idea of individuation, even if von Balthasar does not make this very explicit. It is not until his theo-logic that perhaps he comes closer to the Levinasian sense of "super-individuation":

> The dead Son's passage through hell—when everything seemed already "consummated" on the Cross—is the expression of his "*super-obedience*" to the Father. The "super" means that hell did not appear

within the incarnate Son's visible horizon; that here "even obedience" receives "an impossible form," which produces the "feeling" "that there is some mistake somewhere"; that obedience is, one last time, "overtaxed," since the Father sends the Son into the farthest extremities "in order to answer the craft of the devil with the super-craft of love.... The Son's obedience even in death, even in hell, is his perfect identity in all contradiction." (*TL* 2:353–54)

There are times where von Balthasar's theology almost touches upon a theology of alterity itself. For example, von Balthasar develops a profound theological transcendence of Christ's encounter of hell. Through an "overtaxing" of obedience and love, Christ achieves the impossible, going beyond the limits of identity towards perfection. "Super-individuation" therefore witnesses to the depths of Trinitarian love — to a love that remains in spite of sin.

Question 4: How might we perceive the action of the Spirit on Holy Saturday?

In the theological aesthetics, von Balthasar is comparatively reticent on the subject of the Spirit's action in his account of the mystery of Holy Saturday. His theological aesthetics indicate that hell is a christological concept. However, in the theo-logic he develops hell as both christological and pneumatic. Von Balthasar's statements on Christ's doing "the living will of the Father"[72] offer an opportunity to explore a nonphenomenal view of the Spirit's action in Christ during Holy Saturday. Take the following statement: "Yet this act of seizing fate and destiny, and wrenching them out of their axes, takes place in the deepest silence of death. The Word of God has become unheard, and no message forces its way upwards to speak of its journey through the darkness: for it can do this only as not-word, as not-form, through a not-land, behind a sealed stone. And this 'doing' itself is no longer active, but is only something that is done" (*GL* 7:234). At this important juncture, von Balthasar does not speak of the Spirit's action on Holy Saturday. Nevertheless, he describes hell as "the deepest silence of death" and of Christ's doing as more a passivity and as an effaced trace. In an ethical-metaphysical sense, the Holy Spirit seems to use such silence to communicate not only the Father's will to Christ, but also Christ's absolute passivity in relation to the dead. This "deepest silence of death" appears as the impossibility of leaving the dead to their lostness and God-forsakenness. If hell is the place of the impossibility of Christ's abandoning the dead, hell must also be a place that defies the notion of presence and of what might be said.

Von Balthasar's almost invites us to seek out the nonphenomenal realm of Holy Saturday. He reflects: "On Holy Saturday the Church is invited rather to follow at a distance. Gregory of Nyssa exhorts us to participate in the spirit of the Lord's descent: *an eis hadou katiēi, sunkatelthe gnōthi kai ta ekeise tou Christou mystēria.*... It remains to ask how such an accompanying is theologically possible—granted that the Redeemer placed himself, by substitution, in the supreme solitude—and how, moreover, that accompanying can be characterized if not by way of a genuine, that is, a Christianly imposed, sharing in such solitude: being dead with the dead God" (*MP* 181).

Levinas's ethical-metaphysical idea of glory can be pressed into service to relate the Spirit's role to Christ's super-individuation. Levinas speaks of glory as the very communication of the face of the Other that designates a unique and chosen responsibility beyond the ontological perseverance of being-toward-death. Glory is the realm of "beyond being and death" (*EN* 147). On Holy Saturday, the Holy Spirit helps to super-individuate Christ's being to the will and glory of the Father: "Just so, I tell you, there will be more joy in heaven over one sinner who repents than over ninety-nine righteous persons who need no repentance" (Luke 15:7).

In the depths of hell, the Spirit orients Christ's being toward a unique and chosen responsibility beyond his state of lostness and abandonment and rejection of God, as one dead among the dead. The Spirit's animation of Christ's being produces a state to seek out the God-forsaken in hell. The God-forsaken, lost in the horror of existence without being an existent, portray a state of being-without-a-face. So Christ himself—super-individuated through the Spirit's plan for salvation history—must become the face of otherness and salvation for the damned. Christ disturbs their nonbeing and sense of lostness with a bodiliness of Christian existence: of being hurt by their hurt, wounded by their wounds, and forsaken by their forsakenness. Through the glory of revealing his face even in the depths of hell, Christ articulates a language of otherness "beyond being and death." This is the eschatological prose of Luke 15:7, a statement of glory identifying the hidden work of the Spirit and the drama of salvation history. While we must follow this drama at a distance, the distance should not prevent us from wanting to share with Christ the solitude of his glory among the dead. The revelation is that through the Spirit's super-individuation of Christ's being-among-the-dead, the meaning of the form and splendor of divine beauty become apparent: God's determination to seek the lost and the greater joy of bringing salvation.

The Nonphenomenal Other and the Resurrection

But the narrative does not end here. For von Balthasar, the resurrection is the event in which the true significance of Holy Saturday is revealed (*MP* 189). Von Balthasar finds this significance in the disciples' encounter with the risen Christ in John 20:19–23, which reads:

> When it was even on that day, the first day of the week, and the doors of the house where the disciples had met were locked for fear of the Jews, Jesus came and stood among them and said, "Peace be with you." After he said this, he showed them his hands and his side. Then the disciples rejoiced when they saw the Lord. Jesus said to them again, "Peace be with you. As the Father has sent me, so I send you." When he had said this, he breathed on them and said to them, "Receive the Holy Spirit. If you forgive the sin of any, they are forgiven them; if you retain the sins of any, they are retained."

Von Balthasar explains this sending as "an existential participation in Jesus' self-abandonment, in which the Holy Spirit 'blows' (John 3:8) or is (John 7:39)." The participation is connected with a sacramental experience of the Eucharist and reconciliation. In this, the reality of the risen Christ surpasses that of a mediator because his identity is the Eucharist: the forgiveness of sins in the condition of self-abandonment. The Holy Spirit blows or is in Jesus' eucharistic identity, enabling the disciples to receive the Easter gift of the power to forgive sins (*GL* 7:151–52). What does this suggest about the way von Balthasar structures his language of theology?

Behind so much of von Balthasar's presentation of Christ—from the incarnation to the resurrection—lie the analogies of Being and of the transcendentals. Reflecting on the analogy of the transcendentals, von Balthasar writes, "God does not come primarily as a teacher for us ('true'), as a 'redeemer' for us (good), but to display and to radiate himself, the splendor of his eternal triune love in that 'disinterestedness' that true love has in common with true beauty. For the glory of God the world was created through it and for its sake the world is also redeemed."[73]

Von Balthasar gives us three terms that are almost interchangeable: true love, true beauty, and disinterestedness. Although he naturally privileges the transcendental value of beauty, von Balthasar implies that it must always be in an "indissoluble perichoresis" (*GL* 7:242–43) or unity with the other transcendentals. The three terms imply the interplay between beauty, goodness, truth, and unity (and also the theological transcendental of glory). Particularly for the language of alterity, the term "disinterestedness" is a sign of how theological aesthetics could benefit from a greater study of its application to Levinas's ethical metaphysics. The major question here is: How might theology be developed by heightening the sense of the good in relation to the beautiful? For von Balthasar, this may seem like a reversal of his trilogy into the manual tradition of scholasticism. There is no doubt that von Balthasar's theological aesthetics advocate ethical transcendence; disinterestedness is the fruit of adoration and true love. The nuance or difference, following a Levinasian perspective, is to search for new categories to reflect on the true beauty of disinterestedness. For example, given that there is an indissoluble perichoresis between beauty, goodness, truth, and also glory what is the nonphenomenal character of such unity?

In the resurrection narrative, the disciples are faced with the Otherness of the risen Christ. Christ's Otherness in its fullest dimensions signifies the Holy Spirit in the depth of the risen One. In their approach to Christ in his risen appearance, the disciples are described by John as rejoicing when they see the Lord, perhaps because they have been faced by him in a metaphysical sense. Although they encounter the bodiliness of the resurrection, they also encounter an ethical metaphysical bodiliness. The disciples are also encountering Christ's rejoicing with them. Yet behind (on the hither side of) the theological aesthetic of rejoicing and savoring Christ's presence among them and of participating in it with the eyes of faith, there is an ethical metaphysical encounter of bodiliness and otherness. The otherness of Christ's face overflows in his bodiliness, revealing to the disciples—through the reception of the Holy Spirit (John 20:22)—his experience of Holy Saturday. Through the bodiliness of rejoicing also in Christ's rejoicing of victory over death and sin, the disciples encounter the true beauty of his disinterestedness: "If you forgive sins of any, they are forgiven them; if you retain the sins of any, they are retained" (John 20:24).

Their encounter with Christ (John 20) is beyond phenomenal experience, thus presuming an unveiling of Christian existence and truth. At this point the question arises: How might the disciples express the risen Christ's Otherness? The resolution of such a quandary lies in the sacrificial action of their desire to participate in Christ's self-abandonment. In other words, the Otherness or the nonphenomenality of Christ's face commands the disciples to exist beyond the care for their own death (*jemeinigkeit*) like the risen Christ himself. Summoned beyond the limits imposed by their own death to a morality of being otherwise, the disciples are able to consider the incomprehensibility of Christ's abandonment to the Father's will. Their experience and thought demands a language of alterity by which to express the desire to participate in Jesus' self-abandonment through the Spirit to the Father.

Extending this line of thought, the disciples' desire for Christ unfolds as a plot of individuation and expiation as identity and alterity are united. Like Christ's individuation on Holy Saturday, the disciples' individuation depends on the nonphenomenality of an encounter.

Levinas's concept of a Third speaks of the trace of *illeity* and of a tri-adic structure between the I, the Other, and God. In such a Levinasian frame of reference, the resurrection appears from a different angle. Even though the disciples are face to face with Christ, the non-phenomenal aspect of the encounter draws them toward the language of faith, allowing the Spirit to work in the depths of their soul in hidden ways. The trace of *illeity*—the Otherness of the risen Christ—evokes a passivity of openness to the work of the Spirit of Christ, leading the disciples toward a paschal horizon of Being.

The disciples cannot make an authentically individuated response until Christ breathes the Spirit upon them. Before receiving the Spirit, they are in a state of confusion: "They were startled and terrified, and thought they were seeing a ghost" (Luke 24:37). Keeping this Otherness in mind, let us consider how Levinas distinguishes *illeity* from the "there is." He writes:

> Ethics is not a moment of being; it is otherwise and better than being, the very possibility of the beyond. In this ethical reversal, in this reference of the desirable to the non-desirable, in this strange mission that orders the approach to the other, God is drawn out of objectivity, presence and being. He is neither an object nor an interlocutor. His absolute remoteness, his transcendence, turns into my responsibility—non-erotic par excellence—for the other. And this analysis implies that God is not simply the "first other," the "other par excellence," or the "absolutely other," but other than the other [*autre qu'autrui*], other otherwise, other with an alterity of the other, prior to the ethical bond with another and different from every neighbor, transcendent to the point of absence, to the point of possible confusion with the stirring of the *there is.* (*CPP* 165–66)

Levinas states that for God to be drawn out of objectivity, presence, and Being, ethics must be conceived as the very possibility of the beyond. The ethical metaphysical idea of God is otherwise and better than Being. God can only be truly meant in reference to the neighbor's proximity and the self's responsibility for this Other. God's transcendence is an ethical signification of what is beyond Being.

Furthermore, the trace of God in the Other's face is described in four ways: diachronic, immemorial, effaced, and ambiguous.

For von Balthasar, the resurrection, like the death and burial, is "a historically determined event." Furthermore, the idea that Jesus has risen into history amounts to a disclosure of God's Being as love, that is, "the direct presentation of the new eon embodied in Christ" (*MP* 242, 216, 229). Yet we are faced with an ambiguity of what remains beyond representation in historical time, as when Christ rises "into history" after his death on the cross. The event of resurrection is, in some obvious sense, an interruption of historical time; it disturbs synchronic time with an unthematizable deed and word of God. The appointed time, the kairos, of Jesus' rising into history is not measurable by quantitative clock time. It introduces a qualitative change in time as it summons awakening to responsibility to the Other in the light of the incarnation and paschal mystery. The diachronic time of Christ's encounter with the disciples makes up the concreteness of the resurrection event. It is an encounter outside the disciples' capacity to measure or reduce the appearance of the risen Christ to an act of their transcendental consciousness. In place of an all-reductive subjectivity, the disciples are overwhelmed by a time-transforming Otherness. Through the gift of Holy Spirit, time is torn away from its moorings in the structure of self-sufficiency to be drawn into a new time of responsibility. In this state of deep passivity, in the all-summoning proximity of the Other, the disciples are taken out of themselves, and so disposed to be possessed by the Spirit of Christ.

Hence, the diachrony in the resurrection event prohibits the disciples from trying to grasp Christ's resurrection as an ontological unveiling or as a synchronic experience. The objectivity or Otherness of the resurrection is outside of the disciples' transcendental ego, as though Christ were an empirical object or intuited essence. Levinas's understanding of diachrony permits viewing the resurrection through a pure passivity to the Other who comes from beyond the frame of any presence. In this way, Christ's resurrection breaks open the disciples' consciousness and thematizing propensities. Christ's own state of absolute passivity is the mark of super-individuation, effected through the cross and Holy Saturday. He bears the trauma of the wounds of his obedience to the Father. Having risen from the dead, Christ now faces the disciples in the Spirit of a new time, transcendence, and responsibility.

Where the risen Christ breathes the Holy Spirit (John 20:22) on the disciples, he opens their minds to a diachronic understanding of the Scriptures in the light of what God has done and spoken to him (Luke 24:45). Thus, they are equipped to proclaim the Good News and forgive sins. These dramatic events do not produce an experience and objective understanding of Christ's Being. They are the outcome of Christ facing his disciples, marked with the diachronic trace of obedience to the Father's will.

In the Otherness of the face of the risen Christ, there is both a diachronic and immemorial trace. For Levinas, diachrony and immemorial time are interconnected terms. Diachrony is awakening to the immemorial past as an obligation to be responsible prior to any meaning of freedom. On the basis of the Levinasian idea of immemorial time, Christ's Otherness would inspire a responsibility of such far-reaching consequence that it answers even for another's responsibility—for it communicates the power to forgive and retain sins (John 19:23). By receiving the Spirit, the disciples enter time in its immemoriality, beyond the measurements, memories, or representations of history. This time recalls "in the beginning with God" (John 1:1); Levinas likens it to the "in" of infinity (*CPP* 166).

Through this trace of the immemorial past signified in Christ's mission and resurrection, the disciples are summoned to their own kind of individuation or nonindifference in the Levinasian sense. Beyond the systematic comprehensions of ontological thought and intuitions of essence, and further than any project of the ego-consciousness, the disciples are subjected to a responsibility to the point of expiation. Such substitutionary responsibility bears the trace of the crucifixion and Holy Saturday, which are embodied in the wounds of the risen Christ. The disciples, when faced with the risen Other, cannot decline this responsibility. Henceforth, in their new experiences of time, there can be no history that separates them from either Christ or the suffering Other.

The disciples' encounter with the risen Christ also implies an effacement of the Spirit. The Spirit comes from Christ to the disciples without showing itself, beyond all categories, and to the point of invisibility and absence; their encounter is beyond the domain of Being. The effaced trace of the Spirit penetrates the disciples only on the condition of unconditional receptivity and passivity to the will of the risen Christ. The self-surrender they must engage during their encounter with Christ parallels Christ's own individuation or self-abandonment on Holy Saturday. As the dead were able to hear the Father's word of salvation through the Spirit, so in the same Spirit, emanating from the risen Christ, the disciples become witnesses to the offer of salvation to all.

But receiving the Spirit does not come without discernment. This is a new experience that overwhelms consciousness, turning it inside out and rendering it incapable of containing the event of salvation in any present. And given the transcendent and self-effacing character of God's word, there will at times be ambiguity or confusion surrounding its revelation. The ambiguity is that the disciples cannot simply preach salvation to the world apart from their own responsibility. The meaning of salvation must be signified in a place and time when the neighbor's face draws near in all its forsakenness—otherwise God's transcendence will be reduced to essence. Furthermore, the nonphenomenality of the resurrection has resulted in dogmatic statements (*doxa*) of God's beauty, goodness, and truth. Although such statements could be proposed by involving responsibility in the Levinasian sense, theology, if it is intent on appreciating God's transcendent alterity, must grapple with such ambivalence. Theology needs to be critically aware of the ease with which God can simply be thematized as a presence in consciousness. When theology tries to conceive of praxis and dogma together, it must continually pass through ambiguity in the realization that it could fall back into ontotheology and its associated form of presence. Only by way of "a crooked road," as Levinas remarks, can God's word be signified in the world (*OB* 147).

Such a danger, which Levinas encounters with Heidegger, is a danger of wanting to find something "'more originary' (*ursprünglicher*) than ethics."[74] For von Balthasar, it is a danger of preferencing *Dasein* to the point of contaminating eschatological hope and of departing from the Jesus of the Gospel.

HEIDEGGER AND PAUL'S ENCOUNTER WITH THE RISEN CHRIST

Martin Heidegger was the first to study Paul's experience of the risen Christ ontologically and phenomenologically, though many have followed to renew a phenomenological study of Paul, evidencing a number of diverse approaches.[75] Thomas Sheehan, for example, asks an important question: "Was he [Heidegger] interested in St. Paul and the phenomenology of religion for their own sake, or only as a means to working out the fundamental structures of how his own project of elaborating the analogically unified meaning of Being on the basis of a new understanding of temporality?"[76] Anthony Kelly, another scholar in this field, is particularly intent to pursue a "refreshed phenomenological approach" upon Eric Voegelin's "The Pauline Vision of the Resurrected."[77] Kelly directs his attention toward five major areas of Paul's encounter with the risen Christ: (1) openness to the consummation of history; (2) openness to the radically new; (3) an experience beyond the lens of social or cultural interpretation; (4) the generation of a fertile turbulence to produce an exegesis of the experience; and (5) encountering modernity's reductive tendency to reduce Paul's "theophanic" experience to an "egophanic" one, producing "new forms of ideology and Gnostic totalitarianism."[78] In many ways, Kelly's approach invites an impetus to renew a phenomenological approach to Paul. Using for example, Voegelin's term, "metaxic" (in between character) as a springboard toward developing the sense of Paul's "seeing" and "non-seeing faith," Kelly seems genuinely close to Levinas's ethical metaphysics, which is a vision of consciousness otherwise than Being.[79]

In the winter semester of 1920–21, the "young Privatdozent" Heidegger delivered a lecture course titled "Introduction to the Phenomenology of Religion" (*Einleitung in die Phänomenologie der*

Religion).[80] He particularly focused on three of the earliest Pauline epistles predating the Gospels, namely, 1 and 2 Thessalonians and Galatians, to uncover "the original features of Christian *lived* experience."[81] Sheehan sees Heidegger's course in direct regard to Heidegger's *Being and Time.* In other words, the course foreshadows a twofold development: (1) of *Dasein* in terms of factical life-experience, and (2) of the phenomenological method by developing the notion of experience (*Erfahrung*) from the Husserlian shape of lived experience (*Erleben*). In this second development, the Husserlian transcendental apperception of the *noesis* (*cogitatio;* the process by which we experience the object) and the *noema* (*cogitatum;* the object experienced in consciousness), moves to "the experienc*ing* of that which-is-experienced [*das Erfahren, die Erfahrung*]."[82] This suggests that Heidegger deconstructs the "within" or interiority of experience (*Erlebnis*) by drawing out the "how" of experience (*Erfahren*) to seek a genuine and determinate experience (*Erfahrung*).[83] Although Sheehan holds that his question regarding Heidegger's motivation "cannot be answered here (or ever),"[84] the convergence between Heidegger's Pauline study and his developing ontological phenomenology seems to be personally driven. Something is brewing between a lack of satisfaction with Husserlian phenomenology and a restless yearning to awake to a deeper experience *in* Being.[85] Part of determining whether Heidegger is more interested in *Dasein* (or his developing ontological phenomenology) rather than Paul is also considering whether the young Heidegger saw Paul as one who could lead him toward an experience of the meaning of Being and of ontotheology.

In the lectures on the First Letter to the Thessalonians, Heidegger uses the term "having become" (*Gewordensein*).[86] The term is drawn from the Greek verb *genesthai,* which is found in various forms "within the first twelve verses of the epistle."[87] The Thessalonians have fallen into the dimension of Pauline Being (*genesthai*): "And you became imitators of us and of the Lord, for in spite of persecution you received the word with joy inspired by the Holy Spirit, so that you became an example to us all the believers in Macedonia and in Achaia" (1 Thess. 1:6–7). Within Pauline "Being," there is the witness of the bodiliness/affectivity of Paul enjoying the joy of the Thessalonians and of Paul being wounded by the wounds (tribulations and persecutions) of the Thessalonians. Heidegger seems to imply such affectivity in his lecture: "We put forth formally the state of the relation of Paul to those who have 'given themselves over to him.' Paul experiences the Thessalonians in two determinations: 1. He experiences their having become. 2. He experiences that they have a knowledge of their having become. That means their having become is also Paul's having-become. And Paul is co-affected by their having-become.... Knowledge of one's own having become is the starting point and the origin of theology."[88]

But to what extent does Heidegger allow himself to enter into Pauline bodiliness and affectivity? Or rather, is he more interested in the knowledge of Being's essence? At this stage in the early part of his development, does Heidegger evidence, like Paul, a living faith in "our Lord Jesus Christ" (1 Thess. 1:3)? Or has Heidegger set out to imitate the Thessalonians' sense of "already having become" in the search to develop a phenomenology of the religious life?

A few years before his lecture, in October 1917, Husserl, responding immediately to a letter from his colleague Paul Natorp, wrote: "It is certain that he [Heidegger] has confessional ties, because he stands, so to speak, under the protection of our 'Catholic historian,' my colleague Finke." The context of the comment comes in response to Natorp's desire to secure a teaching position for Heidegger in medieval philosophy. At this stage, Husserl did not know Heidegger so well, although he would become his "favorite student" (*Lieblingsschüler*).[89] By the time Heidegger gives his lectures on Paul and phenomenology four years later, his faith is being carried forward by philosophical study—the very search for the meaning of Being. It is possible, however, than rather than equating God and Being, Heidegger at this time explored an equation between Being and God shrouded in "some obscurity."[90] Heidegger's course of that time called Phenomenology of Religious Life speaks of a "theoretical-philosophical" development. Husserl commented in a letter to Rudolf Otto on March 5, 1919:

> Mr. Oxner, like his older friend, Dr. Heidegger, was originally a philosophy student of Rickert. Not without inner struggles did both of them gradually open themselves to my suggestions and come closer to me personally. In that same period, both of them underwent radical changes in their basic religious convictions. Truly, both of them are religiously directed personalities. In Heidegger it is the theoretical-philosophical interest which predominates, whereas in Oxner it is the religious.
>
> My philosophical effect has something remarkably revolutionary about it: Protestants become Catholic, Catholics become Protestant.[91]

By the time Heidegger had given his course on Paul and phenomenology, he had ceased practicing the Catholic faith and had married a Lutheran woman, Elvire Petri. By 1923, his conversion to Protestantism may well have almost been complete, as he sought to actively engage into dialogue with Protestant theologians at Marburg, "including Rudolf Bultmann, Paul Tillich and Rudolf Otto."[92] From a Levinasian perspective, it appears that the whole momentum is leading Heidegger into the contamination of ontotheology and a terrible, almost apocalyptical journey toward shutting out Christian hope in favor of existential uncertainty. But for now, Heidegger is doing theology with phenomenology. At this stage in his life, his worldview has not been stained by National Socialism. His faith is seeking understanding. And perhaps he is trying to make sense also of his turnabout to Protestantism (his "having-become" a Protestant through Paul). Paul lived between two worlds of Judaism and the new Jewish Sect of the Way; Heidegger, a Protestant ambiguously claiming "that he never left the Catholic Church," discovers the world of a "presence-by-absence...allowing [him]self into (*Gelassenheit*) the prior absence."[93]

Heidegger's religious identity at this time seems, at least in part, to be the theoretical-philosophical presence of the Protestant mind through the absence of the Catholic Spirit. While Sheehan underlines the aporetic nature of the question regarding Heidegger's Pauline studies, Heidegger's Catholic past and his developing Protestant perspective both open a path of hermeneutics. Much later, in 1954, Heidegger writes, "Without my theological origin, I would never have attained to the way of thinking."[94]

Is it possible that Heidegger, similar to Paul and the Thessalonians, is encountering a second journey of having become (*Gewordensein*)? According to Heidegger, the having become testifies to the knowledge of one's despair (anguish of life) and joy (1 Thess. 1:6). Such knowledge has been "learned" (1 Thess. 4:1) and testified as a "living connection with God." Elucidating his phenomenological perspective on Paul, Heidegger emphasizes, "The being-present of God has a basic relationship to the transformation of life.... The acceptance is in itself a transformation before God."[95] Yet there is an important distinction between Heidegger on one hand and Paul and the Thessalonians on the other. It is almost obvious: Heidegger is intent on developing a phenomenology of religious life, while Paul and the Thessalonians are striving to live out a theological (christological) habitus and praxis. To use Sheehan's words, Heidegger is "interested in Paul and the phenomenology of religion" because he has found a fertile context in which to articulate his developing language of ontological phenomenology. He has journeyed from theology to the phenomenology of religion to envisage a horizon of "primordial temporality." For example, he retrieves "the classical Platonic-Aristotelian meaning of *parousia* as a word for beingness as presentness (*ousia*)" as a way to return to Paul's "unique eschatological meaning." For Heidegger, the parousia unveils its authentic eschatological meaning in the presentness of our being-awake and taking upon ourselves a "necessary uncertainty" rather than "looking forward [awaiting] to a future event." This brings to mind 1 Thessalonians 1:9–10: "and how you turned to God from idols, to serve a living and true God, and to wait for his Son from heaven, whom he raised from the dead—Jesus, who rescues us from the wrath that is coming." More and more we are beginning to see how Heidegger sacrifices the language of hope (and the resurrection) for ontotheology. For Paul, the parousia is an immanent future (1 Thess. 5:10) that must—in Heidegger's phenomenology of religious life—be leashed by a temporality of uncertainty structuring our becoming and Being.[96] The how almost seems to conceal the when. The how—"What is decisive is how I comport myself in actual life"—is Paul's response to when the parousia will take place (1 Thess. 5:1–12). The when suggests something like a super-obedience and confidence in the Holy Spirit or — to use Levinas's sense — the when speaks of a nonphenomenal phenomenon or a *noesis* without a *noema*. Heidegger elaborates:

> The "When" is already not originally grasped, insofar as it is grasped in the sense of an attitudinal "objective" time. The time of "factical life" in its falling, unemphasized, non-Christian sense is also not meant. Paul does not say "When," because this expression is inadequate to what is to be expressed, because it does not suffice.
>
> The entire question for Paul is not a cognitive question (c.f. 5:2: "For you yourselves know very well"). He does not say, "at this or that time the Lord will come again" — rather, he says: "You know exactly." This knowledge must be of one's own, for Paul refers the Thessalonians back to themselves and to the knowledge that they have as those who have become.[97]

Heidegger's phenomenology of religious life tells us that Christian life is to have the courage and confidence to live out our unique temporality. In the process of becoming in the uncertainty of the future (the ungraspable "when"), there is the very search to face eschatological problems in regard to the meaning of God's Being and God's eternity.[98]

Paul's conversion, calling, and testimony reveal a "resurrection effect"[99] upon his life and being. In the passivity and otherness of the gift of the risen Christ's being upon his life, something extraordinary has transfigured Paul's consciousness. Paul's experience of the risen Christ is very close to him. The pastoral theologian Henri Nouwen points out that when such a spiritual experience is so close, it is very difficult to articulate and understand it. The presence of the experience does not leave any space to deconstruct it.[100] Paul, rather than becoming lost in transcendence and transfiguration, descends from the mountain, so to speak, to allow his calling to make sense of his encounter with the risen Christ. Remember that the Apostle Paul tells us in his letter to the Galatians that he went immediately to Arabia for three years (including his return to Damascus) after the vision (Gal. 1:17). Voegelin warns that it is fatuous to reduce an experience of transfiguration as a split between personal explanations and "critical doubts."[101] Perhaps, in phenomenological terms, Paul needed his time in Arabia to bridge the gap between the subject and the object. In other words, he needed to take a step back into the language of faith to empty the intellect and make space to welcome a new vision of the other with a "learned ignorance" and "poverty of mind."[102]

It is inviting to wonder whether Paul in Arabia approached a neuralgic stage of his life, uncovering the severe pain along the nerve of his persecuting ways. His question would not then have been of a Heideggerian awaking (*wachsem sein*) to the parousia and the 'how' of life, but of a terrible movement from the horror of being to ethical subjectivity.[103] In the bodiliness and forgiveness of encountering the risen Christ, Paul's experience is now one of insomnia: "the sleeplessness which is not yet consciousness."[104]

In the bodiliness of being wounded through the woundedness of Christ, in the bodiliness of being emptied through the kenosis of Christ, and in the bodiliness of enjoying the joy of Christ, grace has transformed and ruptured Paul's ontological being. Beyond the essence of caring for his own possibilities and of discovering his essence in his own existence,[105] Paul discovers the good truth of grace. Permeating his existence, we may term such grace a "gifted passivity." Allowing himself to be seen by Christ, Paul's being has experienced an extraordinary ontological change. It is so extraordinary that his being cannot contain it. An In-finite change (God-encountered-in-the-finite) has taken place. Yet this change or mutation or metamorphosis, although ontological, is also nonontological. An ethical metaphysical metaxy of living in-between the worlds of the ontological and the nonontological comes to mind. The metaxy unveils an immemorial passivity and otherness; a time bracketed by the resurrection and the parousia. Hans Urs von Balthasar reflects that such paradox and incomprehensibility is the power of the Father and Son's gift, namely, the indubitable (or unquestionable) presence of the Holy Spirit "identifying himself as the synthesis of past tense (the history of Jesus) and future tense (his return), and making both believable by virtue of this synthesis" (*GL* 7:177). Such a synthesis of the ontological and the nonontological—the metaxy of the resurrection and the parousia—seems likely to lead to a state of insomnia. Indeed, the conscience may find it hard to sleep when it has been stirred, ruptured, and awoken by a divine visitation.

The resurrection effect has unveiled the Christian input of grace upon Paul's life and being. Such an experience is demanding to the point of facing the anonymous night and darkness of one's own demons and past. Following Levinas's development of the notion of insomnia from the experience of the oppressive, anonymous and depersonalized nature of existence to an ethical vigilance, Paul's time in Arabia represents first a theo-drama of fear, vigilance, and threat. In the turmoil and passivity of having encountered the Christ, Paul forsakes his old self. Another metaxy comes to mind: he exists without being his old self and he exists in search of his new self as a person-in-Christ. Paul—after encountering the Christ—is plunged into a dark night of suffering. There is very little sense of the ego. Paul cannot acknowledge his I. Thus, it is not so much that Paul can utter, "'I am afraid' or 'I am vigilant' or 'I am threatened.'" Paul is thrown into the terrible horror of existence without existents. He has followed Christ into hell, as it were, which he knows "*as* fear, *as* threat, *as* vigilance."[106] In Arabia, having incorporated Christ's paschal experience into his own, Paul must learn to rise from the dead with Christ. Ironically, his old life of violence and persecution (1 Gal. 1:13) is not finished and past (it will be more inverted into the suffering of humiliation and persecution for the truth of the Gospel [Acts 9:16]). Having seen the depths of God-forsakenness to the point of extinguishing his own hellish effigy or "hollow impression, as when a body has lain in the sand" (*TL* 2:356), he takes on, with the risen Christ, a new existence. The movement or hypostasis from egoistic and self-interested insomnia to ethical and prayerful insomnia has begun.

According to Acts 9:8 (not Paul's own account), Paul experienced a stupor or blinding for three days. In ontological and phenomenological terms, Luke takes the risk of thematizing and representing Paul's experience. And in Paul's own words, he describes the encounter in the passive sense of Christ letting himself be seen.[107] Paul offers the raw reality of his testimony. Like Luke, we also must also take a risk to understand Paul's encounter with the risen Christ. For Luke, the mystery of the divine-human participation stays intact; we must also discover the paschal framework of the resurrection effect upon Paul rather than the attempting to reduce the incomprehensibility of God's action-in-us to subjective explanations or critical doubts.

In Luke's account of Paul's overwhelming experience of the risen Christ, Paul's senses are not able to contain it, which results in a stupor or blinding. Given that Levinas mentions that insomnia is prior to stupor, might Paul's encounter of the risen Christ suggests a diachronic inversion: from the anonymous night of insomnia (*il y a*) to a wakefulness without intentionality (that is, beyond the categories of the object and subject) (*BPW* 132)? Paul, inspired by the resurrection effect, is gifted with passivity and otherness to testify to Christ as Lord and to his preexistence in and as God, that is to Christ's immemoriality (Phil. 2:6). More than just *awakening* to the metaxy of the resurrection and the parousia, Paul encounters an ethical intersubjectivity beyond the subject and object divide. Something ruptures the *noematic-noetical* (or everyday) structure of consciousness, namely, a vigilance and disinterestedness stirred by the turbulence of encountering God's Son-in-the-finite. And as Paul takes up the courage and confidence to return to Being and consciousness, he may also finally return to "sleep," that is to say to a "welcome disburdening"[108] of his old life.

It is conceivable that this disburdening would not happen overnight. The trace and memory of Paul's past must remain with him. It is through remembering one's weaknesses that one may have the "power to be made perfect in weakness" (1 Cor. 12:9). Paul is challenged to remain in and retain a certain humility before the mystery of encountering the Christ. Again, something extraordinary has occurred. However, "the mystery of divine-human participation" must be safeguarded from self-absorption.[109] Heidegger is eager to point this out:

> II Cor. 12:2–10 gave us a preview of the self-world of Paul. The extraordinary in his life plays no role for him. Only when he is weak, when he withstands the anguish of his life, can he enter into a close

connection with God. The fundamental requirement of having-God is the opposite of all bad mysticism. Not mystical absorption and special exertion; rather withstanding the weakness of life is decisive. Life for Paul is not a mere flow of events; it *is* only insofar as he *has* it. His life hangs between God and his vocation.[110]

For Heidegger, Paul experiences knowledge of his having become through entering himself into the anguish of his life. This is not a solitary experience but a co-experience. Heidegger points to Paul's relation to the Thessalonians (1 Thess. 1:5–7) to emphasize this: "Paul experiences the Thessalonians in two determinations: 1. He experiences their having become,...2. He experiences, that they have a knowledge of their having-become,...That means their having-become is also Paul's having become." Insightfully, Heidegger has underlined the raw nerve of anguish in Paul's experience, and it is a religious experience that has taken on meaning. Paul can write to the Thessalonians, "And you became imitators of us and the Lord, for in spite of persecution you received the word with joy inspired by the Holy Spirit" (1 Thess. 1:6). Heidegger's sense of having become does not speak of a past event, but the resounding of their present dimension of their facticity, namely their "alreadiness."[111] It is through "factual life experience"[112] of for example, "distress," "suffering," and "anguish" that the "when" of the parousia can come to mind as "uncertainty" or "constant insecurity." Heidegger explains, "Paul's answer to the question of the When of the [parousia] is thus an urging to awaken and to be sober."[113] The young Heidegger lays out a convincing phenomenology of religious experience. But from a Levinasian perspective, Heidegger "subordinates every relation with existents [beings] to the relation with Being" (*TI* 45). In other words, Heidegger gives priority to the ontological over the ethical. It is not surprising, in contrast, that Levinas writes, "To be oneself [*pour soi*] is already to know the fault I have committed with regard to the Other....To know God is to know what must be done" (*DF* 17).

For Heidegger, it seems that knowledge is first related to its state of Being (existence and reality) in the modes of having become and uncertainty, for example. In contrast, as Levinas suggests, to be oneself and take up a moral existence, one needs to go beyond Being to the Other, reaching a vigilance clothed in justice and a state of insomnia. This positions the Levinasian "to be oneself" (*pour soi*) against the Heideggerian "having become" (*Gewordensein*). Levinas's developing sense of alterity explains that a Heideggerian affirmation of "the priority of Being over existents" speaks of a "relationship of knowing" rather than one of justice (*TI* 45). This suggests that Heidegger's perspective of Paul's religious experience, namely, his relation to the risen Christ and to the Christian communities, reflects more a relation to an impersonal Being; it is as if Heidegger's image of God is one of a totality of knowledge. For example, commenting on "those who find rest and security in this world" in regard to 1 Thessalonians 5:3 ("When they say, 'There is peace and security,' then sudden destruction will come upon them, as labor pains came upon a pregnant woman, and there will be no escape!"), Heidegger states, "They cannot save themselves, because they do not have themselves, because they have forgotten their own self, because they do not have themselves in the clarity of authentic knowledge."[114] In contrast, a Levinasian-inspired commentary would rather try to remain faithful to the mutation or metamorphosis of Paul's encounter with the risen Christ, recalling a movement from impersonal Being to the primacy of ethical relations. For Levinas, Heidegger's phenomenology is too beholden to "the 'egoism' of ontology" as it searches obediently to unveil Being's truth (46). In effect, this places a Heideggerian priority upon Paul's religious experience of "power" over "withstanding the weakness of life."[115] Ultimately, a Heideggerian ontological phenomenology of religious experience must neutralize Paul's metamorphosis to be oneself (*pour soi*) in Christ in favor of Paul comprehending himself as "already having become" (*Gewordensein*) a person in Christ.

Taking the Levinasian perspective further, how might the state of insomnia (in its higher, ethical sense) describe Paul's encounter with the risen Christ? The value of bodiliness and forgiveness attached to Christ's word are so deep that they are preconscious because they give way to sensitivity, empathy, and compassion. In a nonphenomenological way, they help to transform Paul's life, leading to conversion and the call to be an apostle of Christ. Levinas's description of

insomnia[116] seems somewhat like the effects of humiliation or persecution (coring out the ego) and being called to move from humiliation to humility, a state of holiness in which the hollowed state of
the ego unveils a hallowed state of the soul. At least the ego is now
empty to peer through to the soul! And what does the ego now find
in the soul? The revelation of bodiliness and forgiveness comes to
mind. Such a revelation speaks of Paul's encounter—transfiguration,
metamorphosis, or mutation—of Christ allowing himself to be seen
by Paul. Levinas does not deny the application of the term insomnia
to theology. He writes, "But perhaps this theology already announces
itself in the wakefulness of insomnia, in the vigil and troubled vigilance of the psyche before the moment when the finitude of being,
wounded by the infinite, is prompted to gather itself into the hege-
monic and atheist Ego of knowledge" (*BPW* 159).

The Levinasian phrase "wounded by the infinite" speaks of the
essence of theology. By the infinite, we can speak of God-working-
in-the-finite. The encounter with God is a wounding one. Wounded
by the woundedness of the risen Christ, Paul encounters the revelation of forgiveness in the deepest and most hidden part of his soul.
Where the risen Christ unveils his word and being, Paul's troubled
soul begins to finally hemorrhage. Bleeding out the memory of violent persecutions to destroy "the Church of God" (Gal. 1:13), hatred
now finds a place in the love of God (see Ps. 137:8–9). The moment
of encounter with the risen Christ is enough to outlast all hatred
and all God-forsakenness. The bodiliness of Christ descending into
the hell of Paul's indifference and hostility ruptures and disturbs his
"absolute loneliness" (*VBR* 152). Rising with Christ, Paul finds his
calling as the wounded prophet and healer. He must now let go of
his knowledge and preconceptions of the Church of God toward a
language of faith, a darkening of the intellect, to behold a new vision
composed of: "What no eye has seen, nor ear heard, nor the human
heart conceived, what God has prepared for those who love him"
(1 Cor. 2:9; cf. Isa. 64:4).

This Levinasian emphasis on Paul may be critiqued in several ways:
as too "impressionistic and authoritarian," as demonstrating "a lack
of genuine consideration of what is being said that borders on irre-

sponsibility," or as intruding by introducing a subtle form of violence upon the young Heidegger's phenomenology of religious life rather than giving it a "just hearing."[117] These questions are valid ones, but this study chooses not to seek a middle ground between Heidegger and Levinas.

Pursuing other possibilities leads us to von Balthasar's reflection on the metaxy of the resurrection and parousia. This will help us to show first why we need a departure from Heidegger in favor of a Levinasian-inspired perspective gives rise to a new Pauline one. Von Balthasar writes, "It is noticeable how little the original expectation of Paul, that he would experience the return of Jesus (1 Thess. 4.17), became for him a problem with the later prospect of his own death; for he himself, like Jesus, had already spoken at 1 Thess. 5.1ff. of ignorance of the hour and of the coming of the day 'like a thief in the night.'" In contrast to von Balthasar's reflection on Paul's attitude to the parousia, Heidegger seems to make quite a problem out of it by slicing the chronological (quantitative) immanent expectation of the parousia from its "qualitative 'shortened time' (1 Cor. 7:29)" (*GL* 7:178). Furthermore, he cannot accept that the immanent expectation of waiting for the parousia is an anticipation of hope. For example, Heidegger writes, "One could think, first of all: the basic comportment to the [parousia] is a waiting, and Christian hope... is a special case thereof. But this is entirely false!"[118] Here Heidegger reinterprets the qualitative aspect of the parousia to exemplify how Paul's perspective is dependent upon one's having become. And by ignoring the quantitative aspect of the parousia, Heidegger has effectively placed an emphasis on the parousia over the resurrection. This suggests that the hope of the resurrection is subordinate to factical life experience (or the existential analytic of *Dasein*) of becoming in the uncertainty of the parousia. Thinking otherwise by keeping the metaxy of the resurrection and parousia in place, von Balthasar underlines the necessary connection between the quantitative and qualitative aspects of the parousia.

This qualitative character, an essential aspect of which is the anticipation of hope in the end, was first understood as a chronological (quantitative) imminent expectation. Such an understanding was inevitable because Jesus spoke above all on the basis of his own time, in which resurrection and parousia are included together in the same act. Moreover, before Easter, he urgently introduced the disciples into his own attitude of waiting confidently for "this hour" (*GL* 7:179).

Heidegger, in contrast to von Balthasar, "thinks from the outside" by "affirming the priority of Being over existents" (*GL* 7:179; *TI* 45). In other words, Heidegger's ontological phenomenology empha- sizes Being over personhood, or, in Levinasian terms, existence over existents. The young Heidegger's philosophy, if left unchecked, will ultimately consume or mislead theology and the engaging charac- ter of personhood, leaving an anonymous and depersonalizing world of searching for the meaning of Being. As a result, Heidegger's commentary on Paul's relation to the risen Christ is limited by his accent upon Paul's and the Thessalonians' relation with Being as temporality, facticity, and uncertainty. For Heidegger, Pauline reli- gious experience reflects more a testimony to enter the presentness of "being awake" (*wachsam sein*) to the parousia (the "incalculable Coming").[119] Bodiliness seems to be severed from the language of hope. In the bodiliness or mood (*Befindlichkeit*) of *Dasein* finding itself in the present, how might forgiveness find a place to settle in the existential time of the moment (1 Thess. 5:4–8)?[120] Where is the resurrection effect? Has Heidegger forgotten the subjectivity and bodiliness of the Thessalonians incorporating Christ's witness of his own time? Why does Heidegger prefer to speak of an existential being awake (*wachsam sein*) rather than the immanent anticipation of hope? In other words, is Heidegger more interested in *Dasein* than Paul? It is not surprising that von Balthasar will critically write, "Then [the modern constructions] turn to the equally misleading existential interpretation with its use of the present tense, which logically leads away from the Jesus of the gospel to a Platonism of the eschatological 'taking leave of the world'" (*GL* 7:179–80). Perhaps Levinas himself would eagerly insert a trace of "paganism" to the young Heidegger's developing phenomenology of religious life.[121]

Working with Levinas and von Balthasar, we could dare to judge that Heidegger was more interested in developing the concept of

Dasein, which would later find its home in *Being and Time* (1927). Yet this judgment could be too one-sided. Heidegger's focus has proved of great value for theology as a means to develop theological anthropology and theological method, as well as a phenomenology of Paul's encounter with the risen Christ. Perhaps Levinas himself is not so far away from Heidegger: though they are brought together through conflicting positions, each philosopher is concerned with the mystery of our human being, whether we name it *Dasein* or an existent. Sheehan's question reflects the need to see synthetically and sympathetically: Heidegger's search for *Dasein* is a search to understand Being and the ontological world of Paul. But we must witness to a Levinasian caution of falling victim to the pull and power to an anonymous and depersonalizing Being.

The horror of Being draws us away from existential truth. However, in the ethical insomnia of humility, humiliation, and persecution, a time and place for existential and theological truth may come to mind as bodiliness and forgiveness. The journey toward forgiveness may bring us to the vulnerability of our bodiliness, which becomes a place and time in the metaxy of the Resurrection and parousia. Enduring as a gift, forgiveness unveils an epiphany of Christic bodiliness, a resurrection effect through which we are able to encounter, like the apostle Paul, a time of transfiguration and hope. By taking an interhuman path toward the world of the Other, both bodiliness and forgiveness teach us that life is a transfiguration beyond necessity and need; a revelation beyond objectivity and cognition. Paul's experience of the risen Christ asserts that passivity and humility, or bodiliness and forgiveness, are "things God has revealed to us through the Spirit" (1 Cor. 2:10). Could we not then foresee bodiliness and forgiveness as first theology?

FOUR

Von Balthasar's Theological Dramatic Theory

There can be something quite dramatic about a theology of alterity; it can seem like a commentary on the tragic state of human being-in-the-world. To forget the face of the Other's needs, fears, feelings, and desires portrays a self-interested ego bent on being for-itself. Naturally, people are "allergic" to one another. The Other's face of suffering and loneliness, or even fear of death, can be readily objectified in ego-consciousness as something not so important. This may explain why our ordinary consciousness seems to register a problem with suffering. We do not want it, and we do not like how consciousness excessively causes confusion among our experiences and thoughts of the world and of others. However, on the hither side of consciousness, a nonphenomenal drama is awaiting to rupture consciousness with an overwhelming and utmost surprise—an unheard-of encounter that has never been present to experience. This is the surprise of the drama and theology of alterity. On the hither side of consciousness, in the innermost depths of the human soul, there is the moral conscience.

Levinas works hard to describe the non-phenomenology and transcendence of the conscience. Where the self awakes enigmatically to encounter the word of God in the face of the Other and in the inner depth of the soul (transdescendence), it is ordered into a state of responsibility for others (transascendence)—a responsibility that exponentially seems to grow. Such a hyperbolic state of responsibility endures as a difficult freedom of radical otherness. So we witness the drama or liturgy or work of responsibility for the other. Somewhere between the gravity of agapic love and the eros of being-in-the-other's-skin, a touch of ethical melancholy may begin to simmer until it boils over as compassion, prayer, vigilance, and expiation for the Other. The melancholy is no depression, but a feeling associated with radical alterity to help the self envisage something otherwise, namely, a compassion or substitution for the Other to the point of expiation. Levinasian ethics signifies a kenotic drama and passion, provoking an unthematizable realm of hope and promise in the dramatic revelation of the Other.

Von Balthasar also presents God's self-revealing role in dramatic terms, but in a far more overt and obvious way. A theological drama unfolds: God is the author, the director, and an actor in the drama of the world's salvation.[1] The action always unfolds in a Trinitarian framework. Believers are at once the audience and the actors, as they are represented by Christ and share in his mission (*TD* 3:527–35). Theo-drama is a first theology for von Balthasar, in which theological conceptions can be developed in different theological forms such as soteriology, eschatology, christology, pneumatology, and Trinitarian theology.[2] These themes gain depth through a phenomenal and ontological conception of analogy (triads).

Von Balthasar treats God's action in the world drama by way of two triads: "the triad of dramatic creativity (author, actor, director); and the triad of dramatic realization (presentation, audience, horizon)" (*TD* 3:532).[3] The triad of dramatic creativity employs metaphor to suggest that the author, actor, and director together resemble the economic Trinity. As the author, the Father is most profoundly involved in the play. His creative action arises from his responsibility to illuminate the meaning of existence. His action guides and accompanies the actor, Jesus Christ, to act out his role and thus to fulfill his mission. The directional role is assigned to the Holy Spirit. The divine director has the task of bringing together the author's creative vision and the actor's abilities to realize it perfectly. But in a sense, both the author and actor are prior to the director in that their freedom and creativity are in no ways limited. The director is more like a veiled phenomenon, present only as the play's atmosphere. He is the one prompting the actor to perfectly realize the original meaning and words of the author.[4]

Thus, in the first triad, dramatic creativity depends on the interplay of the author, actor, and director. But given that the play must move from rehearsal to live performance, von Balthasar conceives of a second triad related to dramatic realization: presentation, audience, and horizon. In the task of presentation, the director's role is to infuse the integrity of the author's text, not only into the actor's performance but also into the response of the audience. For von Balthasar, the people in the audience are not purely spectators; they see their reactions and reflections represented by the actor on stage. Through their emotions, in their thought and imagination, they are involved with the actor's performance; they want it to succeed. They enter into the play's horizon of meaning as it has been created by the author, articulated by the actor, and inspired by the director. However, the horizon of the theo-dramatic play is God's own. On stage, it can only have redemptive meaning in a fragmentary and broken way. When death intervenes, the play is a tragedy. When the drama depicts the struggle for the good, it is a comedy. Exposed to judgment, it appears as tragedy, comedy, or tragicomedy. Von Balthasar interprets the theo-drama's horizon of meaning as neither comedy nor tragedy, but a mixture of both. As the play alternates between weeping and laughter, it portrays the highest good of forgiveness.[5]

The two triads ultimately merge into each other. If the first reveals the economic Trinity in the world drama, the second shows how that drama is a sharing in the life of the Trinity. Here, three questions emerge concerning the relation between the Trinity and the world drama. First, von Balthasar asks whether God can appear in the play. The question arises from a concern to safeguard the divine transcendence and not to reduce it merely to immanence in the drama. The Christian answer is, "that God has actually appeared in the play: in Jesus Christ, the Son of the Father, who possesses the Spirit 'without measure'" (*TD* 3:535, 506). The divine appearance is based therefore on the phenomenon of God's revelation in Christ. By seeking to show how God might appear in the play, von Balthasar has in mind the relation between the economic and absolute Trinity. Within this relationship, Jesus Christ points both to the Father and to the Spirit. He is both the definitive interpretation of the Father (John 1:18) and the one who admits others to the sphere of the Holy Spirit.

The play presumes an objective phenomenology inasmuch as the play becomes a play by being seen and being known. In the presentation of such a play, the drama between God and the world is enacted as the Father unveils the objective phenomenon of Christ as the manifestation of Trinitarian love. In this dramatic phenomenon, Christ is allowed to be seen and heard, just as the Father's word is understood through the Spirit in order to make personal sense to the audience in a supremely significant way. God's self-revealing and self-giving love is offered to the other to provoke a free response, and such love impacts the salvation of the whole world. God can enter, therefore, into the world drama based on the role and mission of Christ in the Spirit.

In conclusion to the question of whether God can appear in the play as a spectator or actor, von Balthasar states, "He [God] is *above* the play in that he is not trapped in it but *in* it insofar as he is fully involved in it. The Father seems to remain above the play since he sends the Son and the Spirit; but in fact he could not involve himself more profoundly than by sending them both: 'God so loved the world that he did not spare his only Son, but gave him up for us all' (John 3:16 and Rom. 8:32)" (*TD* 3:514). Christ, then, does not appear in the world drama in isolation from the Father and from the Spirit. It follows that with the witness of the Spirit, both the Father and Son dedicate themselves eternally to the world's salvation.

The second question asks whether God as Trinity can be revealed in the person of Christ. Von Balthasar's christology understands the idea of Christ's person as the coincidence of his *processio* and *mission* (*TD* 3:533). Logically, this suggests that Christ's self-giving is identical with his personal being. Before the beginning of the world, Christ has proclaimed his readiness to accept the mission. However, the logic is approached from the theo-dramatic viewpoint. All possibilities are grounded in God's freedom, since, in the tradition of negative theology, God is under no necessity in creating and redeeming the world. Nonetheless, von Balthasar locates the world drama within the eternal dramatic interactions of the three divine persons so that one flows from the other (*TD* 4:327; 3:509, 516).

Von Balthasar's explanation of this point takes into account the character of the mission of Christ: he knows himself to be the Son of the Father in manner, which contrasts with the rest of humanity. More deeply, Christ's mission is divine and eternal: "Only a divine person can measure up to 'God's cause' and be God's 'agent' on earth." The person of Christ is equal to the Father in divinity and co-eternal with the Father's purpose and decision. In this eternal, intradivine exchange, the Spirit witnesses to the Father's will and to Christ's willingness to follow it. Accordingly, on the basis of Christ's obedience to the Father in the Spirit and his desire together with the Father to send the Spirit, von Balthasar discerns the divine essence as three-personal. Only God can reveal the intratrinitarian relationships by entering the world. Because the Son is hypostatically united to human nature, there exists the possibility of coming to some under-standing of God's eternal life (*TD* 3:510–11, 523).

In relation to the third question, concerning the Trinity's presence in the world drama, von Balthasar writes, "Finally, we can ask whether God's inner, vital, triune life, which is the archetype of all being and hence of all history, finds expression as the play unfolds. Can it, must it be mirrored there?" In terms of God's transcendence and immanence, he gives three responses. First, in creating the world, God chooses freely to be bound to it from its beginning to end. In so doing, he also leaves the world to its own process and confusion otherwise, as von Balthasar points out, "he would have to redeem himself." As a result, he is free to guide and to intervene to the point of offering salvation. Second, within the distinction between Father and Son in the Spirit (the personal relationship within the *immanent* Trinity) there is a secondary and economic form, namely, that the Father is the central actor. Although it might seem that the Father is a spectator, he is in the play in the same measure as the "acting

Son" and "mediating Spirit" because of his willingness to forsake his Son for the world (John 3:16). Third, Christ's descent to hell signifies that God can simultaneously be immanent (stepping forth from God's self) while remaining transcendent (in God's self). This is possible through Christ's absolute response of obedience to the Father. Hence, through Christ's descent into hell (God's own reality), God experiences the abyss of hell (*TD* 3:505, 529–30).

Furthermore, implied in the third question is the consideration of how a human consciousness can be related to the eternal personhood of Christ. Von Balthasar here keeps the salvific purposes of the Trinity in mind. It can fully enter the world drama only when the human subject is assimilated to the divine personhood of Christ. Underlying the subject's personal conformity to the person of Christ is the notion of the trace or created image of an eternal, divine Being. The further gift of grace transfigures and elevates this created image of God into a higher level of likeness. The human subject thus realizes its true purpose through the self-surrender of faith in Christ. Von Balthasar's idea of faith assimilating the conscious subject to Christ's divine, triune life finds expression in the Pauline notion of Christ dwelling in the believer's heart through faith (Eph. 3:17). This mode of indwelling derives from the mutual indwelling that characterizes the life of the Trinity itself (John 14:23) (*TD* 3:525–29).

Together, the two triads point to two foundational theological themes in the presentation of von Balthasar's theo-drama: (1) the unity between Christ's person and mission, and (2) the unity between the Father's self-giving and the Son's receiving. Both themes presume the person and role of the Holy Spirit as the very intimacy existing between the Father and the Son.

For von Balthasar, the identity of the person of Christ and his mission is the condition for the world-drama to become a theo-drama.[6] Because the Trinity has actually appeared in Jesus Christ, the Trinity is fully involved in the play. Von Balthasar states, "As we penetrate the consciousness of Jesus—as it expresses itself in his words and deeds, in his unique claim and his humble submission—we encounter the radiance of the mystery of his own divinity and of God's self-subsistent tri-personality. And the concept that included both is that of 'mission'" (*TD* 3:515). Christ's mission is not only identical with his divine person, but also implicates the triune identity of God. It manifests the paradox involved in the synchrony of sublimity and lowliness in which Christ's powerlessness is indivisible from the divine omnipotence (4:335; 3:515).

This simultaneity of Christ's sublimity and lowliness inspires the effort to discover the meaning of divine Being. In this regard, the identity of Christ's *processio* and *missio* would entail the unveiling of God's Being. It is clear that von Balthasar does not confuse the verbal sense of Being with the nominal sense of beings; rather, this is an ontological difference in the context of the assertion that Christ's person and mission are identical. The verbal sense of Being would refer to what sanctions the identity between Christ's person and mission: "this mission has always been present in [Christ's] consciousness *as mission* [*sendung*, (sending)]; in other words, it is not primarily something he himself has conceived and taken upon himself as a private individual. Rather, he is the one who, from before all time, has had the task—indeed he *is* the task—of fulfilling this universal design" (*TD* 3:167–68). On the other hand, the nominal sense of beings refers to the subject.[7] Hence, Jesus Christ (the nominal sense) is distinguished from his essences of person and mission (the verbal sense). Fittingly, von Balthasar does not confuse them; he integrates them with an emphasis on the verbal aspect of Being, that is, of defining Christ's person as one with his mission.

Von Balthasar criticizes Heidegger for not firmly answering the question of God in his fundamental ontology, especially Heidegger's construction of the ontological difference as a reduction of the difference between the finite and infinite. Such a reduction is a failure in intellectual courage to address the question of God. In contrast, von Balthasar understands the ontological difference to be a sign of humanity's creaturehood. Given this understanding, God offers to humanity a share in the abundance of divine Being, as this is represented in Jesus Christ.[8] In other words, it is not the gift of Being, but God's gift of Being in the person and mission of Jesus Christ that enables God to become immanent in the world drama. Von Balthasar even points to the need to go beyond "Heidegger's formulations" in regard to the gift of Being. Because Heidegger's formulations are without "the complement and correction of a philosophy of prayer," they lead ultimately to tyranny and exploitation. Von Balthasar thus reads a sense of isolation in Heidegger's notion, " 'there is' Being" (*TD* 4:159); this bears a striking resemblance to Levinas's conception of Heideggerian Being as depersonalizing. Von Balthasar, against Heidegger, rightly seeks to explain that the identity existing between Christ's person and mission is not a given finality, and therefore can never be exhausted by human thought.

Von Balthasar explores the kenotic interrelationships implied in the Trinitarian life, explicitly focusing upon the relations existing between the Father and Son in their common spiration of the Spirit. The unity between the Father's self-giving and the Son's receiving is presented as gift-as-given and gift-as-received. The aspect of gift-as-given speaks of the Father's generation of the Son. The aspect of gift-as-received evokes the Son's thankful and self-surrendering openness toward the Father. The distinction between these two aspects of the gift is kept open by the Holy Spirit. However, the distinction is transcended in the life of the Trinity. Von Balthasar writes:

> It [Christ's thanksgiving] is a Yes to the primal kenosis of the Father in the unity of omnipotence and powerlessness: omnipotence, since he gives all; powerlessness, since nothing is as truly powerful as the gift. Here, spanning the gulf of the Divine Persons' total distinctness, we have a correspondence between the Father's self-giving, expressed in generation, and the Son's thanksgiving and readiness (a readiness that goes to the limit of forgiveness). It is a profound mystery of faith. Thus the absolute is manifest as "We" in the identity of the gift-as-given and the gift-as-received in thanksgiving, which can be such by attesting, maintaining and fueling the infinite distinction between Father and Son. Thus, within the distinction, the gift is not only the presupposition of an unsurpassable love: it is also the realized union of love. (*TD* 4:326)

In this passage, von Balthasar develops the notion of gift in the interests of a more profound understanding of the primal drama of the Trinity. The self-giving exchange between the Father and Son is

manifested through the Spirit. Kenotic difference is the basis for perichoresis. The event of the Father's generation and the Son's thankful disponibility to the claims of the Father, along with the Spirit's
bridging of the two, is one with God's Being. In contrast, therefore, to Heidegger's idea of the ontological difference between Being
and the nominal entity, God's Being is identical with the event of
Trinitarian self-giving. Here, the reality of the gift enacted in Jesus
Christ connects essence and hypostasis, love and otherness, unity and
difference, kenotic self-emptying and reciprocal indwelling.[9] Bringing out the sense of reciprocal indwelling, Miroslav Volf offers further clarification to the notion of perichoresis: "The Son is the Son
because the Father and Spirit indwell him; without this interiority of
the Father and the Spirit, there would be no Son. Every divine person
is the other persons, but he is the other persons in his own particular
way."[10] Unity and difference within the Trinity bears forth a Trinitarian praxis of gifted passivity.

In the play of unity and difference, the gift or gifted passivity
implies the diastasis between the Father and Son in the Holy Spirit.
But it also envisages the overcoming of this distance or difference as
the divine persons dwell in one another in love. Indeed, the primordial kenotic events of generation and spiration within the Trinity are
identical with God's Being as love. Von Balthasar speaks of an absolute gift as the "We" that the Father and Son have in common, which
transcends their difference in the Godhead. It could be argued that
such a conception of gift represents its metamorphosis, as if the goodness of kenotic giving is metamorphosed into God's Being. However,
von Balthasar speaks of transcendence rather than metamorphosis
or even absorption (*TD* 4:333). Indeed, his sense of transcendence
includes a consideration of suffering in God. Because of the transcendence of divine self-giving, omnipotence and powerlessness are
united; and from this unity issues the perichoresis, which includes
exposure to suffering.

A further link between transcendence and suffering is found in the
diastasis existing between the Father and the Son in the Holy Spirit.
Von Balthasar writes:

We cannot say that the Father is involved in "risk" by allowing his Son to go to the Cross, as if only then could he be sure of the earnestness of the Son's indebtedness and gratitude. However, if we ask whether there is suffering in God, the answer is this: there is something in God that can develop into suffering. This suffering occurs when the recklessness with which the Father gives away himself (and *all* that is his) encounters a freedom that, instead of responding in kind to this magnanimity, changes it into a calculating, cautious self-preservation. This contrasts with the essentially divine recklessness of the Son, who allows himself to be squandered, and of the Spirit who accompanies him. (*TD* 4:327–28)

Von Balthasar's idea of gift depends not only on the unity of kenotic otherness and God's Being, but also on its phenomenality in suffering. The "something in God" refers to the self-giving of the Trinitarian recklessness of divine love. Such recklessness has no limits; it must bear the unbearable. Within God's Being of love, there is a defenselessness in which God endures the sinfulness of humanity. Hence, the Son, following the Father's will in the Spirit, must squander himself so that the creature's "No" can be left behind by the Son's all-embracing "Yes" (*TD* 4:329–30).

TRINITARIAN AND SOTERIOLOGICAL INVERSION

Von Balthasar's analysis of Trinitarian and soteriological inversion covers themes of Christ's person and mission as well as of gift-as-given and gift-as-received. The category of inversion is developed in relation to Jesus' soteriological obedience. More specifically, it underscores the active role of the Holy Spirit in the incarnation.[11] Von Balthasar here is at his most original in that he gives the Spirit a primary role in the operation of the Son's humanity and mission. The inversion occurs in the Spirit's movement from passivity to activity in the Incarnational event.

Von Balthasar clearly presumes that the activity of the Spirit is both subjective and objective. He reflects:

The Spirit does not prevent the Son from receiving his mission directly but makes it possible for him to receive it obediently. An

> infinite variety of possibilities is available to the Spirit: he can act more
> as the subjective Spirit who is common to Father and Son or as the
> more objective "third person," as the witness, the product, and the
> pledge of their mutual relationship. Accordingly, the Son experiences
> his mission on earth, now as something more personal, now as some-
> thing more impersonal. Knowing himself to be identical with this mis-
> sion, he sometimes sees the generating and sending Father in it more
> immediately; at other times, he worships the Father in more veiled,
> objectified form and "believes"—albeit in a unique sense that goes
> beyond all analogies. (*TD* 3:522)

As subjective, the Spirit is the personal expression of the Son's obedience to the Father's will, as in Christ's knowledge that he is the Son
of and has been sent by the Father. In contrast, the Spirit seems to
occupy more of a transcendent position as the one who witnesses to
the mutual relationship of Father and Son. This is especially the case
at the climax of Christ's mission, when, during the crucifixion, the
Father's presence is completely veiled.

The subjective and objective contexts suggest that the Son
encounters the Spirit's activity at extreme points, either in the immediacy of Jesus' experience of the Father's love or in his experience of
God-forsakenness. Von Balthasar, in his presentation of Trinitarian
inversion, in fact, stresses the objective action of the Spirit over the
subjective. For it is the role of the Spirit, as the divine director of the
drama, to bring into effect the Trinity's salvific design, culminating
in the drama of the passion. The active role of the Spirit in the passion leads the Incarnate One to undergo suffering, death, and God-
forsakenness.

Von Balthasar assumes that subjectivity and objectivity are aspects
of the eternal constitution of the Spirit. He writes: "After all, the
Spirit has a twofold face from all eternity: he is breathed forth from
the one love of Father and Son as the expression of their united freedom—he is, as it were, the objective form of their subjectivity; but at
the same time, he is the objective witness to their difference-in-unity
or unity-in-difference" (*TD* 3:187). The two aspects of the Spirit's
face show, in Levinas's language, a nonphenomenal drama of passivity coinciding with activity. The Spirit's passivity takes the form of the

Father's and Son's common spiration of the Spirit. In comparison, the Spirit's activity witnesses to the fact that while their difference is kept open, it is also transcended in the Godhead. Together, both aspects are described as a "twofold face." But there is a further consideration: the twofold face could be named otherness. Such otherness, as the domain not only of relationships but also of kenotic self-dispossession, signifies passivity and activity. But the Spirit's active role interrupts and veils the Spirit's passive role. The interruption occurs because the Spirit exists in and over the Son. This suggests that the Spirit's passivity must be veiled so that it can take up its active role to take over the function of uniting Jesus' I-consciousness with his mission-consciousness. When activity veils passivity in this way, it is as if, in the witness of the Spirit, the first aspect is more akin to a "trace" within the second. However, the eternal twofold face of the Spirit anticipates both the passive and active elements in every aspect of the mystery of Christ.

Describing the Spirit's active role, von Balthasar states, "It is as if the Spirit, now embodied in the form of a rule, says to them both: This is what you have wanted from all eternity; this is what, from all eternity, we have determined!" In the incarnation, the passivity of the Spirit's face inverts, as it were, into an activity of gift: direction and rule. But its active role must include the trace of passivity in relation to the Father and the Son, in bringing God's gift—salvific plan—into effect. In this passive guise, the Holy Spirit must witness "the hard facts that must be" as the Son is sent into the world in the likeness of human flesh. The communication of the rule is more impersonal (objective) than personal (subjective) in von Balthasar's presentation. Above all, it is the role of the Spirit to maintain the diastasis/difference between the Father and Son during Jesus' earthly mission (while transcending it in the Godhead). It allows for kenosis and suffering, as the Son suffers the Father's abandonment during the passion.

"The point of identity," von Balthasar writes in reference to Christ, "is his mission from God (*missio*), which is identical with the Person *in* God and *as* God (*processio*)" (*TD* 3:533). In a discussion of Trinitarian inversion, the implication is that in order for the Trinity to be projected onto the economic plane, the Spirit's second aspect must veil Jesus' awareness as a person from his awareness of his mission. This is because, as von Balthasar explains, the demands of mission take the uttermost priority: "In the Passion, the crucial priority is for Jesus to take upon himself the sinners' situation of God-forsakenness; in such a case, immediacy (which always remains a fact) is veiled to the highest degree" (3:522). This provides the possibility for the Spirit to take an active, leading role in the Son's humanity. For example, the active role of the Spirit during the crucifixion becomes the hard fact of demanding what has been determined in the mutual will between the Father and Son; in other words, the Spirit demands what the Father has commanded (John 14:31). For von Balthasar, this point implies a theology of gift. The Father's self-giving expressed in generation (gift-as-given) unites with the Son's thanksgiving and readiness (gift-as-received) (3:187–88, 522; 4:326, 335).

There are three ways in which von Balthasar's notion of Trinitarian inversion bears upon his theology of gift. First, the passive role looks to the union of the Father and Son in self-giving love. Second, the Spirit's active role or inversion reveals that their difference or kenotic otherness is more a veiled union of self-giving love. It is veiled in the economic plane of the world because the Father must make his will known to the incarnate Son through the Spirit. If it was not veiled, there would be no point for the Father to make his will known. Third, the union of the Father and Son in the Spirit takes the form of a rule commanding what has always been determined from all eternity.

Looking at these three points together, there is a sense that the Father's gift of the Son's generation depends on the action of the Spirit enabling the incarnate Son to give himself for the world. This suggests that a gift is given through generation, through the kenosis of the Spirit's inversion, and through the Son's self-giving in death. In other words, we could speak of God as gift in three senses: as generation, as an inversion of passivity to activity, and as kenotic otherness.

LEVINASIAN REFLECTIONS ON CHRIST'S PERSON AND MISSION

The notions of person and mission each provide a window through which to enter into a search for the meaning of divine-Being-with-and-for-us. Von Balthasar provides a soteriological and pneumatological perception of the drama of the inner-Trinitarian relations. There is a whole momentum leading to the Spirit's active role in the production of Christ's person and mission. He speaks of Christ's person and mission coinciding through the activity of the Spirit under the two aspects already mentioned. He writes:

> There can be no question of the Incarnation interrupting the common spiration of the Spirit by Father and Son, otherwise the Spirit could not exist in and over the Son. Rather we must say, with regard to the *first aspect* of the Spirit, that the identity...in Jesus between his I-consciousness and his mission-consciousness, or (what comes to the same thing) Jesus' consent to the Father's wish to send him, the coincidence of his fundamental free will with that of the Father, points back to a mysteriously supratemporal event that can be nothing but the unanimous salvific decision on the part of the Trinity, according to which it was resolved to send the Son "in the likeness of sinful flesh" (Rom. 8:3). (*TD* 3:187)

The action of Spirit commands and directs the Trinitarian decision. Since the decision is immemorial, that is, it has been determined from all eternity, it is now up to the Spirit to take the form of a rule. As a result, the incarnation must interrupt the first aspect of the Spirit. It becomes clear that the Spirit exists in and over the Son to such an extent that it interrupts and veils the common spiration by the Father and Son. Von Balthasar's sense of pneumatic interruption seems to have some parallel to Levinas's idea of disinterestedness, an idea referred to in a variety of ways, including divine comedy, otherwise than Being, desire for the good, incarnation, exposure, and maternity (*BPW* 85, 139). Often, Levinas writes disinterestedness (*désinteressement*) as *dés-inter-esse-ment* in order to show the break with Being (*esse*). The challenge is to see how a Levinasian language of alterity might help continue von Balthasar's theology in new and further directions.

Levinas's conception of divine comedy focuses on the ethical plot between the I, the Other, and illeity. This threesome signifies that love for the other is the true measure of humanity. Levinas states that the subject becomes a heart (*IR* 133, 143; *CPP* 168). In the ethical plot, the subject, I, is the moral self or a self that is a hostage for the Other. As a hostage, the self is in a state of kenosis, extreme passivity, or exposure toward the Other's destitution. The Other in this case refers to the face of the neighbor drawing near. Illeity signifies the way in which God or the infinite is indirectly in the midst of the moral self and the Other. Levinas states, "The subject is inspired by the Infinite, which, as illeity, does not appear, is not present, has always already past; it is neither theme, telos nor interlocutor" (*OB* 148).

Levinas's sense of comedy has behind it a sense of the tragic. The Other's destitution abruptly stifles the laughter before it breaks out. In Levinas's words, "the laughter sticks to one's throat."[12] It follows that the laughter signifies the extent to which one's conscience is called into question through exposure to the Other's destitution. Behind the laughter that symbolizes the desire for the Good is the absent presence of God in the Other's face. This absent presence is what Levinas names as the trace of illeity. He also states that illeity is a disturbance that can be confused with the stirrings of the "there is." This disturbance evokes a sense of tragedy: the subject is frightened out of its spectatorial attitude, producing a course of action in union with the absolute good.[13] Such responsibility is not the product of theoretical consciousness but is due to an extreme passivity of responsibility.

Accordingly, behind the comic dimension where the moral self puts his or her conscience into question is the tragic dimension that shocks the human soul and inverts it from interestedness to disinterestedness. The tragedy lies in the realization that the self is always too late to give responsibility for the Other. It is a shock to the soul. In an example that brings out the tragic dimension, Levinas quotes Dostoyevsky's *The Brothers Karamazov*, "Each of us is guilty before everyone, for everyone and for each one, and I more than others."[14] Such a signification of responsibility is the tragedy of the human soul because, for the most part, it lacks responsibility. Levinas stresses that responsibility is beyond consciousness, hyperbolic, and before one's freedom to exist in and for oneself. This seems to affirm that infinite responsibility for the Other has never been present to consciousness. Any realization would likely shock and disturb the human soul by overwhelming it with such an idea. Consciousness would not be able to contain such a thought of infinite responsibility. Levinas's ethical plot presents, on one hand, a tragedy of having been already late for the encounter and, on the other, laughter that sticks in the throat of the moral self when the Other approaches in his or her destitution.

Taking these two sides together, it may not be surprising that Levinas describes the sense of being affected by the Other as a "trauma that has surprised me completely" (*OB* 148). The trauma refers to awakening to the immemorial past of God having ordered the self to be responsible. The common conception of trauma often refers to madness or mental disorders. From a psychiatric perspective, the nature of trauma is both catastrophic and overwhelming to such an extent that it can shatter one's whole view of the world.[15] It seems that trauma is like a hyperbolic experience of reality, so overwhelming that one is no longer able to cope with reality. It might also seem that trauma is like an aporetic experience, an encounter with a problem (reality) that cannot be solved. In this regard, the Levinasian aporia could well point to being unable to fulfill responsibility before the Other or, in contrast, of not being able to cope with the horror of human behavior. Where the self has allowed pride and vanity to consume its substance, an ethical challenge could perhaps cause the trauma of having to face its conscience. Conversely, where the self is broken-hearted and crushed in spirit (see Ps. 34:18), the surprise of experiencing goodness could be enough to heal or rehabituate the traumatic ways in which the self processes suffering. This suggests that the activity of the Spirit can be enough to rupture the self's re-representation of suffering, allowing God's grace to take the place of the *noema* of consciousness. The self, then, is left with the good truth of God's love beyond representation and thematization. In simpler terms, the self, traumatized by suffering, receives the eyes of faith, giving hope for God's grace to heal. So something otherwise than human knowledge unveils God's grace and transcendence.

Significantly, Robyn Horner, in her discussion on negative theology has pointed out, "We are reminded that the only way through an aporia is through decision, a decision that passes through madness."[16] In this regard, Levinas's idea of trauma, like his notion of otherwise than Being, reveals a similarity to the aporetic nature of negative theology. For example, there is madness (tragedy) that ultimately leads to an ethical decision (comedy). Levinas's thought might well offer a new twist to negative theology by describing how an immemorial past safeguards God's transcendence from presence.

Levinas emphasizes that trauma cannot be identified as lived experience: "The order has never been represented, for it has never been presented, not even in the past coming in memory" (*OB* 148). The trauma signifies that there has been an encounter with the Infinite, or God, or even perhaps with the stirrings of the "there is." He explains that the traumatic encounter breaks up the unity between the *noesis* and *noema* (representation). This would entail a *noesis* without a *noema* or transcendence to the point of absence (*EN* 175; *CPP* 166). In less complex terms, the encounter speaks of awakening to an order of obedience that has never been present in any way. But because the encounter is immemorial, that is, never been represented and therefore unheard, it is a complete surprise, a trauma. This suggests that it is an absolute trauma to signify God as desire for the good. In a sense, such an encounter is also frightening; Levinas describes the order of obedience as that which "slips into me 'like a thief'" (*OB* 148). In a similar manner, the Trinitarian inversion causes the Son to have an overwhelming and even frightening encounter with the Father's will. Thus, the Spirit's traumatic action causes an interruption of the Son's consciousness as he submits to its rule; it has surprised him completely. The drama of Trinitarian inversion can be likened to an effaced trace or inner secret that the Spirit commands through Christ's paschal life. Christ encounters the unknowable as the Holy Spirit accompanies him through the madness of the cross.

Levinas uses incarnation to describe the moral self's extreme passivity toward the Other. For example, he states, "This exposedness is not like self-consciousness, this recurrence of the subject to himself, confirming the ego by itself. The recurrence in awakening is something one can describe as a shudder of incarnation through which *giving* takes on meaning, as the primordial dative of the *for another*, in which a subject becomes a heart, a sensibility, and hands which give" (*CPP* 168).

This reflection finds Levinas describing incarnation in relation to exposedness and the recurrence of *ipseity* (selfhood or the oneself), where exposure refers to the inversion of the ego from being for-oneself to being for-the-other. Exposure, then, is the very possibility of giving, encountering suffering and trauma, and of even taking responsibility for the persecutor's abuse and wounding. Levinas further speaks of exposure as maternity, the gestation of responsibility for others in the self. The idea of exposure also speaks of incarnation as the penetration of otherness (the Other's look of destitution) to the extent of deposing self-consciousness. Exposedness is therefore not like self-consciousness because the self cannot represent or think of itself as a self. Rather, the self, removed from the present (from representation), is torn from itself in order to offer its soul to another (*OB* 48–50, 76–79). Furthermore, Levinas's idea of the self as a body (incarnation) is not a biological one. He writes, "The fundamental concept of *ipseity*, while tied to incarnation, is not a biological concept. (Indeed, must not the original meaning of the 'lived body' be sought in the 'in itself' conceived as 'in one's skin?'" (*BPW* 87).[17] To be in one's skin signifies substitution to the point where the self inverts itself into a responsibility for another. Here, the self is exposure to the point of substituting for another (*OB* 115). Levinas's nonphenomenal idea of incarnation is not necessarily in contradiction to von Balthasar's Trinitarian theology on this point. For example, his treatment of Trinitarian inversion examines the nonphenomenal or immanent Trinity and how it has its economic form.

In order to explore Levinas's sense of incarnation to continue von Balthasar's theology, it is helpful to begin by looking at von

Balthasar's idea of gender difference. The idea contains not only the complementarity of men and women, their separation from God, and their being an image of the Trinity's inner-divine life, but also an order: "Both are created by God, but the woman is made from the man."[18] This order, based upon a literal interpretation of Scripture (Gen. 2:21–23), can suggest woman's subordination to man. Von Balthasar parallels the sexual difference with Christ and the mystical body of the Church, describing the Church as "Christ's 'helpmate,'" and explaining, "When he is no longer on earth as an historical person, she will represent him and continue his work" (*TD* 3:341). Further, von Balthasar's Mariology approaches the male/female polarity through a single principle of secondary duality, where the woman's essence is dependent upon the man's word and look.[19] Even though, von Balthasar insists that both "man and woman are first and foremost equal persons," his "order of sexual differencing appears to have been fixed and over-determined as a difference in a way which either depends upon or grounds...a misunderstanding of the sacred order of creation and the divine *kenosis.*" The key question, then, must be how to give the maternal a voice in theology so that it is not reduced to an "ancient logic" and "structural silence" of order.[20]

Levinas's analysis of incarnation and exposure offers a means to approach the language of sexual difference in theology and avoid its polarity. If Christ's person signifies an 'I-maternity,' then, an ethical complementarity between man and woman in Christ might be achieved or a more contemporary theology might be developed, more sensitive to (at least Western) cultural experience.

Levinas's idea of maternity expresses an awareness of subjectivity beyond experience and knowledge. It implies responsibility for others, even to the extent of bearing responsibility for the persecutor's abuse. Maternity speaks of an incarnation of otherness in which the subject exists beyond the totality of its lived experience. This sense of incarnation specifically refers to being bound to others before being tied to one's own body. Levinas therefore parallels the feminine image of maternity with bearing responsibility for the Other and characterizes it as the preontological and nonthematizable responsibility of a subject. This conception suggests that maternity is before and beyond the limits of self-consciousness. To describe the identity of an I in relation to consciousness in the sphere of Being is to suggest that the I is the origin of itself. However, for Levinas, the I is more preoriginal; it rests on bearing responsibility for others rather than on itself. In other words, the I is anarchic (without origin), belonging to an immemorial past of having been obliged to be responsible. In this regard, Levinas writes about "an irrecuperable pre-ontological past, that of maternity. It is a plot which cannot be subordinated to the vicissitudes of representation and knowledge, openness upon images, or an exchange of information" (*OB* 78–79).

This sense of maternity is beyond essence. It signifies an immemorial past of having been obliged to bear responsibility for others. In relation to conceiving of Christ's person *in* God and *as* God (*processio*) as I-maternity, this idea offers a new perspective of how the Son—since time immemorial—is God, and is with the Father in the Spirit. The doctrine of eternal Sonship bespeaks more of an infinity of responsibility for the Father. The Trinity's inner divine life must be expressed in terms of alterity rather than essence. Further, the idea of Christ's I-maternity signifies Christ's person, in God and as God, as substitution for others *par excellence*. For example, the Son substitutes for the Father with a spontaneous stirring of ethical emotion. The Son is therefore beyond essence as a divine hypostasis focused infinitely upon doing the Father's will in the Spirit.

The sense of beyond essence stresses the Son's recourse to his preoriginal past of alterity: within divine paternity (the Son being begotten by the Father) there is maternity (the Son gestating alterity). This Levinasian approach sheds light on the relation between the status of the Son as a person *in* God and his personal status *as* God. The relationship in question points to a union of the masculine (paternity) with the feminine (maternity): the divine person of the Son is *in* God infinitely bearing the Father's will, and *as* God beyond essence and the experience of it in consciousness. In more simplistic terms, this suggests that the uniqueness of Christ should be understood as

inclusive of both the masculine and the feminine and as the revelation of a new humankind, a new Adam and a new Eve. Such an
approach facilitates a deeper reading of von Balthasar's treatment of
the feminine in God, "The Old Covenant spoke of God's [womb]
(*rachamim*) trembling with compassionate love: this is precisely
what is revealed to the world when the Father surrenders all his love,
embodied in the Son" (*TD* 3:519). Along Levinasian lines, we could
conceive that the Son's maternity within God gestates compassionate
love in the world. This is a drama beyond representation and knowledge as Christ's subjectivity is always one of being bound to others
since time immemorial.

The idea of Christ's I-maternity can also be applied to von
Balthasar's idea of the sexual difference ("the bifurcation of the sexes")
as a likeness of the divine life of the Trinity. He states, "The fact that
the creature is 'over against God' is itself an image of the divine life
within the Trinity (in the opposition of hypostases); this imparts a
new dimension of the significance to the man/woman polarity" (*TD*
3:340). In contrast, the woman is the force by which man finds his
identity of alterity. Therefore the sexual difference can be articulated
by the woman's gestation of alterity over against the man rather than
woman's subordination to man. This gives rise for a maternal voice
and a sense of complementarity rather than ordering. The male and
female exist for and before one another. Thus, von Balthasar's claim
that "woman, as answer and answering face, is not only a delightful
encounter" (2:262), can be extended: woman is also the gift and revelation for man to encounter himself.[21]

Furthermore we can note that the idea of Christ's I-maternity
offers a new twist to the Trinitarian doctrine of perichoresis. We can
conceive the three divine persons indwelling one another in an act
of self-dispossession for the sake of the other. As each divine person
is overwhelmed by the other, each exists beyond its own essence.
Perichoresis, therefore, is like a mutual, maternal bearing of alterity in
which each divine person transcends its own essence in order to pass
over to the other. In an interesting comparison, Volf describes how
Trinitarian perichoresis overflowing into humanity through the cross

gives rise to a unique look at gender identity. He summarizes, "I have tried to describe what the process of mutual 'creation' of men and women would look like if we assume that they are to be 'created' out of a 'rib' of the triune God and the 'wounded-side' of the Crucified." Volf seems to suggest that gender identity has a Trinitarian and christological context giving rise to an inherently relational definition of what it means to be a man or a woman: "To be a woman means to be a human being of the female sex who is 'not without man'; to be a man means to be a human being of the male sex who is 'not without woman.' "[22] We could perceive that such mutual indwelling bears a trace of Christ's I-maternity.

The Levinasian idea of maternity is drawn from the sense of exposure. The meaning of exposure can be examined in four ways. First, exposure is the inversion of the ego's identity, from being for-one-self to being for-the-other. In the inversion, the self pushes its ego-identity to the limit, to the point of suffering for the Other (*BPW* 121). Levinas describes this as the recurrence to oneself, that is to say, the self contracting to its secret identity of alterity. He writes, "The recurrence of ipseity, the incarnation, far from thickening and tumefying the soul, oppresses it and contracts it and exposes it naked to the other to the point of making the subject expose its very exposedness" (*OB* 109).

Second, exposure points to the very possibility of giving up one's self for another. Specifically, Levinas is referring to a life of devoting oneself to the Other in spite of having the adversity of suffering ("an exposedness always to be exposed the more"). Third, exposure refers to a subjectivity of extreme passivity ("a passivity more passive than any passivity"); the self is kept from being for-itself. Lastly, exposure signifies a state beyond self-consciousness and cognition of essences. Levinas states, "The neighbor excludes himself from the thought that seeks him, and this exclusion has a positive side to it; my exposure to him, antecedent to his appearing, my delay behind him, my under-going, undo the core of what is identity in me." This suggests that responsibility for another does not come from any represented present, but from a time with no beginning, no history, and no memory.

For Levinas, such exposure is the sense of the nonphenomenal, an anarchic obligation to be responsible commanded by the Other's face (*OB* 50–51, 89).

These four senses of exposure taken together form a nonphenomenal context in which to approach von Balthasar's idea of Christ's consciousness of his mission. In the language of alterity, of the notion of "the exposure of Christ's mission" helps us to think anew about the correlation of the Trinity's eternal salvific plan with the incarnate Son's self-giving mission. Take, for instance, the Spirit's active role in the Son's humanity. We can see that this contrasts with the Son's hyperbolic passivity in regard to the Father's will. The consequence of this activity leads to Christ to an immemorial obligation—an overwhelming passivity—of being exposed to his mission. Christ is directed by the Spirit to be exposed more and more to sin, to the point of laying down his life for the world. In this way, Christ's human existence is overwhelmed by others to such an extent that the Spirit inverts the temptation to be for-himself (see Matt. 4:1) to suffering and dying for humanity. If we are to make sense of Christ's suffering, we must discover it in the expiation he offers on behalf of all. To take this nonphenomenal analysis of mission in terms of "exposure" further, Christ's kenotic state is not only activity, but also an extreme passivity toward doing the Father's will. This passivity can never be represented in the present, for, like the filial relationship between the Father and Son in the immanent Trinity, it is an overwhelming and hyperbolic reality that Christ's human consciousness cannot contain. As a result, the Spirit's operation of the Son's humanity acts in such a way as to veil divinity from him, lest the incarnate Son be tempted by the magnitude of his Being and lose his humanity. Simply possessing knowledge of divinity and its profundity does not initiate salvation. This can only occur by being exposed to others beyond one's own limits of suffering, giving, and trauma.

Is Christ's *processio* as I-maternity identical with his *missio* as the exposure of mission? For von Balthasar, the identical nature of Christ's *processio* and *missio* (or the Father's and Son's economic spiration of the Spirit) is a given. However, through the Spirit's operation of the Son's humanity (Trinitarian inversion), Christ's *processio* must be veiled from his *missio* for reasons of salvation history (*TD* 3:188). To develop this understanding, the Levinasian ideas of maternity and exposedness offer a nonphenomenal context to describe how Christ's *processio* and *missio* are identical. For example, both the Levinasian ideas of maternity and exposure describe different aspects of the encounter with otherness outside consciousness. In maternity, the subject gestates otherness to the point of being bound to others before being tied to his/her own body. Through the exposure of being for-the-other, the subject transcends his/her own limits of suffering, giving, and trauma. Both the ideas of maternity and exposure point to the subject's identity as an Other or an incarnation of otherness.

Therefore, the concordance of Christ's *processio* (I-maternity) with his *missio* (the exposure of mission) signifies an incarnation of otherness. For example, the incarnate Son, living beyond the limits of human giving, suffering, and trauma (the exposure of mission), bears responsibility for the Father's will as a person *in* God and *as* God (I-maternity). In the incarnation, the Spirit must veil divinity from the Son so that his mission is the breakthrough of the eternal, triune plan into the realm of humanity. The effect of Trinitarian inversion, therefore, is to produce the Son's humanity without letting his divinity be contaminated by experience, knowledge, explanations, and proof.

A possible parallel exists between the two theological themes of Christ's *processio* and *missio,* and gift-as-given and gift-as-received. Specifically, the themes of gift-as-given and Christ's *processio* share the common ground of the Son's generation. The themes of gift-as-received and Christ's *missio* share the common ground of kenosis, obedience, and thanksgiving. Both parallels point to the union of love between the Father and Son in the Spirit (*TD* 4:326). By developing von Balthasar's understanding of gift-as-given and gift-as-received, we may arrive closer to a nonphenomenal perspective on the mystery of Christ's *processio* and *missio* in Trinitarian inversion. On the point of why the Spirit must veil Christ's divinity from his earthly mission, von Balthasar is rather vague: "For reasons of salvation history, however, this spiration has to go into hiding behind the Spirit's *second aspect*" (3:188). In order to take the matter further, it is helpful to examine von Balthasar's "Dramatic Soteriology." An isolated passage in the midst of his reflection upon the Son's willingness to carry out the mission given to him by the Father speaks of Trinitarian inversion and the omnipotence and powerlessness of the gift:

> But because, in the economy of salvation, the trinitarian decision can only be carried out by the Father making the divine will known to the incarnate Son through the Holy Spirit (in the "trinitarian inversion," cf. *Theo-Drama* III, 183ff.), the impression is given that the Father—*cooperante Spiritu Sanctu*—loads the Son with the sins of the world (to the annoyance of all Anselm's opponents). However, as Thomas rightly says, it is not a question of God overpowering either the Suffering Son or vanquishing worldly powers, but of that powerlessness that is indivisible from the divine omnipotence. *As such,* because it is God's truth and righteousness, this powerlessness is more powerful than all worldly power. (4:335)

Von Balthasar stresses the indivisible unity between omnipotence and powerlessness and speaks of the correspondence between the Father's self-giving (gift-as-given) and the Son's thanksgiving and readiness (gift-as-received) (4:326). The passage indicates that the Spirit's active role in the operation of the Son's humanity (Trinitarian inversion) is to make the omnipotence and powerlessness of God's love "as such" interpenetrate Christ's mission. Although "as such" is a difficult term to clarify, Heidegger's *Being and Time* provides insight into its possible meaning.

For Heidegger, "as such" is a phenomenological description of the Being of a thing (entity or essence) that is in itself (*an sich*). In other words, the thing as such/in itself can refer to either a substance (entity) or substantiality (essence). In *Being and Time*, "*an sich*" is usually translated as "in itself," especially in regard to Heidegger's conception of "Being-in-itself" (*An-sich-Sein*). However, there is one instance where it is clear that *an sich* refers to not only "in itself," but also to "as such." Heidegger asks, "How is it all possible to grasp a substance as such, that is, to grasp its substantiality?"[23]

Von Balthasar uses the term "as such," to describe God's essence as it is "in itself." Nichols holds a similar viewpoint; for example, he offers this translation from von Balthasar's *Theologik*, "Truth is not just a property of knowledge, it is above all a transcendental determination of being as such," and then states in his own words, "Crucial to *Theologik*, then, will be the character of being-itself."[24] Hence, God's "powerlessness that is indivisible from his divine omnipotence" is conceived like the transcendentals, that is, as mutually immanent qualities of God's Being "as such." For example, in the same way that the transcendentals of the beautiful, the good, and the true can never be exhausted by any human definition, so God's powerlessness is more powerful than all worldly power (*TL* 1:15). This objective proposition of God's essence likely gives an all-pervasive character to God's Being—to the extent of going beyond human concepts.

Von Balthasar clearly treats the transcendental qualities of God's Being "as such." The correspondence between the Father's self-giving (gift-as-given) and the Son's thanksgiving and readiness (gift-as-received) is conceived in the same manner. Moreover, the unity of omnipotence and powerlessness identifies the drama (kenotic difference and perichoresis) within the gift: it encompasses the distinction between the Father's self-giving and the Son's thanksgiving and readiness, and also importantly, their realized union of love within the distinction (*TD* 4:326). Here, the gift "as such" can be likened to the philosophical transcendentals of the beautiful, the good, and the true. In short, the gift has the quality of being itself or of being interrelated with Being. Further, while von Balthasar is aware that God alone can truly speak about divinity, he assumes that the idea of a God-Man safeguards the transcendental qualities of God's Being from all the ruin that human freedom might cause (*TL* 1:17).

We can now begin to understand why von Balthasar points to the unity between omnipotence and powerlessness *as such* in relation to divine self-giving. The incarnate Son, having received the unity of omnipotence and powerlessness from the Father, reveals God "as such" to humanity because he can give all to the Father (omnipotence); at the same time, he shows by going to the limit of forgiveness that nothing is as truly powerful as this gift (powerlessness). Accordingly, the Son reveals "God *as God*" to humanity (*TD* 4:326; *TL* 1:17). This is conceivable because the Son's gift of consubstantial divinity with the Father (*processio*) is identical with his willingness to do the Father's will (*missio*). In other words, the Father's self-giving in generation is prolonged through Trinitarian inversion as the Son's mission in the world.

For von Balthasar, the action of the Holy Spirit gives the Father complete freedom over Christ's mission (*TD* 3:522). However, this freedom develops into suffering on two contrasting levels. When the Father recklessly gives all away without regard for himself, he encounters a freedom that changes into "a calculating, cautious self-preservation." Additionally, the Son, accompanied by the Spirit, allows his own life to be squandered. These two levels emphasize that God both suffers and will not suffer humanity's refusal of divine love. Both extremes also exemplify the Trinitarian recklessness of divine love, namely, that the Father must send his Son to the world to suffer and die, and that the Son and Spirit must give themselves to fulfill the Father's will (4:328–29).

So for von Balthasar, the phenomenon of God's suffering points to the unity between powerlessness and omnipotence: "It is irrelevant to suggest that the Father's generation of the Son involves no risk and is therefore 'undramatic': a world that is full of risks can only be created within the Son's *processio* (prolonged as *missio*); this shows that every 'risk' on God's part is undergirded by, and enabled by, the powerless power of divine self-giving.... There is something in God that can develop into suffering" (*TD* 4:327–28). As omnipotent, God the Father is freed from suffering. However, God's powerlessness (which must not be separated from his omnipotence) allows God to suffer the perversion of humanity's freedom by locating it within the Son's ultimate self-surrender to the Father's will. For von Balthasar, the passion exemplifies how suffering in God reveals the dramatic interplay of Christ's *processio* and *missio* in the world. However, in a context reaching beyond essence in the Levinasian sense, the Spirit's operation of Christ's humanity in the passion is an event (like "madness") that overwhelms theoretical consciousness. By producing Christ's kenosis, the Spirit also gives rise to the triune gift of salvation in a space and time beyond essence. Such space and time speaks of Christ's suffering of being forsaken by God on the cross. The implication of such suffering signifies the withdrawal of the Father's transcendence and also the incarnate Son's sense of transcendence in the Spirit. Thus, a gift can be given. Christ himself is not weighed down by the gravity of his divinity; Christ humbles himself and becomes obedient to the point of death (Phil. 2:8) because he is the Gift. This is made possible due to the Spirit's active role in producing the Son's humanity and veiling the Son's divinity. Hence, the Son is a gift of self for the world's salvation.

In an essay written in homage to Emmanuel Levinas, Jean-Luc Marion has spoken of the "as such" as rendering "oneself as an unsubstitutable other."[25] This perspective perhaps points to the suggestion that the "as such" also refers to Christ's suffering through humanity and for humanity as the unique one. For example, in the time and space of the passion, Christ as such (as an Other for all others) is the Gift of God expiating and suffering. The Gift exemplifies Christ being exposed to the hither side of consciousness. This is the space in time in which lies the Spirit's command of the mutual will of Father and Son. We can now conceive that Christ's *processio* is identical with his *missio* through the Spirit's action of giving Christ a sense of God, the Gift, in his earthly life. This sense permits the Spirit to veil Christ's divinity from his self-consciousness, which is necessary because any knowledge of being the divine Logos would have overwhelmed Christ's humanity. Thus, it is left to the Spirit to inspire the incarnate Son to do the Father's will.

Furthermore, the self might begin to theologize the extent to which Christ *as such* "lives in me" (Gal. 2:20). This is where Christ's kenosis in the Spirit gnaws away at the self's identity, breaking up the temptation to reduce God, humanity, and the world to an essence in consciousness. Given that Christ's kenosis turns consciousness away from itself, the christocentric gift awakes the concordance of language and acts in the self. The self, now a person in Christ, is an incarnation of otherness (an Other as such). And if Christ provokes the self into a life of kenosis, a space and time might well exist to theologize God/Gift with the language of alterity. There is always the temptation, however, to pronounce the word "God" within the categories of objectivity, Being, and presence. Thus, is left to the action of the Spirit to inspire the theological person to be like Christ: humble and obedient to the point of expiation. It remains always a difficult freedom for theology to learn from Christ's life of kenosis in the Spirit: a very language and life of alterity in which *theoria* concords with praxis. In this regard, Levinas reflects in "A Man-God?":

> On the one hand, the problem of the Man-God includes the idea of a self-inflicted humiliation on the part of the Supreme Being, of a descent of the Creator to the level of the Creature; that is to say, an absorption of the most active activity into the most passive passivity.
> On the other hand the problem includes, as if brought about by this passivity pushed to its ultimate degree in the Passion, the idea of expiation for others, that is, of a substitution. The identical par excellence, the noninterchangeable, the unique par excellence, would be substitution itself. (*EN* 53–54)

Levinas's major aim is to show how the Christian theological meaning of a Man-God/God-Man contrasts with the Greek man-gods. He further reflects: "The appearance of man-gods, sharing the passions and joys of men who are purely men, is certainly a common characteristic of pagan poems. But in paganism, as the price for this manifestation, the gods lose their divinity. Hence philosophers expel poets from the City to preserve the divinity of the gods in men's minds. But divinity thus saved lacks all condescension" (*EN* 54). The philosophers, such as Plato, Aristotle, and even Hegel, show the depth of how God manifests the divine self in the finite. Here we see a philosophical portrait of God as impersonal and indifferent to the world. For Levinas contends that that we cannot learn from these thinkers how God relates to the world. This challenge thoroughly engages Levinas and von Balthasar. Theology can be inherently theoretical, yet von Balthasar's theological dramatic theory manages to breaks open the incarnation, the paschal mystery, and the Trinity in a way that underlines the meaning of revelation to humankind.

He writes, "In Christ, through grace, creaturely man can become a (theological) person, that is, the Father's child, who has been given a share in a qualitatively unique way in Christ's mission; this takes place through the indwelling of the Holy Spirit in him, whereby he becomes a dwelling place of the divine Persons (John 14:23; 1 Cor. 6:19; Eph. 3:17)" (*TD* 3:527).

These words forge, as it were, a dramatic and theological path to reflect upon how a God-Man relates to the world. The Christian is called to a theological personhood or existence and, further, to find a way not to reduce the story of salvation history to pagan and impersonal ways. This presents the Christian theologian with the obligation to give theology a voice in the world, that is to say, to find a practical way to speak about God in society.

PHENOMENOLOGY, THEOLOGY, AND PSYCHOSIS

In the world of communication, we are often taken over by a language of fear. We desire to discover truth while trying to escape from it. We search to understand reality through language, meaning, and reason. However, there are times when reason is too present and too overwhelming. This is because we can never totally conceive the meaning of our own existence and reality; we remain at most a partial and momentary presence to ourselves. In our attempts to search for meaning and truth, our articulations may become distorted, unreal, and imaginary. Experiences become too close to articulate with meaning. Psychosis, an extreme reaction, is an existence cut off from reality.[26] In such horror, fear is the dominant emotion and becomes so suffocating that it takes the form of an idol. As a result, the self is turned inside out by being removed of subjectivity. It exists in an anonymous vigilance toward the idol or thing. In this regard, delusions and fears take on a terrifying role; they deny the possibility of death, leaving the self to be ravaged by a past devoid of hope and life.

The World War I poet Wilfred Owens wrote a haunting poem titled, "Mental Cases." He awakened readers to the "men whose minds the Dead have ravished." They cannot escape their "Memory" as it "fingers in their hair of murders." We cannot but feel a sense of responsibility as we watch their hands "pawing us who dealt them war and madness." The memory of their murders in the trenches collapses into an abyss between experiences that never die and the dead who ravish their minds. Owens asks his readers to engage with the questions, "Who are these? Why sit they here in twilight?"[27] And if we listen to von Balthasar, he engages similar quandaries, in a way that leads away from meaninglessness and human suffering and toward hope in God: "The world's suffering exceeds our human powers of comprehension. As such it points in the direction of two things: in the first place, there can be depths, in creation itself, that man has no power to dominate; and, in the second place, God can react to human conduct—that is, sin—in a way that is far more divine than man can imagine" (*TD* 4:193).

Like Owens and von Balthasar, we need a language to find a way to encounter and unearth our preconscious feelings and memories as well as those repressed in the darkness of the unconscious mind. Poetry and theo-drama offer potential routes along which to develop a language of alterity. Poetry plucks at the melancholy and vigilance lying in our soul, and theo-drama deepens an ethical awakening toward imagining God otherwise.

Von Balthasar reminds us how deeply we are plagued by limits imposed on life and love:

> The fight for one's place under the sun; the terrible stifling of the individual by the surrounding relations, the clan, and even by the family; the struggle of natural selection, for which nature itself provides the strength and the arms; the laws of time's decay; friendships, once thought to be forever, grow cold, people grow apart, views and perspectives and thus hearts too become estranged. Geographic distances create an additional burden, and love must be strong and single-minded in order to withstand it; pledges of love, meant to be eternal, get broken, because the rising wave of eros gave way and another newer love came in between; the beloved's faults and limitations become unbearable, and perhaps even worsened because the finitude of love seemed to be a contradiction: Why love just one woman when there are thousands that could be loved?[28]

Von Balthasar's existential analysis is compelling, yet noticeably he fails to give the example of war. For Levinas, the memory and suffering of World War II and the Shoah are ever-present in his writings. War itself highlights the temptation to reduce the Other to an impersonal existence and deny his or her dignity of being an existent. Von Balthasar's reflection gives insight to the inner-contours and brokenness of everyday relations. Together, these two thinkers point to the limitations of love, leaving language and reason disturbed by the horror of life and "the abyss of selfishness" (*LA* 66).

In the search for reason, language may also become impersonal and objectified. As a result, it takes a destructive and depersonalizing turn, to the extent of becoming lost in a cold horror of objectivity (the "there is") (*EE* 64). Where the horror of life is so piercing, fear begins to gnaw at the personal and subjective. The self, lacking courage, cannot touch its deeper level where "man is aware of his heart's paralysis, fallenness, and frigidity, his incapacity to meet the demand of any law of love, no matter how generally postulated" (*LA* 67). The self then, ironically, intimately knows fear more than its own self. Moreover, fear's presence consumes its courage to discover truth, leaving an aftertaste of an anonymous and depersonalizing presence of objective reality, knowledge, and reason. Such fear or presence is anonymous because it is too horrible. It is also depersonalizing insofar as it destroys subjectivity and the ability to relate with others.

It is not surprising that the self, fearful of the world, might become lost in darkness and chaos. And here in the night, the ghostly presence of fear sets out to evoke division. The altered self, divided from reason and truth, from relational personhood, is reduced to fear and death. For Levinas, this speaks intimately of the breakdown of the interhuman; and perhaps the extent of how one's being-toward-death alienates others and evolves into a terror of being lost to the "fullness of the mine—a 'mineness' of *Jemeinigkeit*, in Heideggerian terms" (*EN* 212). Also evidencing an anti-Heideggerian polemic, von Balthasar speaks otherwise than such an "abyss of selfishness" by emphasizing, "We can go beyond Heidegger's formulations and assert that all the philosophy of the scope of human power and reason that is based on Descartes lacks the complement and correction of a philosophy of *prayer*" (*TD* 4:159). For example, where von Balthasar emphasizes Heidegger's notion, "[Man] is ultimately nothing but gratitude for the gift of being, for the very fact that 'there is' being" (4:159), something is missing: the meaning and practice of prayer. In Levinasian terms, "Heidegger's formulation" signifies the horror of the "there is," a phenomenology of fear and death rather than of freedom and of "fashion[ing] the earth in a meaningful and fruitful way" (4:159).

Levinas and von Balthasar criticisms uncover the darkness of a world threatened by fear and death, yet also inspires a way to positively think through Heidegger and ultimately beyond him. For the most part, the objective world is a partial presence in consciousness; there is so much that we do not know about. Such unknowing produces fear. In other words, the world is not only present by way of knowledge, ideas, and imagination, but also through fear.[29] The self is both in relation to itself and the world, yet the extent to which the relation is governed by being conscious of something is the extent to which the self remains caught in its own possibilities and fears (the Heideggerian care for Being). In von Balthasar's sense, this is the plague of limits imposed upon love.

As Levinas and von Balthasar deconstruct Heidegger, four points emerge here representing a phenomenology of fear. First, every act of consciousness is a search for the presence of meaning. Second, every act of consciousness is also a relation and response to Being, that is, the presence of things in the world (real or imaginary). Third, the act of consciousness signifies the fears of nothingness and anxiety. Fourth, granted that the self is usually centered on its own possibilities, fears, and desires, the act of consciousness grounds experience as objective in the sense of making it "mine." In this pattern, the conscious self responds to the presence of other things in the world by objectifying them in a possessive and egoistic way, thereby imposing limits upon love and friendship. This could well lead the self to fear a menacing presence in the world: something unknown that disturbs, seeks us out, and aims at us (*CPP* 181). We might experience this as fear in the form of anxiety and uncertainty. If the fear is too consuming, existence becomes shattered; we lose a sense of our personal self. We are left with a consuming darkness that leaves the self unable to engage normally with others in the pursuit of a philosophy of love.

When fear becomes so overwhelming, we face a "horror of the night": an inability to ascertain the presence or absence of anything. In this horrible eternity, there is darkness in and around the self that calls into question any attempt to derive meaning and truth. The darkness creates illusion. In such an existential state of being cut off from itself, the self undergoes a thrice-altered state of existence. Reflecting on transcendence and the Levinasian idea of the "there is," John Caruana describes: "The state of mind, or more precisely, the destructed or unraveled mind that the *il y a*—the invisible forces that grip the self—effects can be simultaneously terrifying and enthralling.... Lévinas suspects that the sacred entails a *confusion* of the absolute or divine with the elementary powers of the *il y a*." It is in regard to such confusion that a sense of ethical escapism leads on to an experience of "terrifying and enthralling" transcendence. Caruana continues:

> Rather than having to face up to the consequences of the profound ambiguity of existence—indeterminate being provides us with no signposts that might help us to lead a purposeful life—our fear, Lévinas contends, can drive us to establish idols that we imagine can arrest the incessant ambiguity of being. We associate idols primarily with human-made objects of veneration, such as totems or natural objects like the sun. But idolization is not restricted to physical objects; it also encompasses complex psychological states of mind like those that Freud aptly characterizes as magical thinking or "omnipotence of thought."[30]

The states of "idolization," "ethical escapism," and "terrifying and enthralling transcendence" provide another horizon by which to understand a phenomenology of fear. They also offer a set of categories to develop and find a way for God's word of compassion and friendship to speak to the world. Von Balthasar, however, presents a warning about understanding human existence and the failures of love: "The stages of the journey are impossible to map out; they trail off immediately into the impenetrable night" (*LA* 67). Given this warning, an analysis of the three states seems a prudent way to explore altered, divided existence.

Idolization is an illusional state that results in the depersonalization of the self. The idol in this case is the self's experience: all its ideas, thoughts, imagination, and fears. In this state of being separated from reality (truth, meaning, and relationship), a suffocating type of existence takes hold: any resemblance of reality "as such" (as it truly is) is rejected and blocked. In fact, existence is so suffocating that the idol (the experience itself) shreds the self of any value. No amount of suffering and hemorrhaging of wounds will rupture the state of such depersonalizing existence. The self's experience of suffering bleeds fear to such a degree that the self becomes lost, numb, and divided from reality. Furthermore, the fears (delusions and illusions) depersonalize the self to the point that the self takes an anonymous form; it becomes a nothing in the horror of existence. What is left is the idol—the cold and heartless experience of fear itself—revealing an antitheo-drama: the idol, distorting the "fundamental act" of prayer, grows in power "until it becomes a tyranny over the earth, exploiting it and heedlessly laying it waste" (*TD* 4:59).

In the darkness of existence, the self is idol, fear, and tyranny. Accordingly, all ideas, thoughts, and imagination are brought into servitude partaking of fear, idolization, and manipulation. Here, there is no role of the self; the self is but a trace to itself, lost in darkness. Nevertheless, the idol commands a response, an overshadowing experience that must always negate the self: its fusion with the idol. This response cannot be heard, seen, or sensed in any way. Traces of the response take a nonpersonal form, pouring into reality in delusions and illusions. These traces of horror seek to evade ethical responsibility. The idol, having reduced the self to anonymity and anxiety, can now aim at the good by seeking it out and corrupting it with the heart of evil. Taking on a closed and suffocating existence, idolization is the first movement and experience of delusion. Once it is formed like a haunting ghost in consciousness, the self is tied to manipulate the good to its delusional state of fear and horror.

The suffocating embrace of experience can be so overwhelming that it causes the self to lose sense of its reality. The "threat" of a "quasi-anonymous annihilation of personal existence" has taken form (*TD* 4:59). So the self loses control of its ideas, thoughts, and imagination to the idol. And the idol emerges as a trace in reality as it seeks to give itself meaning and significance by seeking out the good. But its attachment to the good is destructive. Moving through fear and anxiety, the idol or "thing" expresses itself in relation to the good because it must hide its difference from it. Furthermore, by seeking to relate to what is good, the-self-as-idol confuses itself with the good, and thus finds a way paradoxically to escape the ethical life. This is because the idol dwells in the totality of Being; it can never embrace a life of transcendence as it cannot divest itself of the anonymous and depersonalizing nature of Being and pass over beyond toward ethical subjectivity. In other words, the totality divides the self from knowing freedom and justice. No one can ask the self to be accountable. The idol-self has closed the door to the "outside" (*EN* 30), locking in a "context for evil" to "explode" through "the tension of personal and social existence" (*TD* 4:160).

So the self, consumed by the idol, not only sets out to escape the good but also seeks to strike at reality with its totalizing presence and gaze. For example, delusional thoughts and behaviors are naturally attracted to the good, but not being able to subjectively approach the good, the idol objectifies it as an experience. The experience is so all-consuming and overwhelming that it leaves no room for the infinity of the good. However, believing itself to be in the realm of the good, the idol reduces the good to its presence of fear and delusions (a bad infinity). A dramatic "struggle for the primacy to be genuine unfolds" to the point where the idol now believes itself to be "better" even than the "good" (*TD* 4:160). Calling this a state of ethical escapism acknowledges that while the idol seeks to merge with the good, it escapes from it by way of its hidden intent to negate (reduce) the good to its better experience, namely, its existence of fear, manipulation, horror, and alienation. Such experience necessarily finds its expression through language, behavior, and even in the realm of transcendence.

The idol that has consumed the self with fear is ready to participate in the sacred: "heresy and obscuring our view of the absolute, normative good" (*TD* 4:160). The experience of the sacred, as Caruana has pointed out, can be both terrifying and enthralling.[31] Further, by approaching the sacred, the anonymous thing (the idol of presence and fear) seeks an enthralling and terrifying experience above all experiences: the impossibility of death. This is the final consummation for the idol to strip subjectivity inside out. In the guise of "infantile religious feeling" and mystical experience (*DF* 142), the idol is both fear and horror. In other words, the act of participating in such a false sense of sacred transcendence—such as experiencing awe, enthusiasm, mystery, rapture, and mystical ecstasy—is an illusional state that results in the depersonalization of the self.[32] But this is not to deny a true sense of transcendence that might also bear the effects of awe, enthusiasm, mystery, rapture, and mystical ecstasy. Given such personal encounters of the divine that animate the mind, heart, soul, and body through prayer, liturgy, or having a heart for the Other, these encounters are signs of transcendence or sacred feelings that lead beyond the everyday experience of the senses toward peace, mercy, and justice. To make a distinction between false and true transcendence is perhaps daunting; is it an idol experience or the very word of God?

For von Balthasar, the "holistic encounter" transcends human emotions while transforming or grounding them into "a Christian 'attunement' to or 'consonance' with God." So von Balthasar points out: "Constant contemplation of the whole Christ, through the Holy Spirit, transforms the beholder as a whole into the image of Christ (2 Cor. 3:18)" (*GL* 1:242). In contrast, Levinas points to the love of the Torah "even more than God." If one has to make a distinction here, to be filled with "high thoughts" of the Torah speaks more of a "difficult adoration" than "constant contemplation." Levinas is wary of "direct contact" with the "sacred mystery" outside of reason; instead the self needs to rebel against and reproach God as an equal. This is not to deny God's greatness, but to enforce a hidden kenosis of God so that God "may show His face" (*DF* 145). In effect, to love the Torah more than God creates a space for humanity to demonstrate a personal relation with God—to reproach, rebel, and die for God. In view of the Shoah, to reproach God is to demand that God reveal the divine face in the form of justice and the messianic era.

Together, von Balthasar's and Levinas's critique of the sacred imply the extent to which the idol almost inverts the relation with God into a solipsistic darkness. For example, where the idol has overcome the self with fear and the delusion of the good, reason has lost its hold, leaving the self in "constant contemplation" to the idol; the self loves the idol-experience more than God because nothing is more enthralling and more terrifying than the impossibility of death. Death, the greatest fear that ends all fears, is made impossible because the idol must negate its reality and mystery. In other words, the idol must divide the experience of death from death itself. Although the idol denies the event of death to the self, the self nevertheless experiences a death turned inside out: a terrible horror of being abandoned to a solitude without end and a shadowy life of anonymous personhood. In this sense, the idol is also the self turned inside out. Its relation to the self is one that denies the possibility for the self to die and thus to be in a world of well-being.

By seeking a terrifying state of transcendence, the idol can more powerfully divide itself from the true self and allow its being to approach the world with the language of fear and horror. Having no face—as the ghostly self is anonymous—there is the impossibility of death. While the self is depersonalized, the idol is free to transform ideas, emotions, and the imagination into behaviors of fear and horror that ultimately might become also enthralling. It is not surprising to think of such a state of horror and/or hell.

The three states of altered existence emphasize that the self is vulnerable to experience in everyday life. Any experience could overwhelm the self with trauma. Such trauma can consume the reality of the self, turn it inside out, and throw it into an impersonal vigilance of fear and horror. To maintain such a state, the idol of fear must not only deceive the good but transcend the possibility of death and thus ever deny its reality and mystery to the self. In effect, the idol prevents the self from engaging in meaning, insight, and personhood. Or in another sense, the idol-experience maintains the divide and abyss "between God and the created natures." The *analogia entis,* Christ, must therefore set out to bridge "this abyss," disarming ("rendering speechless") the horror from the idol "through the presence and mystery of his person" (*GL* 3:220). In a practical sense, this suggests that those who provide pastoral care for persons suffering the moods and difficulties of psychosis are to be bearers and reminders of Christ through compassion and friendship.

Where the self is locked in servitude to its idol-experience, it is surrounded by fear and is denied the possibility of death. Just as these overwhelming experiences have denied the self of personhood, so something of equal or even greater force must allow the sense of self to be renewed. If at best we can only respond to traces of the self and, moreover, traces that continue to efface the memory of the self, how then are we to respond? The idol, by its very depersonalizing nature, seeks to make the self faceless, beyond memory, and eternally fearful. In contrast, the face of the Other suffering the moods and difficulties of psychosis should be viewed as a graced space and time for healing and compassion. This means responding to the word of God in our neighbor's face of misery, loneliness, outrage, and fear of death. We can begin to appreciate that the face of the poor one awakes within us, like a great and terrible wind, graces of exposure and maternity (mercy).

These Levinasian terms, exposure and maternity, signify the extreme alterity of a life of genuine otherness. For von Balthasar, this is partaking of *analogia entis* christology: "Jesus' Trinitarian mission" is the analogy for the christological life of life in the Holy Spirit and doing the Father's will. Of course, in practical terms, human existence is a "partial or inchoate" christology. However, like Levinas's sense of unlimited responsibility for the Other, Christ (the *analogia entis*) unveils "the superabundant expression of anthropology" (*GL* 3:222–24). Hence the mission (von Balthasar) of responsibility for the Other (Levinas) is hyperbolic (von Balthasar and Levinas). To draw from this a Trinitarian ethic and praxis of pastoral care, we are commanded toward a difficult adoration of exposure to Christ in the face of the Other.

Exposure to the Other is inherently a christological encounter. Through exposure to Christ and the suffering Other, consciousness takes on a maternal and ethical character: it bleeds for the suffering Other. Consequently, we become deeply affected by his or her wounds, outrage, and insult. What occurs first is not necessarily an activity of responsibility but of acute passivity and mercy. The uncaring ego in ourselves begins to contract; our sense of the Other moves from one of pity or even heartlessness to compassion, having a heart, and even friendship. An inchoate christology takes hold in the innermost part of the self, inviting fusion with the suffering reality of the Other. In this new identity of openness, our own imperialistic ego is broken up. As a result, the Other's fear opens a sense of responsibility and kenosis. We find ourselves entering a new discourse that effaces the stigma of the Other's delusions and suffering. Bearing forth a language of openness, compassion, and friendship, the responsible self takes an expiatory stance.

The self experiences overwhelming surprise in moving from a state of objectivity to a state of passivity. In other words, when the self becomes a gift to the Other, Christ enters human nature (*OB* 79, 147, 151; *GL* 3:234). The objective self in its experience of the suffering Other will always seek to treat this Other as an object, a presence in consciousness, or a fact of knowledge. But the Other is a person whose face we cannot truly know by the lens of objectivity and theory. In contrast, the Other's face is more an enigma exposing one to his or her suffering, wounds, and outrage. Furthermore, as an enigma, the Other's face identifies the trace of God as the inspiration that commands us to be responsible. Even though there will never be enough responsibility to answer for the pain and destitution of the suffering Other, the enigma of the face inspires expiation and kenosis. We become faced by the Other's fear of loneliness and death to such an extent that we begin also to bleed with them and take responsibility for their wounds with a heart and as a friend. In this sense, we can imagine alterity as compassion and friendship: a donation of oneself for the Other suffering the moods and difficulties of psychosis.

Compassion helps us to understand that the face of the suffering Other speaks of fear and death. Everyday experience (*my* experience) will try to hide this reality. But when we are exposed to the face and its very enigma, we become exposed to this persecuted truth, namely, that the poor one is suffering the outrage of persecution and humiliation. Whether or not the wound is real or delusional, any attempt to objectify it with the presence of knowledge and experience will perhaps deepen the wound. If we are to hear the word of Christ in the face of suffering others with compassion, we are called and ordered to develop a sense (of transcendence) in which we listen to their fears of loneliness and death and attend to them in humility, even to the point of taking on responsibility of those who have caused them pain. This is a great burden; it calls us to a Trinitarian praxis, which invites the grace of encountering Christ's offer of friendship in the face of the Other (John 15:15).

As a starting point for responsibility (as friendship would be the very fruit of a relational personhood with the Other), there would be a need for a compassionate discourse. Experiences of paranoia, delusions, disorganized thoughts and behaviors, and fear are in some ways responses to overwhelming experiences of existing in the world. The suffering Other is a person in whom the word of God can be testified. But if our testimony is to be heard beyond empathy, then the Other's pain and suffering must also be heard. No amount of explanations (objectified empathy) may help to assuage their suffering. However, where others in pain encounter a face of friendship inchoately bearing Christ, perhaps there is hope that they truly might feel free to voice their fear, pain, and outrage.

The fear of death, the very fear in which the self-as-idol tries to conceal, is one which needs to have a sacred time and space to be heard. If then the suffering Other trusts and believes that we have a heart, then there is a chance—albeit at a risk of falling into objectifying them even with empathy—to resuscitate their lives from their world of darkness and chaos. In the Gospels, the silence surrounding the experience of Holy Saturday teaches us courage and openness: to be faced by the silent fear of death. We are called and moreover commanded to witness to such silence with compassion and a heart. Perhaps in such silence and witness, we might see, a crooked path to well-being, unfolding with passion (compassion) for the Other.

At the very moment where everything seems lost, everything is possible if we can have a heart and a sense of otherness for our suffering neighbors. Their delusions, pain, and suffering is not useless if there is humility and a willingness to bleed and grieve with them. This is no doubt asking too much. But when we allow for a sacred space and time for the fear of death to express itself, we might find ourselves within a theo-drama or theological existence of working to bring God's grace and love to the world. The Other's face is an enigma, but if we make it our desire, we can discover our heart and soul encountering the Other's grief and fear of death. Then perhaps, like the powerlessness of the Father giving his Son to the world, we might be able to enter into the "true beauty" and "good truth" of the theo-drama. We can learn that the Father's self-giving and the Son's thanksgiving and readiness commands and ordains a language (and theology) of alterity: the giving of compassion and friendship to those suffering the moods and difficulties of psychosis. We can allow also for a little Trinitarian inversion in our own lives, so that the Spirit might actively choose and call us toward the difficult freedom and path of alterity.

FIVE

Von Balthasar's Theological Logical Theory

There is a profound human need to understand suffering. This is not surprising, given that understanding has the potential to effect relief and well-being. But what happens when understanding is put to the test by violence or insults? Such a question points out that the state of uttering truth exists not just in the pleasant discovery of unconcealment (*aletheia*) or in the realization of trust, but in the tragedy and stuttering of humiliation and persecution. Any logic that has something to do with truth invokes a grave existence and reality. To think otherwise beyond the presence of facts and the temptation to interpret them with illusions about reality requires a certain vigilance. Facts do not necessarily unveil truth; they convey important information and promote discussion and interest. Yet in regard to truth, there is something ethical, eternal, and theological about it. And where ethical metaphysics concords with theo-logic, "the most rigorous of theological conceptions" comes to mind (*AT* 182). Here we are borrowing a phrase that Levinas uses in his reflection on kenosis and prayer. He suggests that the most rigorous of attempts to find a rational way to speak about the mystery of God cannot be done without the language of prayer. For Levinas, ethics is prayer, and this provides a key insight into the nature and elements of a theo-logic.

The ethical metaphysical aspect of prayer seems to exist in a horizon of truth. This horizon is veiled by suffering, distress, and perhaps even horror. If some clearer picture of truth is to emerge beyond the corrosion of "time and conventions," there will have to be a new gravity of existence ethically and even cosmologically. Truth demands a different way of being. Attuning to a new atmosphere or gravity of existence reflects the challenge to forget oneself, to hemorrhage for the Other and to meditate upon the biblical word and the revelation it holds. For Levinas, the logic of a language and even a theology of alterity is to receive the Torah or Scripture in the life of "ethical behavior" (*NT* 47).

Where there is suffering, loneliness, and distress, the horror of life can break the human heart and also crush the spirit. But we can learn how God is with us in our suffering (cf. Ps. 34:18, 91:15). In Christian theological terms, the person and mission of Jesus the Christ teaches humanity how to have a sense in Being—to love and to take on kenosis and expiation. So truth speaks of revelation through hardships, humiliation, and even persecution (2 Cor. 6:4–10). We know that the logic of truth can be hidden by proofs, facts, explanations, and interpretations. But in the very moment where the word of God awakes the moral conscience, a call is made to remind the self of its vocation of working toward the promise of peace and healing (Isa. 57:19). Levinas's own grave and rigorous theo-logic of prayer and ethics offers a biblical and a radical entry point through which to consider and engage von Balthasar's theo-logic in the hope of coming toward a theology of alterity.

Von Balthasar's theological logical theory poses the question: "What role does 'truth' play in the event of God's revelation through the Incarnation of the Logos and the outpouring of the Holy Spirit?" In von Balthasar's mind, this is a search for truth and Being, and underlying this search is an ontotheological inquiry that attempts to give some insight into the relation of Being to truth. Von Balthasar emphasizes truth in the following way: "The two constitutive features of truth—its unconcealment, and its trustworthiness—have this in common: each is an opening, an opening beyond itself. In its unconcealment, a being opens and proffers itself in knowledge. It does not, however, open itself simply as this or that individual thing but also as being in general. It follows that every opening of a particular being includes the promise that all being can be made manifest" (*TL* 1:7, 39).

Von Balthasar's reference to "being in general" projects an onto-logical foundation of truth. However, by speaking of truth in two senses, not only as *aletheia* (unconcealment) but also as *emeth* ("fidel-ity, constancy and reliability"), he has stepped toward a combined conception of ontology and theology. Von Balthasar, bringing out the theological horizon, states, "Where there is *emeth*, there is some-thing we can rely on, something to which we can hand ourselves over," and later affirms, "The creature's will is open to be disposed of according to God's will, and it is here that we find the creature's ultimate attitude before God and the quintessence of all perfection." The truth (*emeth*) of the creature's faithfulness unfolds as the uncon-cealment ("self-surrender") of the creature's being as love (*TL* 1:38, 39, 270). Truth as love has finally found a way to return to God.

We know that von Balthasar borrowed from Heidegger the sense of "the truth of being as disclosure or revelation (*aletheia*)."[1] However, von Balthasar goes beyond Heidegger to think of Being and God together, in other words, philosophy and theology are inseparable. For Heidegger, the idea of truth as unconcealment is not a quest for understanding things present-at-hand in the world. It is a quest of understanding hidden things within the world based on the factic-ity of *Dasein* and care for its possibilities.[2] In this sense, Heidegger is pleased to separate philosophy from theology. Levinas contends, however, that Heidegger ultimately fails to do this because he con-taminates theology with his ontological phenomenology. Perhaps Levinas would find more resonance in the way von Balthasar brings philosophy and theology together; a theo-logic emerges in which the creature's openness to God's truth as love "is the sole a priori of ethics" (that is to say, of "holiness"). Testifying to such a theo-logic of holiness, von Balthasar relates truth in terms of mystery and the intimacy of love: "In this way, the love that God has lavished on the world in freely turning to the creature is returned to him in the form of reciprocated love. God shares his truth with creatures inasmuch as he makes his ever deeper mystery visible *as mystery;* and the creature shares its truth with God insofar as it acknowledges this mystery and gives it back to God." The more von Balthasar reflects on the mystery of truth, the more he encounters a sense of wonder and curiosity in the experience of divine Being as love. This is expressed theologically as the search to discover the ontological meaning of how God can become flesh or, alternatively, how the creaturely *logos* can harbor its divine essence (*TL* 1:39, 270, 23–24, 8). In proceeding with this search, von Balthasar studies truth in two parts in his *Theo-Logic*. In the first volume of this work, he investigates worldly (finite) truth as the object of philosophy. In volumes 2 and 3, truth becomes the object of theology, inquiring into God's self-revelation in the incarnate logos and God's pneuma.[3]

In volume 1, *Truth of the World,* von Balthasar speaks of worldly truth as categorical revelation, suggesting that we encounter truth in the world in a variety of forms or categories. He divides this volume into four parts: Truth as Nature, Truth as Freedom, Truth as Mystery, and Truth as Participation. These four categories of finite worldly truth are not mutually interdependent, unlike the transcendental (*TL* 1:13, 15). However, because for von Balthasar the world is embedded in the supernatural sphere of God's grace and revelation, the "Christian option" is to accept the presence of God's grace and revelation at the center of philosophical thinking (1:31). In other words, von Balthasar chooses to study the truth of worldly Being with the help of the doctrine of the transcendentals (1:30–31).[4]

But there is another twist. While recognizing that worldly phenomena contain divine elements, he focuses on human reason alone to describe the appearance of worldly truth without taking the position of whether such truth is grasped by natural or supernatural light. In addressing the question of whether worldly truth is illumined by natural or supernatural elements, von Balthasar encounters an aporia, meaning a problem resistant to any logical solution and demanding a decisive option. It would appear that the first volume of *Theo-Logic* pursues a philosophical method at two levels. On one level, it is a matter of dividing worldly truth into four categories. On another level, von Balthasar wishes to speak of truth as a transcendental in relation to the other transcendental qualities of Being. On that presumption, volume 1 seeks to use natural or human reason to show that a philosophical route toward worldly truth eventually leads to a theological horizon. The connection between human reason and God is at least a logical necessity in the first volume of *Theo-Logic*. After all, von Balthasar emphasizes that the supernatural permeates the deepest structures of Being and that it would be utter folly to divorce supernatural truth from philosophical inquiry (*TL* 1:12, 31).

The inherent relationship between philosophy and theology opens to a horizon in which there can be no theology without philosophy. In this regard, von Balthasar chooses to discuss the structures of creaturely and divine truth by reflecting explicitly on the interplay of the transcendentals. This unlocks reflection on the most fundamental questions of Christian life and faith. Theology is not possible except by way of making ontological sense of God's beauty, goodness, and truth and unity in the world. Von Balthasar writes, "In order to be a serious theologian, one must also, indeed, first, be a philosopher; one must — precisely also in the light of revelation — have immersed oneself in the mysterious structures of creaturely being. . . . Insofar as he is a philosopher, the authentic theologian by definition is struck by the boundless amazement at the structural complexity of the transcendentals in contingent being, whose bottomless mystery defies all claims to have definitely mastered any problem" (*TL* 1:7–8).

The totality of Being cannot be exhausted by our reflections. In fact, it demands a sense of awe at its infinite mystery. In the light of revelation, the theologian might come to understand a deeper insight of truth, namely, that the hidden ground of love underlies the interplay of the transcendentals. But because the theo-logic presupposes ontology, it must first focus on the problem of the logos or the truth of Being itself. As von Balthasar admits, it is necessary to grapple with the laws of thought and discourse. Such a course of action gives greater depth to the proposals contained in his theological aesthetics and theological dramatics (*TL* 1:7). His ethics and aesthetics of truth are understood to convey a "true" knowledge of Being. To this end, the structural complexity of the transcendentals — their indissoluble perichoretic relation — is a phenomenon grasped by faith and knowledge. In this sense, von Balthasar must always position truth in relation to the other transcendentals so that everything begins and ends in love (1:272).

Von Balthasar explains that there is an order in God's essence of love: love proceeds to Being, Being proceeds to knowledge, and knowledge ends in love. In this sense, love, not Being or knowledge, is the ultimate ground of eternal truth. There is an eternal circulation in which the beginning and end are joined in the unity of love. The eternity grounds the truth and the meaning of Being (*TL* 1:272). Franz Rosenzweig wrote similarly of eternity: "To live in time means to live between beginning and end. He who would live an eternal life, and not the temporal in time, must live outside of time, and he who would do this must deny that 'between.'" The ultimate ground of eternal truth is where the revelation of divine love (redemption) merges into the ever-renewed beginning of creation. And so human experience, Rosenzweig explains, is guided by the light of eternal truth.[5] Von Balthasar ultimately places a caveat upon Rosenzweig, though: "on account of the centrality Rosenzweig gives to the inter-personal dimension, even the Old Testament's understanding of revelation becomes a universalized philosophical-theological logic in which the Christological concept of truth has no place" (2:53).

PARTICIPATION AND REVELATION

The challenge remains to give a place for Christ in the interhuman realm, first using Levinas and then going beyond him. To this end, this analysis is limited to von Balthasar's understanding of truth as participation (the relation between worldly truth and eternal truth). By taking this further, through engagement with Levinas's language of alterity, a context may be found in which to show how supernatural truth must not be divorced from philosophical or other types of enquiry. A definite goal of a language and theology of alterity is not just to walk around the truth, but to do something radical by setting out responsibly to encounter the truth. For example, there can be so many competing metanarratives within the age we live in, but there is one defining Christian narrative that overarches all others. This must always remain primary so that the "Christian option" can communicate the true beauty and good truth of God's grace and revelation.

Von Balthasar considers that the relation between worldly and divine truth must be developed thematically. He begins by examining how participation in God and God's revelation is related to Being and consciousness. After that, he considers the properties of truth—unconcealment and faithfulness—in relation to the horizon of Being. When the essence of truth creates a sense of certainty and trust, an endless search begins. This, he suggests, signifies an a priori quality of truth, of always being more. Hence, it would follow that for truth to be truth it cannot be exceeded by any human definition or intelligibility. Von Balthasar wants the reader to understand that truth is infinite and that any human knowledge of it is contingent upon such a proposition. It follows, therefore, that eternal Being and eternal self-consciousness coincide within truth's infinity as the condition of possibility for human cognition. When God's infinite consciousness unveils the meaning of God's Being within the sphere of absolute truth, the finite subject must touch on such divine consciousness; all finite truth is dependent upon this same sphere. Commenting on the infinite consciousness as the condition of possibility for finite consciousness, von Balthasar reflects: "In this way, there opens up an analogy of self-consciousness, whose inmost, irrefragable certainty is the non-identity of finite and infinite consciousness. At the very moment when finite consciousness touches on the sphere of the divine (and, because it is self-consciousness, it *must* touch on it), it is immediately thrown back into an ever greater distance from it" (*TL* 1:227–28). In this sense, the ontological dependence of finite truth is a moment in which the Being of God's truth is unveiled as a presence in theoretical consciousness. And yet it is still to be unveiled, given the horizon of unlimited meaning.

In a passage expressing the analogy between finite and divine truth, von Balthasar writes:

> *Because* divine truth, being the truth of an *absolute* interiority, necessarily remains a mystery inherent in worldly truth in all of its manifestations, all worldly truth has some share in this mysteriousness.

Specifically, the mystery inherent in worldly truth is given into the *possession* of worldly being, which can therefore act freely and spontaneously out of a personal interiority, yet it always remains only a *gift*, the gift of participation in the absolute interiority of divine truth, from which the creature draws its own mysteriousness. However hard it may try, in fact, the creature can never betray and profane its mystery as completely as it might intend by its sin. The mystery, in other words, is never given into the creature's possession in such a way that it ceases to remain, at the same time, in God's safekeeping. (*TL* 1:231)

Here, the idea of participation rests on an ontological understanding of gift; the gift-character reveals something of God's Being, that is, knowledge of God's essence and existence. Furthermore, the search for the meaning of the truth of Being through participation can never ultimately be betrayed. Granted that the mystery is safeguarded in God, to assert that the creature's sin is ultimately powerless in betraying and profaning the mystery presumes that God's divine truth contains something of a diastasis, a separation between God and the depth of human sin.

To hold that the mystery of divine truth remains in God's safekeeping suggests that the gift of participation retains the character of worldly power. The reason that the mystery of divine truth is ultimately protected from the destructive forces of human sin lies in understanding God on the basis of the analogy of Being, for it safeguards the difference between God and the creature. If we take von Balthasar's conception of truth further, it must follow that divine truth is an essence that must be safeguarded from the creature at all costs. We would argue that from a Levinasian perspective that truth is encountered through an extreme passivity or passion of responsibility before the Other. Moreover, divine truth acts in a way to diachronically rupture the self into responsibility, working in such a way to rehabituate the self toward the life of a moral conscience. This is a "difficult freedom," given where truth passes through the passion of humiliation and persecution. Such a situation, in practical terms, can give insight into, for example, why whistleblowers go through so much pain and trauma to unearth the truth. Or in more theological terms, God's word ruptures time with a demanding existence overwhelming reality and consciousness. This perhaps is part of the nature of truth. Truth shocks us, wakes us out of our idealized states of consciousness, and turns our worlds of fantasy upside down when the Other comes to mind in his or her misery and need.

The gift of participation in divine truth also contains a nonphenomenal quality. From a Levinasian perspective, we have established that intentional consciousness cannot wholly contain the gift. So in some way, the gift is also a nonpresent gift or a trace of the proximity of God. And for Levinas, as he breaks open a phenomenology of suffering and truth, his radically transformed ethical context demands a rethinking of truth as transcendence rather than immanence. He points out that truth as transcendence takes the form of persecution and humiliation. Moreover, such a conception challenges the Heideggerian conception of truth as unconcealedness. The idea of a persecuted truth stands as a more radical and painful perspective to von Balthasar's two modes of truth as unconcealedness and trustworthiness.

Still, with the idea of a persecuted truth comes an ambiguity: a sense of transcendence in the withdrawal of transcendence from consciousness. In this regard, ethical transcendence is beyond ego-consciousness. A concrete expression of transcendent truth, then, would speak of substituting for the Other's persecution and humiliation beyond theoretical self-consciousness. So how does Levinas's idea of truth stand in relation to God? Truth derives from God's proximity as an effaced trace in the face of the persecuted, defenseless Other. Truth surfaces as a demand for justice, signified beyond objectivity in the giving of justice. In other words, the truth of God's word is beyond any notion of unveiling and verifying it as a trustworthy presence and experience of Being. Given Levinas's mistrust of presence and Being, it is not surprising that he speaks of the need for the humility that refuses to reduce the word "God" to thought and experience. The response to the first word of revelation is to give thanks for the very fact of being able to give thanks. Levinas writes, "One may wonder whether the first word of revelation must not come from man, as in the ancient prayer of the Jewish liturgy in which the faithful gives thanks not for what he receives, but for the very fact of giving thanks" (*EN* 56).

The ideas of humility and persecution that characterize ethical transcendence constitute a difficult condition, characterized by an ambiguity in which God's manifestation is also a distancing. Divine otherness is not a participation in the world. Levinas writes:

> But the opening of ambiguity into which transcendence slips may demand a supplementary analysis. Can the God who humbles Himself to "dwell with the contrite and the humble" (Isaiah 57:15), the God "of the stranger, the widow, and the orphan," the God manifesting Himself in the world through His covenant with that which is excluded from the world—can He, in his excessiveness, become a *present* in the time of the world? Isn't that too much for His poverty? Is it not too little for his glory without which His poverty is not a humiliation? In order for the alterity that upsets the order not to become at once *participation* in the order, in order for the horizon of the beyond to remain open, the humility of the manifestation must already be a distancing. (*EN* 56–57)

Otherness is given priority over participation. God is neither a presence in the order of Being nor something we participate in, since any such participation seeks to reduce or confuse transcendent truth with the immanence of thought and presence. There is no possibility of creaturely self-understanding—even in relation to the analogy of Being that safeguards God's transcendence from the creature. Analogical thinking certainly seeks to acknowledge God as the ever-greater reality but refers to God in terms of lived experience. Such thought is always an apprehension, a partial knowledge, of divine truth: "The knower knows that the truth he apprehends is only a part or an irradiation of the total truth in which he is embedded" (*TL* 1:261). For Levinas, God cannot be contained in the creature's time. The divine trace is encountered in the countenance of the Other's face. He writes, "I'm not saying that the Other is God, but that in his or her Face I hear the Word of God" (*EN* 110). There is the good beyond Being, a realm of divine transcendence beyond the disclosure and presence of Being and its thematization in consciousness. Where von Balthasar makes reference to Being, Levinas refers to what is otherwise than Being, a place and time in which God's covenant might come to mind.

Von Balthasar argues that the truth of the world is utterly contingent upon divine truth and its manifestations of mystery (*TL* 1:231). Levinas, in contrast, has thought otherwise through his idea of the trace of the proximity of God in the face (*EN* 57). In the passage previously quoted, Levinas emphasizes that the humility of God's manifestation must be a distancing, "a past that was never present" (57). By severing the link in time between God and the world, Levinas directs us to a context of nonphenomenality, wherein the truth of the world might be encountered rather than being unveiled and reduced to immanence. The Levinasian context of the encounter is connected to the nonphenomenality of the face. His context looks to the Infinite (the good beyond Being) and its immemorial past (a past outside of memory and consciousness). Indeed, from such a nonphenomenal starting point, the self is free to discover the truth of the world, inasmuch as it can persevere with the extreme passivity of being faced by the Other.

In the severing of transcendence from immanence, Levinas has shown that the self must be utterly removed from participating from truth in the ego-dominated world. The self must extricate itself from the time of being in-itself and being for-itself. In the absence of the *conatus* of Being, truth is determined by the good, namely the for-the-other: "But isn't what we really call the truth determined by the 'for-the-other,' which means goodness? And not in the first place by the 'in-itself' and 'for-itself' of the truth?" (*IR* 263). Levinas's ethical position depends on a relation with otherness (the trace of illeity), actualized in the act of substitution to the point of expiation. The possibility of truth in the world lies in the self emptying itself of its Being: "To be me is always to have one more responsibility" (*EN* 58–60; cf. *OB* 84). In contrast, as soon as the self begins to seek the meaning of its own Being in the world, it has allowed consciousness to thematize its engagement in the world. The self, by virtue of disclosed truth, translates such experience into the belief that it can participate in divine truth, as von Balthasar contends: "Looked at from the creature's point of view, then, the relation between finite and infinite freedom is one of intrinsic, naturally necessary *participation* (so much so, in fact, that if its relation to God's truth were somehow broken off, worldly truth would instantaneously collapse in on itself and cease to be truth at all)" (*TL* 1:232).

Von Balthasar does not offer examples of behavior to illustrate the relation between worldly and divine truth; neither does Levinas. Nonetheless, despite his complex language, Levinas provides a more vivid picture of human suffering and ethical praxis in relation to God. A helpful example is Levinas's conception of the self as the persecuted one:

> The self involved in the *gnawing away at oneself* in responsibility, which is also incarnation, is not an objectification of the self by the ego. The self, the persecuted one, is accused beyond his fault before freedom, and thus in an unavowable innocence. One must not conceive it to be in the state of original sin; it is, on the contrary, the original goodness of creation. The persecuted one cannot defend himself by language, for the persecution is a disqualification of the apology. Persecution is the precise moment in which the subject is reached or touched with the mediation of the logos. (*OB* 121)

For Levinas, the event of persecution is the absence of discourse, the break with every apology and every logos. The sense of being reached by the mediation of the logos is, on one hand, the susceptibility to the discourse of the world causing pain, outrage, and unhappiness. On the other hand, it signifies the transcendence of self-consciousness, meaning substitution and responsibility even for the persecutor (*OB* 197). Levinas's conception of the persecuted one provokes a sense of self-transcendence as expiation for the Other. If there is to be discourse in which the logos might communicate, the self must substitute for the Other as a persecuted one. Levinas names this the condition of being a hostage. This is a dramatic term, but one that carries enough ethical force to break open what Levinas describes as the "barbarism of being" (*EN* 187).

How does this relate to the deepest problem found in von Balthasar's theo-logic—the relation between God and the world?

The Levinasian position concerning the hostage or persecuted speaks of the extent to which compassion and grace is articulated with the language of alterity: "The self, a hostage, is already substituted for others. 'I am an other'" (*OB* 118). In the humiliation of silence, the hostage does not seek the truth of the world through concern for Being. By contrast, the condition of being a hostage signifies truth as persecuted truth. Levinas understands this to be the self's 'true' responsibility with 'messianic' overtones: "The *I* is the one who, before all decision, is elected to bear all the responsibility for the World. Messianism is that apogee in Being—a reversal of being "persevering his Being"—which begins in me" (*EN* 60). Truth is not any type of participation in the realm of intentional consciousness. It is found in an extreme exposure to accusation, persecution, humiliation, and expiation for others.

Levinas expresses the persecuted one as living in the state of the original goodness of creation and, therefore, not in the state of original sin. Beneath this statement, there is a more ancient and more primordial truth, namely, that responsibility is prior to all finite freedom. In other words, the goodness of creation, prior to all Being, has already claimed the subject and inspired the very desire to be responsible for the ones on the margins of society. In Levinas's account, this state signifies the self as incarnation or as being an Other; an "anarchic trauma" is implied (*OB* 122–23). The self is wounded, vulnerable, overwhelmed with responsibility for the Other. The subject has been called since time immemorial to be responsible for the Other. A response of disinterestedness cannot be reduced to propositions about the event and truth of Being. Accordingly, the outcome of the relation between God and the world is the subject who, in the depths of self, can never escape God's command to be responsible for the Other.

Transcendence slips into ambiguity; it unsettles the very idea of truth as an unconcealed presence in consciousness (*EN* 56; *OB* 126). Immemorial and nonphenomenal, truth appears in the nakedness of the Other's face as a trace of God's proximity. In Levinasian terms, this is the truth of diachrony: "an unbridgeable difference between the

Good and me, without simultaneity" (*OB* 122). Diachrony describes the self's responsibility for the Other as a past without any memory of prior commitment. The good, therefore, cannot be reduced into a theme as it precedes cognition and commitment. Indeed, the good, the word of God, articulates an unrepresentable past: a commandment to be responsibility for the Other to the point of expiation (122; *EN* 170–73; *CPP* 120).

For von Balthasar, the gift of participation in divine truth remains in "God's safekeeping" (*TL* 1:231). This supposes that the mystery of divine truth is safeguarded from the destructive forces of human sin within the goodness of Creation. From a Levinasian perspective, the gift of participation is perhaps even more ancient than original sin: "To be persecuted, to be guilty without having committed any crime, is not an original sin, but the obverse of a universal responsibility— a responsibility for the Other [*l'Autre*]—that is more ancient than any sin" (*DF* 225). Such participation defines the essence of the divine gift as agape, the grave responsibility for the Other. Extending von Balthasar's view, the truth would need a divine safeguard within the good creation, but only if the free creature is concerned with its own Being. In contrast, Levinas's account implies that the creature is called to a difficult freedom to be like God, infinitely responsible: "To be responsible over and above one's freedom is certainly not to remain a pure result of the world. To support the universe is a crushing charge, but a divine discomfort. It is better than the merits and faults and sanctions proportionate to the freedom of one's choices" (*OB* 122). The creature, then, finds commitment to the good in the absolute passivity of responsibility for others.

Von Balthasar's analogical divide, set between the creature and God, necessarily undermines the idea of the goodness of God's creation. Rather than a barrier between the creature and God, there exists as an open relationship of communication. Within this interrelationship, God's powerlessness, which von Balthasar names as God's righteousness and truth (*TD* 4:335), could be more appropriately conceived as the alterity or the very goodness of creation on the Other's face. This alterity commands the creature to awake to a life of disinterestedness and leads to understanding truth in the ethical metaphysical sense of coming to responsibility through time. Truth is to be found on the margins of society, in persecution and humiliation, and in the difficult condition of expiation for the poor one. In this sense, truth relates to the divine powerlessness rather than to the divine power of safeguarding. When truth is beyond presence, when it is signified in otherness from an immemorial past, the safeguarding activity from God may not be necessary. Truth, then, is neither wholly a function of the unconcealedness of Being nor the object of the divine safeguard.

Von Balthasar assumes that the analogy of Being bears on the problem of the God-world relation. More precisely, it focuses discussion of the problem of how God might safeguard the divinity in God's self-revelation to the world. He asks whether God's self-communication to the world can transcend humankind's idolatrous images of God: "The *analogia entis* forbids the erection of any overarching third that includes both God and the creature; God cannot fall under any concept. The problem, then, has to do with the relation between God and the world: Can God make himself understandable to the world *as God* without losing his divinity, without falling victim to a (Hegelian) dialectic between God and the world?" (*TL* 1:117).

The problem here is that the desire to understand God "as God," that is, "as such," which is also the search to discover the meaning and truth of God's Being "as such." On the basis of the analogy of Being, von Balthasar is aware that God's appearance in the creature "as such" is not God, for the creature has its own worldly truth that defines its own Being. Von Balthasar is also aware, however, that the creature's truth is sustained and made possible by God's truth. Finitude is the fundamental characteristic of the creature's truth and Being. Only within finite limits can it express the infinity of God's truth and Being: "Moreover, this quality [of finitude] immediately expresses creatureliness and, therefore, immediately expresses the Creator's infinite being and infinite truth" (*TL* 1:244–45).

For von Balthasar, the finitude of worldly truth is best exemplified by the delimitation and definition of knowing. Describing how knowledge can construct a domain of truth, he writes, "Knowledge comes about in the following way: one delimits the domain of what is to be known vis-à-vis other truth, which is thereby excluded, and, by setting boundaries and by delineating their contour, determines the content of this domain" (*TL* 1:245). Both Husserl and Heidegger seem to influence this position. In a parallel to Husserl's idea of the unity of transcendental apperception, von Balthasar uses the example of "the judgment 'the tree is green,'" to emphasize that Being (the object of consciousness) is represented in the knowledge of sensible appearance. He adds, like Husserl, that such an object can never be known "as such": "Being, in this case the tree, is represented within knowledge, not in itself, but in the sensible appearance, which as such, as we have already had occasion to observe, is not yet known." However, he seems to depart from Husserl when he states that the subject must seek the unreachable unity of the anonymous (universal) and personal forms of species in God alone: "Here man is reminded, more clearly than anywhere else, that he must seek the unattainable unity of the personal and of the universal in God alone." Hence, even though the subject can never completely grasp the ground of its ontological mystery, it must nevertheless seek what is "unattainable" (1:247–49).

Like Heidegger, von Balthasar conceives of worldly truth in relation to nothingness and unconcealedness. He extends these concepts from their Heideggerian context of finitude toward a divine horizon. Once the nothingness of worldly truth and value is disclosed, the mind can compare it with divine truth and recognize it in terms of the true divine disclosure of Being. Knowledge for von Balthasar begins by apperceiving worldly truth, proceeds by discovering its nothingness, and finally seeks eternal truth as it is unveiled by God's Being, "the limitless totality of being" (*TL* 1:251–53).

Looking at the relationship between the analogy of Being to its phenomenal and ontological foundations, von Balthasar writes:

> To recognize creatureliness as creatureliness means to recognize God immediately within it. To perceive the limit of worldly truth means to apprehend concomitantly and tacitly what lies beyond it.... The

restricted nature of an individual being shows up only against the ever-present background of the disclosed being as a whole....Man's reason, then, is not shut up in finitude. Rather, it can function as reason, performing its finite work of knowing finite things, only because it is already in contact with the infinite....It follows from this that even the most insignificant act of thinking implicitly contains the knowledge of true infinity and that every judgment made by a finite intellect proves that there is a God. (*TL* 1:252–53)

Von Balthasar emphasizes apprehending the lived experience of what lies beyond the limit of worldly truth. He then highlights that even though worldly truth restricts an individual's Being, it is opened up by the unconcealedness of Being. Reason, says Balthasar, is determined not just by the finitude of worldly truth, but also and more so by the infinite totality of Being. Finally, he notes that human thinking is not just constituted by finitude, but also by knowledge of a true infinity that in essence proves God's existence.

These four points seem to bear some relevance to the deepest problem von Balthasar must face in his theo-logic. Given the dissimilarity between God and the world, how might we appreciate a similarity between them? Von Balthasar has tried to show that the finite person is a likeness and image of God because ultimately the truth of the world is grounded in the truth of God. While such revelation remains indirect—God appears through the creature—it is nevertheless disclosed through thought and, hence, as a presence in consciousness (*TL* 1:244). This reveals a possible limitation of the analogy of Being: because it is the basis for ontological knowledge of God, God is necessarily restricted to the realms of theoretical consciousness and Being.[6] Finite reason itself can only operate because it is indwelt by a living orientation toward the infinite totality of Being: "The very fact that we think at all; the very fact that the finite intellect, under the impact of the limitless totality of being, feels compelled to posit the existence of absolute being and absolute truth...demonstrates that finite reason itself can operate only because it is indwelt by a living orientation toward infinity" (1:252–53). Thus, the finitude of worldly truth is endowed with an ontological trace of divine truth.

In contrast to von Balthasar's emphasis on "the limitless total-ity of being," Levinas looks to the idea of the good beyond Being. In this perspective, transcendence is outside consciousness and its explanations or theological rationality of God. By prioritizing eth-ics, Levinas is continuing a tradition beginning with Plato's *Republic* and *Parmenides* and developed through Kant's distinction between the ethical and the ontological.[7] The good is beyond Being in an eschatological and messianic sense as God humbling the divinity "to dwell with the contrite and the humble" (Isa. 57:15).[8] The overrid-ing influence, however, is his distaste for analogy, particularly the analogy of Being with its attempt to comprehend the transcendent:

> Theology imprudently treats the idea of the relation between God and the creature in terms of ontology. It presupposes the logical privilege of totality as a concept adequate to being. Thus it runs up against the difficulty of understanding that an infinite being would border on or tolerate something outside of itself, or that a free being would sense its roots into the infinity of a God. But transcendence precisely refuses totality, does not lend itself to a view that would encompass it from the outside. Every comprehension of transcendence leaves the transcen-dent outside and is enacted before its face. If the notions of totality and being are notions that cover one another, the notion of the transcen-dent places us beyond categories of being. We thus encounter, in our way, the Platonic idea of the Good beyond Being. (*TI* 293)

For Levinas, the idea of the good beyond Being provides an under-standing of the relation between God and the creature free from the limitations of analogical thought and its reduction to presence. This provides a way for the drama of alterity to unfold: "It is an expiating for Being" (*OB* 118). The unique logic of Levinas's ethical meta-physics now unfolds. Given its biblical, messianic, and prophetic overtones, in many ways it feels more theological than philosophical, which reminds us not to interpret his writings purely on philosophi-cal terms. There are experiences that cannot be deconstructed solely by the logic and play of ontological or phenomenological reasoning. However, major Levinasian commentators like Graham Ward and Michael Purcell are not wholly convinced that Levinas can use his language of alterity to extricate himself from analogy; thematizations; and the categories of objectivity, Being and presence.[9]

Discussing theology and analogy, Ward's position is largely guided by Derrida's argument that the theological is implied in Levinas's thinking. Ward seems convinced that Levinas's language falls close to thematization: "a theological argument for the existence of God." For example, Ward points out that for Derrida, Levinas's idea of the trace of God is in fact a language of presence, and Levinas's idea of the good beyond Being is an analogous rapport between Being and beyond Being.[10] In Ward's reading, Derrida believes that Levinas implicitly espouses the analogy of Being. Furthermore, such a position is dependent on Husserl's analogy of appresentation (intentionality). In fact, Ward, following Derrida, states that the analogy of appresentation is the reason why Levinas implicitly adopts the analogy of Being, for it depends on dialogical philosophy with its analogy of dialogue with God. Consequently, Ward prioritizes Levinas's trinodal economy of illeity (the self, the Other and the trace of illeity) in terms of appresentation: "the Other for Levinas is not simply an appresentation of the Ego, but it, simultaneously, appresents and is appresented by the absolutely other (*autre*)." As a result, Levinas only "modifies" Husserl's intentionality.[11] Such a view places more emphasis on Levinas's "modification" of intentionality than on his movement from ontology to ethical metaphysics (*OB* 115). It is therefore not surprising that Ward describes Levinas's thought as a "language of presence" and that "Levinas is resigned to betraying his own intentions in his philosophical discourse."[12]

Ward is convinced that Levinas's idea of the good beyond Being expresses an analogical relation between being and Beyond Being, that is, between the totality of the existent and transcendence. In this respect, Purcell adds that ethical praxis is not conceivable without ontology:

> The difficulty of the separation of being and beyond is not only the problem Derrida indicates regarding the impossibility of the thought of the absolute other; it is also the problem of incarnating responsibility without ontology. Levinas's stress on the other beyond being to whom

the subject is always and already responsible may affirm the absolute uncompromisable value of the other, but it offers no way of linking responsibility with practical commitment to the other. In place of the gulf between being and the good, we would wish to argue for a wider understanding of being which accommodates the good, and enables the good to be actualized.[13]

Purcell, upon first reading, seems right to point out the charge that Levinas does not give practical examples of responsibility. However, Levinas addresses the danger of exemplifying practical commitment. Just as there is the temptation to thematize the Other with personal experience and knowledge, one can do the same thing with practice. So the faces of those on these margins of society, for example, should never be reduced to experience, knowledge, or practice. The poor one precedes us in the sense that we have already been summoned to a responsibility beyond our personal freedom to choose. Levinas points out explicitly that consciousness is not thematic; it precedes both cognition and commitment (*CPP* 120).

Levinas does not reject practical commitment; his whole corpus of writings suggests otherwise. However, Purcell offers for readers of Levinas a place from which to search for ways to transpose his pure philosophical and biblical thinking into ethical practice, albeit at the risk of thematization. Yet, following Levinas, perhaps we need to spend more time rubbing off the corrosive layers of ontology that seep into the substance of theology. This is not easy; it is a potentially heartbreaking task because, in many ways, a theology of alterity is caught in between two worlds: the world of otherwise than Being and the world of returning to Being with a sense of ethical transcendence. In contrast, Purcell defines the good within Being with an emphasis of "*being* otherwise than Levinas's comprehension of Being."[14] He therefore sets out to "advance" Levinas's thought.

Purcell is fond of using the word "advance" to describe his development of Levinas's thought for the purposes of Christian theology. For example, Purcell writes: "We want to try to advance Karl Rahner and Emmanuel Levinas along the narrow way of convergence. We want to let the thought of Rahner and Levinas speak, as it were, in each other's time in order to recognize, despite their differences, something of each other in the other, to recognize primarily the significance of the Other in what each of them says."[15] Here, Purcell desires to use the philosophical insights of Levinas's thought to reread and deepen Rahner's thought. In a way I am taking Purcell's lead and doing the same with von Balthasar's theology but, rather than advancing Levinas's thought in the language of ontotheology, I ultimately wish to pursue Levinas's language of alterity more acutely.

For Levinas, the ethical encounter with God is beyond Being. But Purcell inquires into the appropriateness of this position, arguing that this encounter takes place not beyond Being, but in the goodness of Being. Purcell engages Levinas's writings critically in order to redeem an ethically grounded ontology from the contamination of ontotheology. He identifies "The ontological question of the meaning of Being" as "the ethical question of the significance of the Other." This suggests the question of whether Levinas's writings have an implicit ontology or a meta-ontology that "accommodates the good, and enables the good to be actualised."[16] In spite of the idiosyncratic semantics of Levinas's philosophy, the ethical dimension in his writings contests the Kantian understanding of ontology exemplified in the question: What can I know?

At the heart of Purcell's experiment with the thought of Rahner and Levinas is the challenge to rethink the question of Being: "The question is not Being, but whether Being is the question." This is an important turning point, whereby Purcell redirects ontological thinking to an ethical context: "The ontological question of the meaning of Being becomes the ethical question of the significance of the Other, the interlocutor, the one who makes significance significant."[17] In such reasoning is an implicit challenge to Levinas's reduction of Being to totality. Purcell is not comfortable with Levinas's rejection of the whole Western ontological tradition:

> What we wish to enquire after in this chapter is whether Levinas's choice for the Good and his privileging of the Good over Being is appropriate. Levinas's choice is a choice between two *alternatives,* which is really no choice. Is there not perhaps what we might term

a *tertium gaudens* which is neither in the alternation of Good and Being, but in the very goodness of Being. Being itself is not opposed to the Good, but is itself good. Being and the Good are One. What we want to argue is that it is not so much a question of the *otherwise than Being* but of **being** *otherwise,* and particularly of **being** otherwise than Levinas's comprehension of being.[18]

In his advocacy for a return to the question of Being, Purcell may fall back into the totality of ontological thinking by revising the notion of otherwise than Being in terms of being otherwise. He implies that the good is not located beyond Being, but is associated with Being." Even though Purcell does not mention association, there is in a sense a movement from accommodation to association, whereby the Good of responsibility within Being is actualized as "practical commitment to the other."[19]

For Purcell, accepting the value of Being as good opens the horizon of incarnating practical responsibility in the world. He will point out that the notion of beyond Being, especially articulated as diachronic responsibility for the neighbor, cannot in fact be practically shown in the sense of being proven or demonstrated: "Levinas's stress on the other beyond being to whom the subject is always and already responsible...offers no way of linking responsibility with practical commitment to the other."[20] Again, Purcell is correct to point out that Levinas, like Rahner, does not offer an adequate illustration of what is meant by responsibility for the other. But on the other hand, as mentioned previously, Levinas emphasizes that the ethical relationship precedes not only thematization and cognition but also practical consciousness or commitment: "Consciousness reverts to obsession.... Obsession is a responsibility without choice, a communication without phrases or words" (*CPP* 120). The whole issue for Levinas is how we can truly be responsible if we are beyond Being or beyond the world of presence.

Granting the divide between Purcell and Levinas, could they nevertheless be emphasizing the same thing, that is, the good, by each uniquely redefining the meaning of Being with a sense of alterity? In other words, does it matter whether Purcell stresses that Being accommodates and actualizes the good, or whether Levinas situates the good beyond Being? Both seek to argue for the connection between the good and alterity through an ethical existence in the world. This is, however, more than a problem of semantics: their difference relates to the fundamental problem of the logos. For Purcell, ontology under the realm of alterity is the ground of the Good. But Levinas has rejected any ontological thematizations of the good. Purcell may have misunderstood his privileging of the good over Being. After all, Levinas points out that the word "God" is nonthematizable because it overwhelms semantics and, as a result, does not enter into any grammatical category (*OB* 162).

So beyond analogy and presence, Levinas's idea of the good is situated in transcendence. This is the space and time in which the logos concords with disinterestedness. Such transcendence is a messianic time of persecution and humiliation or a space of giving oneself for the Other on the margins of society. Here, and only in this space and time, it is possible to theologize in the world. In sum, the idea of the good beyond Being signifies a theo-logic: the logos in God overflows thought and cannot be reduced to consciousness. This is to say that the relation between finitude and infinity is an overwhelming encounter with the good beyond Being, signifying the divine logos as a nonpresent and immemorial trace in the Other's face. This encounter does not contain the proof of God. It is, rather, the space and time of God's transcendence in which the finite can be an image and likeness of the Infinite.

Von Balthasar considers that the creature has truth in so far as it is "kept safe" in the archetype of God. Truth then takes shape as the archetypal form of justice and love. The implication is that truth signifies a relation to God. This relation of the finite creature to the Infinite contains three qualitative aspects of disclosed truth: the form of believing trust (*emeth*), the preservation of the world's Being in God, and the apperception of God in the sphere of the divine truth (*TL* 1:266–67, 261, 264). Von Balthasar posits that only on the basis of the correct analogical connection between the finite and the infinite might the creature know that it is in God's safekeeping:

Which of these two truths about the creature is the true one—the truth of the archetype that God has and beholds in himself or the truth of the image, which distances itself, indeed, falls away, from the archetype? If the truth of the image is its definitive form, the creature is justified and saved, but on the basis of God's creative gaze, which sees and declares what is as if it were ought to be. If, on the other hand, the truth of the image in its self-distancing from the archetype is definitive, then this image has to be declared inadequate and, therefore, rejected.

At this point, we need to recall our earlier remark that the creature's truth extends in a seamless continuity from the immanent idea (the *morphe*) through the idea embedded in the context of the world to the transcendent idea present in God. (1:265–66)

For von Balthasar, the major factor in the event of God's Being is unveiling the truth of the archetype to the creature in God. The creature is ever dependent upon God's creative gaze, which ensures the creature's apprehension of the archetype in its definitive form of love and justice. Hence, von Balthasar maintains that the creature recognizes truth as it is in God on the basis of apprehending it in the sphere of the divine. The implication is that the activity of faith is inherent in the act of knowing. Although von Balthasar stresses that finite consciousness is encompassed by infinite consciousness, the knowledge gained of God's absoluteness and divinity still depends on the creature's self-consciousness: "God is known as mystery in the form of self-consciousness" (*TL* 1:260–61, 272). Such knowledge of God's inner mystery is given only in part. Hence, von Balthasar describes the finite's attitude toward eternal truth in God on the basis of the analogy. But alterity too can provide a language for the creature to testify to God's transcendence.

Like the drama of von Balthasar's theology, Levinas's ethical metaphysics can be quite compelling about human living and the hidden dynamics of our relations to God, others, and the world. However, unlike ontotheology, which remains confined within the category of Being, Levinas's thought takes us out of Being. We can then return to Being with a sense of our radical existence and of what remains unknown, such as the face of the Other or our infinite responsibility.

While God must keep the divine gift safe from human sin (according to von Balthasar), Levinas's idea of the immemorial also seems to convey a sense of truth and trust in humanity despite its sinfulness. The difference compels us to conjecture that God is willing to allow the divine gift to be given generously in human hands despite the risk of it being shattered by sin. But the Levinasian implication is this: from time immemorial we are called to be like God, responsible for everything and everyone.

Perhaps the divine gift needs to be broken by our fragile and vulnerable ways. Through our brokenness, the Infinite may permeate the finite so that God's redeeming ways can eucharistically break open the gift for us all. In the pell-mell of human existence and swaying from one challenge to another, we can be tempted to desire perfection. But perfection will remain an illusion because it is an eternal progress. However, in the perfection of the divine gift humbled by a broken and suffering humanity, "God's creative gaze" commands and ordains a theo-logic of hope and healing. So perhaps the divine gift is meant to be ruptured by human beings in the world; thus, we can learn to be like the Giver, ethical, prayerful, and loving. The logic of God's truth then is not just found in activity—the unconcealment of revelation and a response of faithfulness—but also in the passivity of the giving up oneself to-God and to-others in a fragile, broken, and suffering world. Such passivity defines a hope to allow an immemorial and nonphenomenal word of God to come to mind. This is the overwhelming encounter of the kenotic Christ: "And being found in human form, he humbled himself and became obedient to the point of death—even death on a cross" (Phil. 2:7–8). The truth and logic of the kenotic Christ on the collision toward the cross is the splintering of the divine gift for the world.

Truth, consequently, is not just knowledge and experience but also something beyond Being and understanding. Truth is mystery. It is like a splinter of the cross piercing our souls to be like Christ; it is a gift of self for another even to the point of death. Truth and humility unite to reveal a theo-logic that the soul must answer through participation in the divine gift and mystery of Christ's kenosis.

Christ's kenosis implies that God's divine Being is not just an immanent interest in consciousness or the form of an idea. Christ's state of humility in the presence of the Father signifies openness and passivity to the gift. Put another way, through Christ's death on the cross there is an irreducible difference between the Infinite and the finite. The Infinite remains in the finite while not being the finite. And this depends on the metaphysical idea of radical alterity and on the existential reason of our finiteness (our fragility and being a sinner). Rather than God keeping the divine gift safe from human sin, through Christ's death, the divine gift is saturated by human sinfulness. This allows for the possibility of the radical alterity of Christ upon the cross to unfold as redemption and love for us (1 John 4:16). The Holy Spirit holds these two ends together, actively permitting the Gift and human sin to collide. Christ's death initiates this theologic: the greater the difference is between God and humanity, the greater the opening can be of divine Being, generosity, and the hope of forgiveness to take hold over the world. God permits the divine Gift to enter humanity in the great hope of repentance. God strives to "keep us safe from sin" by entering into our deepest wounds and brokenness in the hope of speaking the promise of redemption and eternal life. Remaining in God's safekeeping, we may then discover the good truth and true beauty of Christ's kenosis: "Just so, I tell you, there will be more joy in heaven over one sinner who repents than over ninety-nine righteous persons who need repentance" (Luke 15:7).

Von Balthasar's theo-logic invites us to reflect upon the ontological unveiling of the mystery of truth and how it initiates the relation between the creature and God. The unveiling takes the form of knowledge and presence. This suggests that the truth of God's subjectivity is found in both self-consciousness and in the sphere of absolute mystery. According to von Balthasar: "The creature is naked before God. But its nakedness is veiled under the vesture of God's mystery. God sees its inmost essence" (*TL* 1:269). In other words, as the creature participates in God's infinite personality, God sees the creature's deepest essence. In von Balthasar's mind, such participation implies an apprehension of the mystery of Being. This, in turn, unveils to self-consciousness the ultimate theological proposition that God is love.

The participation in the disclosure of God's Being is also shaped by an attitude of spiritual and conscious abandonment. The creature must consciously unveil itself before God via confession and acknowledgment. Von Balthasar explains that the creature must not only open its will to understand that its being and essence are in God and seen by God, but also that it must want to be what God wills it to be. This is to say that the creature's self-surrender to God enables a participation in the mystery of God's truth and, thus, in God's Being, unconcealment, and love: "The creature's will is open to be disposed of according to God's will, and it is here that we find the creature's ultimate attitude before God and the quintessence of all perfection" (*TL* 1:270–71).

This theo-logic asserts that the creature's self-surrender to God is the sole condition of ethics. So the creature is not alone before God, but stands together with others. This would suggest that the creature's participation in God is also a participation in the unveiling of the neighbor's truth and Being before God. To reach the heights of holiness, an ethical openness toward the neighbor is necessary:

> If one wants to know another, it must try to contemplate the other with God's eyes; it must, like God, look upon the other's defects through the medium of the archetype and measure, in order to overcome the distance between archetype and image in (an unfailingly just) love.
>
> We can look at our neighbor in this way only in the closest possible reliance upon God, in prayer, and in self-denial.... The confession of one's unveiledness before God and confession of the unveiledness of one's neighbor before us are both only one aspect within the all-ruling confession of God's mystery for every creature. (*TL* 1:271)

Here, then, is a phenomenology of the other's defects based upon an ontological unveiling of the other's truth in God's archetype of justice and love. Yet, by prayer and self-denial, the creature comes to contemplate the Other within God's perspective. Still, this contemplation or confession of unveiledness begins in the form of self-consciousness. A finite subject's understanding of the other's defects is dependent upon representing in consciousness "God's mystery for every creature." In this confession of God's mystery for each and all, the creature has a glimmer of God's eternal truth and love. Von Balthasar's attempt to give an ethical perspective to the confession of God's mystery occurs at the end of his ontological inquiry into the revelation of God given in creation (*TL* 1:271). But to arrive at ethics at the end of such a philosophical inquiry contrasts with Levinas, who would rather begin with ethics. From a Levinasian perspective, the deepest problem reflects how to give the ethical priority over the ontological. This radical move to conceive of ethics as first theology may be called theological logical theory and praxis or, more simply, a theological quest. Levinas's notions of prayer and liturgy help to illustrate how von Balthasar's theo-logic can be extended further into the domain of ethical metaphysics.

If von Balthasar's theology is to be grounded first in ethics, then a practical ethical context beyond Being needs to be elaborated. For Levinas, the praxis and quest of prayer and liturgy makes the height of transcendence reachable. In the language of alterity, prayer is sharing in God's suffering and is the work of redemption. Liturgy, in its original Greek sense, is to accept without thought of reward or compensation the burden of devoting oneself to serving the Other (*DF* xiv; *AT* 181–82; *ITN* 130). Together, both prayer and liturgy exemplify the praxis and the logos of the good beyond Being. Given that prayer and liturgy are necessary components of religion, Levinas, bypassing theology, writes:

> The relation with the other (*autrui*) is not therefore ontology. This tie to the other (*autrui*), which does not reduce itself to the representation of the Other (*autrui*) but rather to his invocation, where invocation is not preceded by comprehension, we call *religion*. The essence of discourse is prayer....In choosing the term *religion*—without having pronounced the word *God* or the word *sacred*—we have initially in mind the meaning which Auguste Compte gives to this term in the beginning of his *Politique Positive*. Nothing theological, nothing mystical, lies hidden behind the analysis that we have just given of the encounter with the other (*autrui*). (*BPW* 8)

Though Levinas does not entirely dismiss theological concepts and symbols, he is suspicious of their ontological foundation. But what if theology were to have an ethical metaphysical foundation? For Levinas, for the most part, only philosophy has such a foundation. His view of theology is a limitation, as he prioritizes philosophy as "the wisdom of love at the service of love" (*OB* 162). There is no reason why theology cannot be called upon to enact the same principle. For to do so, theology must be articulated by way of an ethical metaphysical conception of religion. One may dare pronounce the word "God" or the word "sacred," even at the risk of thematization.

Through prayer and liturgy, the creature may rise to responsibility for the Other, even to the point of substituting for the Other's humiliation and persecution. The creature begins to discover its own theo-logic in the quest to share in God's suffering and be devoted to the service of the Other. Following Kierkegaard, Levinas has explained that persecution and humiliation signify the encounter with transcendent truth. This ethical behavior does not signify participation in immanence, thought, and Being, but an encounter with a trace of God's proximity. Levinas writes, "But the trace is not just one more word: it is the proximity of God in the countenance of my fellowman" (*EN* 56–57). If liturgy and prayer are to be conceived in connection with the modalities of the true, namely, persecution and humiliation, then we must also consider the enigma of the trace of God's proximity. The enigma does not permit participation, since that would reduce God to analogical and ontological representations in consciousness. However, the enigma commands from its immemorial past (a past more ancient than original sin) a state of passivity greater than thought and too overwhelming for consciousness to hold. Such passivity, to the point of substituting for the Other's humiliation and persecution, portrays prayer and liturgy as the very signification of the good beyond Being.

In the realm of the good beyond Being, liturgy and prayer express passivity toward the Other and also toward the trace of God in the Other. This amounts to an obsession with responsibility in which the creature is inspired to transcend its freedom to be in-itself and for-itself. A possibility emerges here for the creature to be in-the-Other and for-the-Other, as an Other as such. In less complex terms, the trace of God in the Other commands the subject or creature to turn itself about radically toward a life of alterity. The discourse between the subject and God by way of the Other's face is not language or ideas available as representations of consciousness, but the sharing of God's suffering and responsibility for the Other. The subject's most available means of encountering the logos of God is prayer. In this respect, prayer transcends self-consciousness and leads to the realm of the good beyond Being through the liturgy of responsibility.

Prayer is an extreme passivity and obsession with regard to the Other. It shares in God's suffering and even assuages it. But prayer does not serve as the ontological unveiling of the subject's responsibility before God; it rather signifies passivity to the point of substituting a self-interested existence for persecution and humiliation. The good, transcending beyond Being's essence and presence, is signified in love, justice, and the trace of God's proximity. If theology is going to articulate such good beyond Being, then its first words must be drawn toward prayer. Such an assertion can be applied to von Balthasar's ontological articulation of truth in the world, as he writes:

> The ontological unveiling of the creature before God guarantees that the truth of this world is in fact true. Truth is the unconcealment of being, while the full notion of this unconcealment requires someone to whom it is unconcealed. This someone is God and can only be God, because not all worldly being can be revealed to every worldly subject. Because it is unveiled to God, it can also be unveiled to other subjects, without needing to be actually unveiled to them. It has its objective truth thanks to its unconcealment before the eternal subject. (*TL* 1:269)

Von Balthasar's theo-logic asserts that "truth is the unconcealment of being," but when divine truth is reduced to the scope of human objectivity and to the plane of presence, the subject is not free to confess its destiny to be what God wills it to be (*TL* 1:269–70). Hence, the subject's self-consciousness is not the definitive place and time to determine the meaning of God's truth. In contrast, if it is possible for the subject to share in God's suffering by way of substituting for the Other's persecution and humiliation, truth is not only the "persecuted truth" that Kierkegaard and Levinas stress, but also a kenosis of God in the praxis of prayer and passivity. Through prayer and passivity—as the world of the suffering other comes to mind—the "beyond Being" of God's kenosis begins to take form in the innermost part of the self. By way of such passivity toward the Other, prayer is not caught up in the ontological play of veiling and unveiling, but opens to the quest of discovering truth of the world in the encounter with God's kenosis.

TRUTH AS BODILINESS AND FORGIVENESS

Von Balthasar's understanding of the destiny of the subject as found in confessing what God wills it to be can be seen also as the prayerful otherness of encounter with the divine kenosis. At the heart of a language of otherness, there remains the challenge to allow ourselves to be incorporated into the story of Christ's kenosis and to witness to its truth in terms of bodiliness and forgiveness.

For von Balthasar, God's glory is the "good truth" and "true beauty" of Christ's disinterestedness in the paschal mystery.[21] The grammar of truth here seems to reveal that its meaning is played out in relation to and between beauty and goodness. We must therefore look at drawing out an ethical metaphysical sense of truth as a means to come to the beautiful and the good. This is important from a Levinasian perspective since truth plays a key role in regard to ethical transcendence. Moving another step toward a theology of alterity—by heightening the sense of the good and also the true in relation to the beautiful—produces an interesting turn of events. Developing von Balthasar's theology via Levinas's philosophy, promotes a greater acceptance of how the transcendental values of the good and of the true find their home in the beautiful. This suggests that von Balthasar's theological perspectives call for the need to go through and beyond Levinas's thought.

Reflecting on Jesus' identity and relation to the disciples in the context of John 20:21–23, von Balthasar writes, "He himself is the forgiveness of sins, with his whole authority to judge—but in the condition of self-abandonment, of his distribution in the Eucharist. It is not so much that on Easter day he forgives the disciples who betrayed him and fled; rather, he is bestowed on them as an Easter gift, the act of forgiveness which has been given the form of the sacrament of pardon" (*GL* 7:152). The two key themes can be taken up into a theology of alterity; bodiliness and forgiveness not only touch upon the mystery of incarnation, but also the paschal mystery (the second kenosis). The "flesh" of Jesus Christ is the condition of possibility of the Christian concept of God's being. This bodily condition of God's revelation takes place through the incarnation and the resurrection. By encountering the earthly and risen Christ's bodiliness, we discover his eucharistic identity: Christ is the "the forgiveness of sins." The truth of Christ's being is unveiled by way of bodiliness and forgiveness. In ethical metaphysical terms, this is the sensibility of otherness creating a relational-ethical bond of bodiliness, resulting in forgiveness, reconciliation, and love. So in bodiliness, we suffer by the suffering of the Other, we are hurt by the hurt of the Other, and we enjoy through the enjoyment of the Other. Forgiveness arises through this bodily and existential journey of deep sensibility and feelings, giving hope for a beatific moment of holiness, love, and transcendence. The encounters of bodiliness and forgiveness together initiate a relational or interhuman horizon to journey toward truth. And it is in this horizon that we want to creatively initiate a practical way to exemplify a theology of alterity—one that draws from the insights of Levinas and von Balthasar.

Truth is a relational discovery rather than a cognitive one. In relation to the Other, we have a better chance to uncover a truth about our identity, existence, suffering, and our need for healing. Iván Böszörményi-Nagy (1920–2007), the Hungarian "psychiatrist, humanist...founder of family therapy and developer of contextual therapy,"[22] found that interhuman relations are more valuable practically rather than for advancing "cognitive solutions to what moral positions should be...about what a family should be." This is because the cognitive solutions "don't as such lead to clinical relevance." Therefore, for Böszörményi-Nagy, "Cognitive efforts at defining ethical values are only tangentially relevant to the requirements of contextual therapy and relational ethics." The major principle of relational ethics is, he concludes, "the balance of giving and receiving [direct and indirect returns] and the dialectic of receiving through giving ['an offering of genuine concern for the other']."[23] In the effort of uncovering truth as bodiliness and forgiveness, Böszörményi-Nagy's insight into family therapy and relational ethics can be roped into service. This leads to a preconscious relation to truth: relating with others in an ambience of solicitude, empathy, compassion, and sensitivity does much more in relation to truth than coming to a "cognitive consensus."[24]

The idea of the preconscious state can be difficult to relate. Levinas provides a revealing account of consciousness between the self and the other. Like Böszörményi-Nagy, he underlines the importance of the interhuman over cognition and self-interest. Levinas's phenomenology can help to deepen and define the drama behind Böszörményi-Nagy's insight into relationality. He reflects: "Consciousness in all its forms—representational, axiological, practical—has already lost this close presence. The fact that the neighbour does not enter into a theme, that in a certain sense he precedes cognition and commitment, is neither a blinding nor an indifference; it is a rectitude of relationship more tense than intentionality: the neighbour summons me" (*CPP* 120).

Levinas realizes that we are not good at interpreting one another through our personal experience, objectivity, and everyday life. He finds a real problem with the "presence" of consciousness because we tend to be so late helping the other in need. The other's condition is literally a past that fails to be present in consciousness because we tend to be so self-interested in our own possibilities, caring more for the way we do our own things. We can easily fall prey to treating ourselves as the most important child, so to speak. The Other becomes more a blur in consciousness or a fact of knowledge, or even a totality of value judgments. We can feel this when we do not like to be inter-preted or branded by objective representations. We do not realize how violent our interpretations can be. Truth, however, is something oth-erwise, in another realm of consciousness—the interhuman relation.

Drawing from Kierkegaard, Levinas posits truth in terms of other-ness and particularly in two almost paschal modes: persecution and humiliation (or humility). In the essay entitled, "A Man-God?," Levinas writes:

> The idea of a truth whose manifestation is not glorious or bursting with light, the idea of a truth that manifests itself in its humility, like the small voice in the biblical expression—the idea of a persecuted truth—is that not henceforth the only possible modality of transcen-dence?...It is doubtless Kierkegaard who best understood the philo-sophical notion of transcendence contributed by the biblical theme of God's humility. For him, persecuted truth is not simply truth approached in a bad way. The persecution and humiliation par excel-lence to which it is exposed are modalities of the true. (*EN* 55–56)

As a means to stretch Levinas's and Kierkegaard's insight into truth as persecution and humiliation, bodiliness and forgiveness again play important roles. Both bodiliness and forgiveness are connected to the drama of being persecuted and humiliated by the perpetrator. The sensibility of truth as humility or meekness evokes a way toward imag-ining truth through the lens of bodiliness and forgiveness. Through humility, the interhuman encounter of forgiveness can evoke an epiphany of bodiliness. However, the bodiliness of moving toward forgiveness—of being hurt by the hurt of the perpetrator—initiates "an entire existential, relational, social and ethical context." Although "forgiveness is neither easy nor impossible . . . [i]t does require patience and humility in order to accept that forgiveness comprises a number of steps, and that these steps cannot always be made in an equally fast and progressive manner." These steps reveal that forgiveness is some-thing we allow to happen to and through ourselves.[25] Forgiveness, then, is like a journey toward discovering God's gift and embracing it in the midst of the perpetrator's struggle for repentance. In a reveal-ing way, Miroslav Volf points out: "As Gustav Jung observed after

World War Two, most confessions come as a mixture of repentance, self-defense, and even some lust for revenge.... We admit wrongdoing, justify ourselves, and attack, all in one breath."[26]

In other words, the interhuman journey toward forgiveness and facing its obstacles gives rise to a transformation of ourselves so deep that it is preconscious. Through the power of love and the work of the Spirit, the self becomes an "Other." The path toward forgiveness can bring us to the truth and vulnerability of our bodiliness. So the gift of forgiveness unveils an epiphany of bodiliness through which we are able to glimpse the way in which the spirit transforms our deeper selves. By pointing to the interhuman and preconscious nature of truth, the two modes of bodiliness and forgiveness teach us that life is a transformation beyond necessity and need; a revelation beyond objectivity and cognition. We are called toward a life of passivity, humility, and being moved by the Spirit of God in us. Analyzing a Mennonite and then a Jewish (talmudic) perspective of forgiveness will help to further illustrate the interhuman and preconscious nature of truth.

Stanley Hauerwas relates a grave Mennonite conception of forgiveness as a mode of truth. It is grave because it highlights the cost of discipleship—the pursuit of truth—that radically realizes the Gospel's call to be countercultural. The individual must seek to rupture the Western embodiment of the priority of the individual over the community so that "forgiveness becomes a community process." In a 1992 commencement address titled "Why Truthfulness Requires Forgiveness," Hauerwas explains: "Mennonites, after all, refuse to buy the idea that forgiveness is simply a matter of being told that God has forgiven us. Mennonites have been about reminding other Christians that forgiveness is a community process that makes discipleship possible. Indeed, the nature of discipleship as the hallmark of Mennonite life was determined by people who had learned that forgiveness was a practice of a community committed to the truthful worship of God."[27]

The Mennonite position on forgiveness engages truth in a way that shapes existence and reality in a realm other than the interests of the self; it is an exacting humility and an act of obedience to a crucified and demanding God. Hauerwas describes the Mennonite path to peace as "painful" because the process of "forgiveness, reconciliation, discipleship and truth" requires a radical turnabout toward the face of Christ in the community. This seems to imply that not only forgiveness but also bodiliness is present because people "are ready to confront one another with the truth so that we will be better able to name and confront those powers that feed on our inability to makes our wrongs right."[28] In confrontation, people face the ways in which they are hurt by the hurt of the Other or wounded by the woundedness of the Other. This journey toward humility before the Other speaks also of a time and place for forgiveness to reveal bodiliness. In other words, confrontation must invoke the promise of peace and healing (Isa. 57:17) of the body (and soul) as much as it demonstrates the eschatological gift of inheriting the earth (Matt. 5:5), embodied in the practice of gentleness and mildness. The truth of forgiveness is ultimately a path to encountering peace as a eucharistic gift. But forgiveness is never easy; it requires a whole existential reality of bodiliness—journeying through feelings and the language of faith and reconciliation.

Levinas's position on forgiveness, drawn from Jewish theology and practice, is that God cannot forgive our sins if first the victim of our evil deed has not forgiven us. In his reading of the Talmud, Levinas finds: "If a man commits a fault toward another man and appeases him, God will be able to forgive; but if the fault concerns God, who will be able to intercede for him? Only repentance and good deeds" (*NT* 12).[29] This reading on forgiveness can help to reveal some important ramifications of the ethical and interhuman relation of forgiveness.

For Levinas, there are crimes or levels of behavior that are unforgiveable. This suggests that the victim has a duty to protect the good and show "the greatest circumspection" (*NT* 23). On the other hand, just as the perpetrator has done something senseless to commit evil, so the victim could do something equally senseless and forgive the perpetrator.[30] The promise and gift of forgiveness is not easy; it is a deep process of journeying through feelings, realizations, and discoveries. We can appreciate Levinas's own "existential" encounter with the raw reality of being hurt by the Other (bodiliness) when he reflects on Martin Heidegger and the Germans in the context of a talmudic reading on Hanina's refusal to forgive Rab:

> One can, if pressed to the limit, forgive the one who has spoken uncon-
> sciously. But it is very difficult to forgive Rab, who was fully aware and
> destined for a great fate, which was prophetically revealed to his mas-
> ter. One can forgive many Germans, but there are some Germans it is
> difficult to forgive. It is difficult to forgive Heidegger. If Hanina could
> not forgive the just and humane Rab because he was also the brilliant
> Rab, it is even less possible to forgive Heidegger. Here I am brought
> back to the present, to the new attempts to clear Heidegger, to take
> away his responsibility—unceasing attempts which, it must be admit-
> ted, are at the origin of this colloquium. (25)

In this reflection, we begin to uncover the important connection between forgiveness and bodiliness. Levinas lives with—"is domi-nated by"—the truth of the "presentiment and the memory of the Nazi horror" (*DF* 291), and is hurt and shocked by Heidegger's pagan turn. The relationship between Heidegger and the National Socialists indicates the temptation and the perils of allowing philoso-phy to be contaminated by nationalism and ideology, Thus, Levinas sets out to protect the good and develop an ethical metaphysics against Heidegger's ontological phenomenology. Levinas finds that he can forgive some Germans, but not Heidegger. For Levinas, even though Heidegger was banned from university teaching for five years after World War II, there has not been enough justice for Heidegger to extricate himself from culpability. In spite of Heidegger's turn toward totality, his writings have had an enduring legacy, even upon Christian theology, as one can see in the writings of Rudolf Bultmann and Karl Rahner, among others.

In response to Heidegger's bodiliness of being inspired and drawn in by the Nazi propaganda manipulating emotions, Levinas demon-strates a bodiliness (sensitivity) of being inspired and drawn to coun-ter Heidegger. Levinas initiates a stance toward forgiveness by not forgiving. The important lesson here is that forgiveness should not be cheap, to borrow a term from Bonhoeffer's discussion of grace: "Cheap grace means grace sold on the market like cheapjack's wares. The sacraments, the forgiveness of sins, and the consolations of religion are thrown away at cut prices."[31] For Levinas, justice has not been fully served due to "unceasing attempts" to take away Heidegger's responsibility. What Christians can especially learn from Levinas's Talmudic stance toward forgiveness is the necessity for crimes against the Other to have an ethical dimension. For Hauerwas, the Mennonite position almost suggests that the place of ethics in community is first theology. These two perspectives together suggest that the ethical relationship (of justice and judgment) with the Other/and or community is the condition for the authenticity of our religious relationship (with God), as we confess in the Our Father: "forgive us our trespasses as we forgive those who trespass against us." If the ethical dimension of justice and judgment is ignored, the sinner or perpetrator risks isolating himself/herself from following through the necessary interhuman path toward forgiveness and reconciliation.

What then does the ethical dimension of justice and judgment signify about religious confession and the divine grace of mercy? It shows that confession itself helps one to savor the "good truth" and "true beauty" of God's glory—that forgiveness and reconciliation are a taste of the reign of God. Through the bodiliness of allowing the self to love through the love of God, new hope can emerge for the sinner to take on the courage and confidence to allow justice and judgment to take its course. This bodily-relational event seems to invite the ego-self into another world: that of gift toward the truth of the face of Christ, in which "he himself is the forgiveness of sins" (*GL* 7:152). The ego-self could feel quite lost and lonely in its own world, and when it encounters another face in community, it will need some "costly" grace or word to help it focus for a moment and rise out of its hurt (sense of sin) and loneliness (sense of being isolated from others). But when something of the eucharistic self and/or the other comes to mind, the self can begin to discover a new way of life and bodiliness, partaking of the eucharistic gift that Christ has prepared for us.

Inside our own world, we can fall into an abyss of worry, anxiety, delusions, and loneliness. When another sacrifices for us in a way that saves us from the horror and anxiety of our ego-self, loneliness does not have to suffocate our soul and being. Solitude (prayer, meditation, contemplation) and solicitude (contrition, love for the other) come together in bodiliness and sensibility, that is to say, an embodied, eucharistic gift of love. And when the body wakes up to its sense of gift and being-for-the-other-in-community, we may begin to sculpture an eschatological form of forgiveness and bodiliness through a gestation of responsibility.

The gestation of responsibility is like a preconscious state of kenosis or an incarnational sensibility. Often we are wounded by the woundedness of another. In an enigmatic and perhaps costly way, the preconscious and vulnerable state of our bodiliness is related to the response of expiation (or substitution and forgiveness) for the Other. There is much that seems concealed about our human identity and inner state. The deep pain we feel could at once conceal and reveal our inner states. The states of bodiliness (passivity) and forgiveness (expiation) for the other seem to point to some preconscious openness of having a heart for the other. In this way, the primary ethical condition and uncondition of being for the Other reveals not just a persecuted truth of uncertainty (*EN* 55), but a response of humility, which is to say, of forgiveness and bodiliness.

Humility does not protect or insulate the self from being wounded and hurt by the Other, but it allows the self to suffer for the Other and journey through the heartfelt existential process of feelings and emotions. Even though we resemble God, there is much about our sensibility that remains unknown. And this unknowing gives us the potential to learn the language of faith and community and to allow the Spirit to work in our soul's depths in hidden ways. Too often we want to rationalize problems; this can be a helpful response and part of the existential process of suffering, but eventually we realize that facts and objectivity are not everything. The interhuman relation with others, God, and the world can help to initiate a voice of the conscience and of the soul groaning to be embodied by another.

Through the humility of bodiliness and forgiveness, the language of faith and community allows us to share a word and a smile and to become a gift of self for another.

CHILDREN OF A LESSER GOD

Films can provide people with opportunities to encounter the sacred and the revelation of God's word through personal transformation. The American theologian Craig Detweiler reflects on the inspiring experience of relating film to theology and revelation:

> This book begins as a personal effort to reintegrate my head and my heart, to unite my feelings about life, art, and God with the facts of faith. It is a study in film as an occasion for general revelation; a meditation on the Spirit of God, which blows where it wills, inspire(it)ing artists and audiences alike. It is also a work of theological aesthetics—an effort to reunite what the Enlightenment separated: beauty, goodness, and truth (in that order!). I want to practice what Jürgen Moltmann has preached: "It is possible to experience God *in, with and beneath* each everyday experience of the world, if God is in all things, and if all things are in God, so that God himself 'experiences' all things in his own way."[32]

While Detweiler dedicated his life to the study of film and theology, one of his major aims is to encounter the transcendental value of the beautiful in film, particularly in the genre of film noir. For Detweiler, films express something beautiful, namely, God's dramatic revelation. And even where films are "ugly," they can nonetheless point to ethics (the good) and truth. Guided by Hans Urs von Balthasar's evocation of the philosophical transcendentals, Detweiler—through a study of twenty-first century films like *Donnie Darko* (2001), *Eternal Sunshine of the Spotless Mind* (2004), and *Spirited Away* (2001)—places a priority on the beautiful (discovering God's revelation in the world) as the starting point for exploring the connection between film and theology.[33]

Keeping in mind von Balthasar's (and Detweiler's) perspective on the transcendentals, I want to look at the "good truth" and "true beauty" of God's glory in the interhuman relation. Like the Mennonite position expressed by Hauerwas, my Levinasian reading portrays a grave view of responsibility and of love for others. But, following von Balthasar's theological aesthetics, the interhuman relation bears the theological aesthetic truth that " if the world wholly belongs to the Incarnation, then it must wholly die with the Son of God in the night of God-forsakenness in order to rise with him wholly in the definitive form which God confers on it." For von Balthasar, to participate in the mysteries of the faith is a relation of conformity to the "divine kabod" (glory) (*GL* 1:674). In contrast to glory, Levinas speaks of holiness. In "The Other, Utopia, and Justice," he reflects:

> What emerges is the valorization of holiness as the most profound upheaval of being and thought, through the advent of man. As opposed to the interestedness of being, to its primordial essence which is *conatus essendi,* a perseverance in the face of everything and everyone, a persistence of being-there—the human (love of the other, responsibility for one's fellowman, an eventual dying-for-the-other, sacrifice even as far as the mad thought in which dying for the other can concern me well before, and more than, my own death)—the human signifies the beginning of a new rationality beyond being. A rationality of the Good higher than all essence. An intelligibility of kindness. (*EN* 228)

Levinas's reflection could be fittingly applied to much of the engaging drama in the film *Children of a Lesser God.* Based on the play by Mark Medoff, the film, directed by Randa Haines and starring William Hurt (as James Leeds) and Marlee Matlin (as Sarah Norman), was in May 2010 used by the University of Oxford Division of Medical Sciences in discussion on faculty and student perspectives on disability.[34]

Children of a Lesser God is a love story between James (Jim) and Sarah. James is the new teacher at a deaf school on an isolated island. Sarah is a beautiful, intelligent, mysterious and angry 25-year old deaf woman. She is a former student of the school who is currently working there as a cleaner. Jim notices Sarah and wants to help. The principal of the school, Dr. Curtis Franklin, is quite content for Sarah to do demeaning work at the school and not to fulfill her potential. Through Jim's openness, determination, and care, Sarah begins to respond, breaking through her anger and allowing her feelings to emerge a little from the protective shell that she has created over the years. The two soon fall in love. Yet Jim feels that there is a barrier in the relationship because the woman he loves refuses to speak. He needs her embodiment of voice, sound, growth, and emotion. He wants to be joyful by her joys, to experience life through her experience, but he cannot get in—she refuses to let people in—so the teacher is hurt by the hurt of the one he loves. The film boils over with emotion and bodiliness. In the inevitable confrontation, Sarah voices a scream of words that evidence her woundedness, humiliation, and shame. Sarah's cry, "Ahh…Hear my voice!…I am such a freak!" stuns Jim, and Sarah runs away to her mother, whom she has not seen in eight years. Eventually Jim discovers where Sarah is by meeting face-to-face with her mother. From a distance, he watches Sarah working as a nail artist, but does not approach her. Later, Sarah feels her loneliness and love for the teacher. At the end of the film, she approaches him at a school concert. After the concert, they come together privately to share moments of deep bodiliness and forgiveness where they confess to one another with heartfelt tears and embraces. Bodiliness and forgiveness become one, almost indistinguishable in the true beauty between Sarah and Jim.

The last scene of the film evokes the culmination of bodiliness and forgiveness, namely, the good truth that love is being a gift for another.

Sarah (Jim interpreting): You have been angry since you were a little girl. You didn't want to hurt so you used your anger to push me away. You were sorry.

Jim: I am sorry for hurting you.

Sarah: But you learned from me. You learned that you can hurt, that you won't shrivel up and blow away. I don't want to be without you.

Jim: I don't want to be without you either. You think that we can find a place to meet not in silence and not in sound?

Sarah (in sign language without Jim's interpretation): I love you.

Jim (in sign language): I love you.

Levinas, in the excerpt from "The Other, Utopia, and Justice" quoted previously exemplifies the rationality of ethical transcendence in five ways. So the path to holiness or the "intelligibility of kindness" evokes a sense of agape, otherness, death, sacrifice, and transcendence. Levinas's five descriptions point to a way of life beyond Being, that is, an existence otherwise than competing self-interest and forgetting the face of the poor one in our midst. These five descriptions of the path to ethical transcendence, truth, and the beautiful can help to guide us into interpreting the drama of bodiliness and forgiveness in *Children of a Lesser God*.

In the film, Jim discovers his own disability in relationship. He cannot control Sarah's bodiliness; moreover, he must follow her pull of emotions. In the growing love for Sarah, Jim is wounded by her woundedness. Sarah shares memories of pain and hurt, her hunger just to be like "hearing girls," and her desire to prove that she can be better than them. But all her efforts have seemed to remind Sarah that she is a child of a lesser God, so to speak. Sarah must withdraw to the silence where anger and depression tragically consume her self-worth. But Jim's love refuses to allow her to wallow in a long night of horror. Through love, he moves her to a sense of melancholy, culminating in the last scene. In the film, Jim is constantly a voice for Sarah, sharing with the audience her thoughts and feelings. He is Sarah's interpreter and lover, but must learn more and more how to interpret and to love. In the end, Jim is beginning to allow his heart to be touched by Sarah's heart.

Throughout much of the movie, Jim seems to listen more to his own needs and thoughts in his attempt to "teach" Sarah how to talk. Conflict can give vent to profound openings of vulnerability, sensibility, and openness. Out of despair and frustration, Jim in a previous scene shouts and commands to Sarah, "Now come on! Speak to me! Speak! Speak to me!" Sarah responds with "passion and shrillness"[35] to finally give pain a voice. She voices several inaudible sentences, but the ones the audience can discern evoke pathos and an overwhelming sense of heartache at the fracture of Sarah's silence. Her utterance of: "Ahh...Hear my voice!...I am such a freak!" is also no doubt present in Jim's broken heart and crushed spirit (Ps. 34:18) when he encounters Sarah in the moving and last scene of bodiliness, forgiveness, and reconciliation.

Sarah's audible and inaudible shrill words are the place where silence comes crashing into sound to speak of the hope of giving pain a voice. Lamentations 1:12 could very well speak for Sarah what has been deeply repressed: "Is it nothing to you, all you who pass by? Look and see if there is any sorrow like my sorrow, which was brought upon me, which the Lord inflicted on the day of his fierce anger."[36] So when Jim reencounters Sarah after her absence, he can see and hear Sarah's sorrow and hear her inner voice. Jim responds, "I am sorry for hurting you." From the otherness of agape, truth unveils in the form of bodiliness and forgiveness: Jim is hurt by the hurt of Sarah, and Sarah is hurt by the hurt of Jim. The mutuality of shared pain allows both to feel the surprise of being touched by the other and to allow this encounter to melt into love.

Sarah's dialogue demonstrates that through love and responsibility, we can learn from one another how to hold our hurt and permit the other to journey into the pain of the heart, mind, body, and soul: "Holding our hurt in a certain embrace—neither keeping it out of view nor clutching it in futile complaint—initiates a process of healing. This saving dynamic does not magically absolve the pain or restore our loss. But depression's hold is broken."[37] Sarah and Jim now begin in unity to voice their pain and to hold their hurt. She learns the valuable lesson from Jim that she can take the risk to let out her pain and feelings from the hidden inner prison of silence. She knows now that by giving pain a voice and holding her hurt, she will not "shrivel up and blow away." And both Sarah and Jim begin to discover something remarkable together, namely, that they are vulnerable and that they can be hurt. Theologically, we can perceive that they are not perfect or ever can be; they are humans, "lesser than God," yet resembling God's love and goodness (Gen. 1:26).

Sarah and Jim learn to die a little for one another. Through a heartfelt devotion and mutual affection, they learn that they do not want to live without each other. Each must learn to die to the negative force of anger, control, and pain. In the final scene, both lovers intone their grief, "singing the blues," as it were, to salve their pain and depression. We witness a "transformation of pain into shared grief."[38] Both are willing to almost die for one another. Levinas describes, "Responsibility for the other to the point of dying for the other!" is a "revelation" or "the fall of God into meaning" as "St. Augustine himself" experienced (*EN* 173). So the love between the self and God or between lovers involves a mutual dying for the other. Saint Augustine teaches that one can die for the other through intimacy ("Let me know you, for you are the God who knows me; *let me recognize you as you have recognized me*") and through confession (allowing "one's conscience to lie bare before your [God's] eyes."[39] And perhaps like Saint Augustine's confession to God, both Sarah's and Jim's intimate confession to one another is a way to transform their forgiveness into the bodiliness of being a gift for the Other.

Sarah and Jim are finally ready to begin to sacrifice their lives and heart for one another. We can appreciate this movement when Jim voices, "You think that we can find a place to meet not in silence and not in sound?" This is the place of learning to hold the hurt, to give pain a voice, and to journey into one another's heart, taking responsibility to the point of "dying for the other." This is a time where Sarah and Jim learn the fragility of their existence, suggesting that when they have reached the point of being able to die for one another, everything becomes possible — for they now have each other. Bodiliness emerges as forgiveness through the mystery of the relation of love to suffering. There is no drug or solution to take away their pain and hurt; they have one another and this is their embodied and loving reality. Suffering for one another can now take on meaning.

There is always one option that remains universal because it is preconscious. This is the option to love. Only love can be bold enough to "find a place to meet not in silence and not in sound." The love for the other will stretch the self's bodiliness to reach "the possibility of dying for the other — a chance for holiness ... opening the order of

the human, of grace, and of sacrifice" (*EN* 202). The joy of forgiveness taking place between Jim and Sarah allows them together to discover a new paradise or Garden of Eden. In *Existence and Existents,*
Levinas writes in relation to "*Time and the 'I'*": "To understand the
mystery of the work of time, we should start with the hope for the
present, taken as a primary fact. Hope hopes for the present itself.
Its martyrdom does not slip into the past, leaving us with a right to
wages. At the very moment where all is lost, everything is possible"
(*EE* 92).

The hope of Jim and Sarah has begun to transform the past of
heartache into the presence of love and forgiveness. In their bodiliness, they remain hopeful through the hope of each other that they
can find a place, an Eden, which exists in the reality of the love for
one another on the hither side of, perhaps, a beatific vision.

Sarah and Jim discover a new epiphany of one another. Where they
both sign language to one another, "I love you," they have touched
upon transcendence, a little beatific vision of one another in all
their weakness, bodiliness, and need for forgiveness. They have now
become each other's truth in their one reality of love. It is no longer
a raw truth of anger, control, and abandonment, but a good truth of
the beautiful love they now hold for one another. In Christian theological terms, Sarah and Jim recognize each other as grace; they have
broken through "the obstinacy of being" (*EN* 202) to discover the
delight of the interhuman and the humility of being-for-the-other.
By participating in the realm of nonphenomenality—"the world that
wholly belongs to the Incarnation" (*GL* 1:674)—they have discovered the good truth and true beauty of God's glory through interhuman love.

Children of a Lesser God is a moving film, bringing together bodiliness, being hurt, language, and forgiveness. It inspires reconciliation between body and soul through forgiveness. It teaches us that in
the mystery of existence, our "embodied" knowledge is different to
objectivity, facts, and representations. We can come to truth through
forgiveness and bodiliness. And the pathway to truth is such a deep
sensibility that it must come from the preconscious. *Children of a*

Lesser God unveils that in the preconscious order of the interhuman, we are capable of suffering through the suffering of the Other, enjoying through the enjoyment of the Other and laughing through the laughter of the Other. The journey toward truth (and forgiveness) is difficult, even terrible, as it is overwhelming for the emotions. But it reveals that we are living in the mystery of our bodiliness. So with the courage and confidence to face each day, and through the humility of forgiveness, a beautiful and good truth may come to mind: that love remains in the gift of oneself (one body) for another. And in terms of theological aesthetics, we can return again to von Balthasar's words, "We can, therefore, say that theological aesthetics culminates in the Christological form (taking the word seriously) of salvation-history, in so far as here, upon the medium of man's historical existence, God inscribes his authentic sign with his own hand" (*GL* 1:646).

Movies like *Children of a Lesser God* help us engage with our "historical existence" to become a person in Christ. The drama of the nonphenomenality of Christ's face on Holy Saturday and in the resurrection can help us to understand the connection between salvation history and our historical existence. Our lives are meant to take on a christological form of responsibility for the Other, even to the point of expiation. So through our interhuman existence of bodiliness and forgiveness, as Jim and Sarah show in *Children of a Lesser God*, we can learn how incarnational and paschal elements can help us to partake of a theological consciousness. By engaging von Balthasar's theology with Levinas's thought, our aim has been to heighten the role and sense of the transcendental values of the good and the true in relation to beauty. This is not to deny von Balthasar's emphasis on the value of the beautiful, but to signify the state of indissoluble pericherosis or unity between the beautiful, the good, and the true. The language of alterity naturally has its own favored horizons, namely, the good and the true. But when placed beside von Balthasar's theology, it can serve to accentuate the vision of God's glory coming to mind through all that is beautiful, good, and true.

Furthermore, von Balthasar's Christian theological perspective has helped to challenge and guide how the language of alterity can be used for theology. We have begun to discover a path toward how to use Levinas's thought and go beyond it while trying to respect its own specificity and limits. For example, by respecting Levinas's limit in regard to the transcendental of the beautiful, I have not set out to enclose his thinking, but to find a way to discover new modes of being like bodiliness and forgiveness. Perhaps like Jim and Sarah wanting to find a place to meet not in silence and not in sound, philosophy and theology too can try to find a way to grow with one another. Von Balthasar's perspective and prioritization of the beautiful has an important teaching for the language of alterity: the good and the true can together find a place in the world where the beautiful comes to mind. From a Levinasian stance, this is not easy to admit because the language of alterity is grave and demanding. But when we think of von Balthasar's descriptions of God's glory as the "good truth" and "true beauty," we discover a certain logic that the good and true must lead us to the beautiful. And therefore we can think of the Other's face as an ethical and true place for the beautiful word of God to approach us. Would this not then be the "breakthrough" of a "definitive eschatological event" of God's love drawing us on to faith, hope, and the love of the Other? (*GL* 7:528).

SIX

Trinitarian Praxis

At the very moment where everything seems lost, everything is possible. The evocative condition of alterity defines a praxis of being for the Other so that the impossible might be breached. Where praxis takes us toward a quest to encounter Jesus the Christ in the face of the Other, we have discovered something Trinitarian about our existence: the passivity and openness of self-giving love. The true beauty and good truth of God's glory in personal encounter, drawing us onward to travel through the limits of human understanding, equips us with a new understanding. We learn that suffering, humiliation, and persecution break open a theo-logic of Christ's kenotic personhood. Such self-giving love for us is a Trinitarian praxis, and it follows that a theology of alterity signifies an encounter with Christ and with the Other in Christ.

There is often confusion and ambiguity in Levinas's style of thought. There are also so many various interpretations of Levinas's thinking, creating some intellectual vertigo and making things more complex. Yet Levinas's writings help to attach sense and meaning to theology to the point of becoming a "guide to life" or a dramatic commentary on the degree to which humanity is an image and likeness of God (Gen. 1:26–27).[1] In the Levinasian comedy of realizing how guilty and responsible we are before the Other, we uncover the tragedy of being too late to respond to the destitution, misery, and loneliness on the face of the poor one. If the human person resembles God's image, then, for Levinas, the image seems to fade when self-interest takes over. However, the more the self or subject responds with a heart toward others, the more its image takes on the goodness and truth of God. And so the subject remains not just an image of God, but further, hypostatically, acts otherwise through being-for-the-Other. To this degree, to resemble God reflects a journey of growing more and more into the likeness of God, responsible for everything and everyone. Such Trinitarian praxis or ethical transcendence will seem almost hyperbolic in the way that it reflects the difficult condition of radical alterity. But the progress of the journey is eternal. There are no limits to responsibility and love. Such thinking can hopefully evoke a passion or an ethical melancholy affecting us before all consciousness. Where philosophy and theology not only forge insight and reflection, but also attach sense and meaning in the world of emotions, there can be much value to be gained. The value here lies in passivity, ethical melancholy, vulnerability, and weakness.

In times of hardship, melancholy, and stress, the self can feel the end of the world has arrived (Mark 13:24–25). However, taking a stance otherwise and inverting this feeling into a sense of passion allows for the potential to respond with prayer and desire to wait on for the good. We may call this grace or the inward word of God working in the soul. Where the self becomes pensive and prayerful in response to its sadness, a feeling of melancholy, vigilance, and even spontaneity may develop and inspire the self to respond in new ways beyond "violence, hate and disdain" (*EI* 89). In other words, imagining the world otherwise signifies the possibility for melancholy and vigilance to unite with ethics. As a result, something merciful and good may come to mind such as prayer and compassion (substitution for others). Even a little ethical melancholy, or a little good—like an "After you, Sir!" or the benediction of "Hello!"—could be enough to produce a change of heart and a hope for the promise of peace and justice (89).

In the way that Levinas's philosophy can be a guide to life, it can perhaps begin to penetrate the center of the self's being, producing a spontaneous passion of ethical melancholy and ethical vigilance. A way to approach Levinas's writings is to encounter it not solely within the totality of knowledge, but as a site of passion, vulnerability, vigilance, and melancholy. In this site we may envision a Trinitarian praxis of holiness, "An original ethical event which would also be first theology" (*IR* 182). Addressing the underlying ethical principle of the Bible, Levinas writes: "Holiness thus shows itself as an irreducible possibility of the human and God: being called by man. An original ethical event which would also be first theology. Thus ethics is no longer a simple moralism of rules which decree what is virtuous. It is the original awakening of an I responsible for the other; the accession of my person to the uniqueness of the I called and elected to responsibility for the other" (182). Levinas makes mention of "an original ethical event" in which holiness and theology might coincide. In this regard, his conception of holiness parallels the Trinitarian praxis I wish to develop. But this requires first analyzing previous attempts to initiate a prolegomenon to a Trinitarian theology or praxis with Levinas.

PURCELL'S ETHICAL TRINITARIAN THEOLOGY

In the article, "Leashing God with Levinas: Tracing a Trinity with Levinas," Purcell introduces his reflection on the Trinity by referring to Levinas's question regarding "the apparition at the Oak of Mamre" (Gen. 18:1–2): "When Abraham receives the three visitors, does he receive the Lord because of the trinity which the visitors prefigure or because of his hospitality?"[2] Levinas is responding to Paul Claudel's Christian appropriation of the Old Testament, particularly to the idea of prefigurement. For Levinas, Claudel's Christian exegesis exemplifies how theology contaminates sacred history, "managing to shock us as Jews, and driving us away from the Old Testament" (*DF* 121). Purcell takes up Levinas's criticisms of theology by developing their connection to the ethical, noting that ethics complements theology. He wishes to argue: "that an ethical reading of the encounter is not necessarily at odds with a theological reading."[3] He has importantly brought out how Levinas's ethical metaphysics may be developed theologically. The access to God is not only in ethics, but also in theology. Even though he is aware of the contaminating effects of ontotheology in the Levinasian sense and seeks to address them, it must be remembered that Purcell returns to an ethical-ontological basis for theology by arguing for "the goodness of Being" and by criticizing Levinas for separating the good from Being.[4]

Pursuing the ethical-ontological basis, Purcell makes use of the metaphor of "leash" to appropriate Levinas's thought for Trinitarian theology. For him, "leash" has a double sense, namely, firstly, to harness Levinas's thought and, secondly, to link God together, "especially in threes." But, Purcell is clear in his intention: "But, going beyond Levinas, we wish to attempt a theology of the Trinity."[5] Practically doing theology with Levinas will mean that we have to go beyond his thinking into other contexts. The way Purcell develops his metaphor exemplifies par excellence what theology needs to do. Theology needs to make a radical move with philosophy—to utilize it but not to be finally constricted by it. If we remain wholly within Levinas's pure philosophical context, we will remain just in ideas about God, the world, and the Other. But the spirit of Levinas's philosophy invites us to use its language and unique ideas in new contexts such as theology, film, psychology and Jewish-Christian relations.

By "tracing a Trinity with Levinas," Purcell employs Levinas's phenomenology of human existence and his notion of illeity. Learning from Levinas, he underlines four principles: the reality of ethical subjectivity is the possession of a moral consciousness; the illeity of the Other sustains the ethical relation; the anonymity of illeity, namely, "the third who is in our midst," affirms the possibility of justice for all humanity; and, finally, as the Other's face signifies humanity as a whole and the trace of God, the Other is a likeness of God's irreducible and incomprehensible mystery.[6]

With these principles in mind, Purcell asks: "Can we leash God ethically? Can we 'think' God in terms of ethical rather than ontological *hypostases?* Can we unleash God from the ontological ties which bind him, and of which Levinas is critical, yet none the less *leash* him ethically in his trinitarian self?" The aim is to "attempt a theological appropriation of the ethical hypostasis." He begins to leash God ethically by emphasizing "the *liturgical nature of God*."[7] So drawing from Levinas's notion of liturgy (a devoted openness to serve) as the "one-for-the Other," Purcell stresses moral consciousness at the center of God's ethical subjectivity. In Trinitarian terms, this is understood as the Father-being-for-the Son and the Son-being-for-the-Father. He therefore concludes, "The divine nature (*ousia*) is the ethical reality of 'for-the-other.' "[8] Therefore, God's divine nature manifests an ethical reality or, in a sense, an infinite liturgy of a self-relating God. So we see how Purcell finds a way to reflect ethically and theologically upon the notion of hypostasis and its connection with *ousia*.

Even though the three divine persons (hypostases) share the same divine nature, they "remain distinct, unconfused, and absolute in respect to one another."[9] To highlight this, Purcell utilizes Levinas's notion of "absolution," emphasizing how the Other (*Autrui*) as other (*autre*) is absolute and thereby able to relate distinctly without being confused with the self. Here, the illeity of the Other sustains the ethical relation. In Trinitarian terms, Purcell writes:

> In other words, the relationship between the Father and the Son is not the same as the relationship between the Son and the Father. The Father and the Son are the same in that they are essentially "for-the-other". Yet, the Son's relation to the Father is responsive, whereas the Father's relation to the Son is initiative or originary. Thus, there is both an identity yet a non-identification of Father and Son. Or again, since responsibility is the ethical hypostasis of "the-other-person-in me", might we also say that the Father is in the Son and the Son is in the Father (cf. John 14:10, 11), in a non-identical way, and that it is precisely this *perichoresis* of the one in the Other which constitutes the hypostasis of each? That each is 'in-the-Other' points to the unity of essence, but that each remains absolute despite the relation points also to the difference between the persons, where the *between* is not only the relations but also the difference to the other.[10]

The hypostases of the Father and Son are brought to light in a way that shows how each mutually indwells in each other "in a non-identical way." Importantly, Purcell has heightened the difference between the Father and Son. Even though each possesses the same divine essence or nature, the difference is exemplified by their different states of dwelling in each other. The Father's ethical dwelling-in-the-Son is active whereas the Son's dwelling-in-the-Father is more passive. Therefore, the Father and Son "remain distinct, uncon-fused and absolute" while bearing the same divine nature as for-the-Other.

In regard to the Spirit, Purcell, although he does not state it explicitly, uses Levinas's notion of the idea of the "infinite-in-me," which he interprets as "the turgescence of excessive responsibility within the self." He identifies the Holy Spirit as the Father and Son's mutual relation of excessive responsibility: "Might we, then, proceed by saying that the relation between Father and Son is one of exces-sive responsibility, which not only involves an absolute distinction between the one and the other, but also a responsibility which is absolute and total?"[11]

The Spirit is described in the context of the "absolute and total" giving of the Father and Son. Proceeding, therefore, from the Father and Son, the Spirit completes the liturgical drama in God: "Thus, in keeping with the liturgical nature of God, we would have as our trini-tarian model the leash of the Father who is utterly 'for-the-Son', the Son who is utterly 'for-the-Father', and the Spirit who is the turges-cence of responsibility between them."[12]

Emanating from this liturgical drama in the immanent Trinity is the christological drama of the incarnation and paschal mystery. Purcell links the immanent Trinity with the economic Trinity by emphasiz-ing that the ethical reality of the triune God finds its expression in the world through justice. This implies that the dramas of the incar-nation and paschal mystery signify God's grace of divine justice and portray "an understanding of God in himself as response and respon-sibility."[13] This is where Purcell's analysis ends. Significant parts of Levinas's thought have been enriched ethically and theologically in pursuing a theology of the Trinity.

Purcell admits that his work on the Trinity needs to be developed further as he has "simply opened up some pathways in the Christian mystery of God."[14] Importantly for our study, Purcell's theological imagination has exemplified the possibility to begin to trace a Trinity with Levinas. However, it is interesting that his more recent publica-tion, *Levinas and Theology*, lends itself perhaps to a more adamant

Rahnerian focus through an emphasis on fundamental theology and eucharistic theology. This is understandable, given Purcell's background in studying Levinas and Rahner together. So then, Levinas's incarnational ethical metaphysics bears a resonating parallel with [Rahner's] theological anthropology; the interhuman is the locus for salvation. Purcell explains: "One could express this in terms of a fundamental theology by quite simply saying that one cannot begin to ask the question about God until one has first asked the question about the one who is able to ask the question about God. The human existential is fundamental to the theological enquiry. Hence the stress throughout on 'fundamental theology' which is, at its most basic, a theological anthropology. Thus do phenomenology and theology occupy the same existential and ethical terrain."[15]

This explanation is marked by an important caveat: "What will need to be resisted is doing violence to Levinas and recasting him as a theologian."[16] So the question Purcell needs to ask about Levinas who is not primarily a theologian is: Should one hesitate to take Levinas further into the world of theology? When speaking of the Eucharist, Purcell goes as far as finding parallels in Levinas's philosophy. The dialogue or conversation ends in discovering that Levinasian "responsibility, as 'for-the-other,' has the same 'for structure' of the Eucharist. 'This is my body' which is 'for you.'" Eucharist as responsibility is also a work of justice, even to the point of being subjected to death 'for-the-other.'" Purcell can go no further because his awareness of "scope and limits of doing theology with Levinas" motions him to take a retreat: "One hesitates here, for this is going further than Levinas might go."[17] In another example of reflection on Levinas's notion of "a Man-God," Purcell offers only a short reflection of its application to Christian theology, ending with a suitable parallel in Levinas's discourse:

> This is perhaps as far as we can go with Levinas. The person of Jesus serves as an example of what the human is and is called to be; the proximity and presence of God in the world can only be articulated in terms of the neighbor and the responsibility and justice which this provokes. Thus, "I alone can, without cruelty, be designated as victim.

The I is the one who, before all decision, is elected to bear all the responsibility for the World. Messianism is the apogee in Being—a reversal of being 'persevering in his being'—which begins in me."[18]

Despite Purcell's assertions, we should not necessarily apply limits to doing theology with Levinas. By going further and deepening the mysteries of Christian systematic theology, for example, is not to turn Levinas into a theologian, but to employ his ethical metaphysics for the benefit of Christian theology. And this is what Levinas wanted. Purcell might then find himself freer to explore Christian theological themes in fundamental theology and eucharistic theology with Levinas, and remain within an ontotheological horizon of thinking Being and God together. Purcell acknowledges the work of "Marion, Henry, and Chretién,"[19] who force phenomenology further, yet he is reticent to force it further toward a systematic theological horizon. Purcell's analysis, on its face, is profound in its insight into and knowledge of Levinas's terms and writings. Yet perhaps it is his Rahnerian legacy that ultimately leads him to structure or force limits upon utilizing Levinas's thought. And this gives greater impetus for study how to use Levinas and go beyond him to develop Christian theology and find some practical applications.

FORD'S THEOLOGY OF BEING TRANSFORMED

The Eucharist and eschatology are key themes in any theology of Christian existence. David Ford places special emphasis on the Eucharist and the self's transformation, drawing also—like von Balthasar—an eschatological connection.[20] The eucharistic prayers contain the liturgical acts of praise and thanksgiving (*eucharistia*), acclamation, the calling down of the Spirit (*epiclesis*), the Last Supper narrative, remembrance (*anamnesis*), sacrifice, intercessions, and doxology.[21] These eight acts precede the reception of the body and blood of Christ in Holy Communion. Given the centrality of the Eucharist in Christian self-understanding and its transformation, it is not surprising that both Ford and Barnes have appealed to Levinasian sources to further their respective understandings of the self in transformation. Ford, by treating the Last Supper as "a meal in the face of death," seeks to develop an aesthetics and ethics of feasting.[22] In contrast, Barnes highlights doxology and its relation to life and experience.

Ford works with the analogy of joyful obligation as means to describe "the worshipping self." Here he is indebted to both "Levinas's prophetic philosophy of responsibility and Jüngel's joyful risking theology."[23] Using Jüngel as a means to think "the unthought" in Levinas, namely, joy, Ford considers: "I now want to open a further dimension by asking a question of Levinas: in his conception of the 'I' separate in enjoyment, vulnerable and suffering in substitution, with the face of the other calling the self from separation to limitless responsibility, what happens if one introduces a conception of joy as extreme as the conception of responsibility?"[24]

Ford argues that there is "a glimpse" of joy found in Levinas's writings.[25] It is akin to Levinas's notion of "enjoyment" and further present in Franz Rosenzweig's "*The Star of Redemption.*" In this regard, he takes up Jüngel's conception of joy to make a case of "'thinking the unthought' in Levinas." So that he also might "do justice" to the concept of "the worshipping self" (the analogy of joyful obligation), he appeals to Levinas's friend and dialogue partner, Paul Ricoeur.[26] Taking up Ricoeur's idea "that in biblical faith 'love is tied to the "naming of God,'"[27] he suggests that biblical faith intensifies and transforms the determinations of "the worshipping self." Developing the biblical perspective, he identifies John the Evangelist as "a Levinasian figure obsessed with the joyful responsibility of obeying the imperative to love."[28]

For Ford, the notions of the Eucharist and the self take priority. The Eucharist is "a condensation of the Christian habitus" for it impacts upon all dimensions of life. Accordingly, the self "embodies a multi-dimensional 'habitus', formed through repeated celebration of the Eucharist and interweaving with the rest of life." In the development of a "eucharistic *habitus,*" Ford identifies four aspects of "a eucharistic self": blessed, placed, timed and commanded.[29] It is not clear how Levinas's conception of responsibility beyond Being enters into Ford's analysis. The four aspects of the self he refers to are more explanations of personal reality and experience in a eucharistic setting. Certainly, Ford employs Levinasian categories ("being faced" and commanded in the encounter with the Other) but not in accord with their original sense. So we see in Ford, as in Purcell, the need to go beyond Levinas to discover practical contexts. For example, Ford writes: "Above all, being timed by the Eucharist relativizes death, and liberates for the ethical, fasting and festal time of responsibility and joy before the crucified and risen Jesus." Ford also asks: "What will help most in acquiring the [eucharistic] habitus? At the practical level, the answer is obvious: practice." Admittedly, Ford is concerned with developing a practice that is "theologically informed."[30] Perhaps more like von Balthasar, Ford seeks to liberate theology with a eucharistic or theological aesthetics. Going beyond Levinas is a necessity to reclaim the value of the beautiful in relation to truth and the good. Levinas's radical grasp of the good begs theologians to find a way to transpose it in relation to the beautiful. Even the feeling of melancholy, even an ethical melancholy, reflects the beauty of the vulnerable human spirit. At the moment where all is lost, the melancholy of the moment speaks of a desire for all that is possible: "Peace, peace, to the far and the near, says the Lord; and I will heal them" (Isa. 57:19).

In the final chapter of *Self and Salvation*, Ford devotes his exploration to the aesthetics, ethics, metaphysics, hermeneutics, and spirituality of feasting. Again like von Balthasar, Ford places a priority on theological aesthetics. For Ford, the "figure of feasting" is the lens by which salvation suggests the relation between selfhood and eschatology. He speaks in terms of the "pure joy" and "infinite felicity" of feasting. Further, he relates the aesthetics of feasting as a place and time in which: "All the senses are engaged in a good feast. We taste, touch, smell, see, hear. Salvation as health is here vividly physical. Anything that heals and enhances savoring the world through the senses may feed into a salvation that culminates in feasting. From prayer for healing, and all the skills of medicine, through the accumulated wisdom of traditions of cookery, wine-making and brewing, to the experiences and habits which refine our sensual discriminations and enjoyments, the requirements of full feasting draw us deeper into appreciation of our embodiment."[31]

Ford holds that the self's experience of God reflects an aestheticization of consciousness. This reflects a need to think beyond Levinas. The Levinasian idea of extreme responsibility is conceived otherwise through the idea of extreme joy, so aesthetics, ethics, and metaphysics converge: "To envisage the ultimate feasting is to imagine an endless overflow of communication between those who love and enjoy each other. It embraces body language, facial expressions, the ways we eat, drink, toast, dance, and sin; and accompanying every course, encounter and artistic performance are conversations taken up into celebration." Ultimate feasting sings of the dizzy joy and ecstasy of being with others. This is important as it relates the gift of everyday life. As the senses are saturated with love and joy, eros unites with agape. For Ford, "feasting allows for [Levinas's] pluralism of being," and "the feast can enact the union of substitutionary joy in the joy of others with substitutionary responsibility."[32] The celebration of a feast reflects then promise of peace and healing (Isa. 57:19). And indeed the feast is a time to bring the promise of peace and healing. At the moment of encountering the sorrow where "the laughter sticks to one's throat when the neighbor approaches—that is, when his face, or his forsakenness, draws near," the "subsitutionary joy" at a feast can take effect as a "substitutionary responsibility." This calls to mind a time that is "sorrowful, yet always rejoicing" on "the day of salvation" (2 Cor. 6:2, 10) (*CPP* 166). And, going beyond Ford's analysis, this is not far from the experience of melancholy, a place and time that brings eros and agape. Von Balthasar writes: "The direct equation of *eros* and *agape* lends to eros new colors and new properties." Indeed, von Balthasar implies that melancholy is the place where eros and agape meet; they become "a veritable place of decision." And the "hidden Christological structure" of melancholy is "the totality of divine beauty" (*GL* 5:267).

Von Balthasar teaches that melancholy has a special place in ethical transcendence, an insight, which also illuminates aspects of Levinas's writings. For example, even though Levinas speaks of love without eros, his writings are not devoid of eros. His affection-laden language employs images such as "having a heart" for the Other and "being in the Other's skin." And Levinas's perspective may not be uncommon at first sight. Benedict XVI points out in *Deus Caritas Est* that the New Testament writers tend to avoid the word "eros" in favor of "agape": "The tendency to avoid the word *eros* together with the new vision of love expressed through the word *agape* clearly point to something new and distinct about the Christian understanding of love." Following the tradition of the Old Testament attitude toward eros, Benedict XVI remarks further, "True, *eros* tends to rise 'in ecstasy' towards the Divine, to lead us beyond ourselves; yet for this very reason it calls for a path of ascent, renunciation, purification, and healing."[33] Levinas, perhaps would have taken a similar view; this could help to explain how his imagery has been transformed ethically through the sense of radical alterity. Additionally, it seems that Levinas's writings as a whole demonstrate a high degree of melancholy, which is not surprising since much of his work is fueled by the Shoah. Given that his language is that of otherness, his writings signify a sense of what can be called an ethical melancholy, or a state of mind associated with ethical transcendence.

BARNES'S THEOLOGY OF DIALOGUE

Barnes's theology of dialogue is likewise influenced by Levinas. Barnes is aware of Levinas's lack of interest in giving practical examples of ethical relations. More radically, he questions Levinas's defense of subjectivity and nontotalizing account of alterity: "The question, however, is whether his project enables him to defend subjectivity *and* establish a non-totalizing account of alterity, or whether it just leaves him locked within the polarities of the same and the other."[34] Barnes considers it impossible to avoid the language of totality when speaking of ethics. Accordingly, he describes Levinas's work as a "project," a word that evokes a sense of totality, a system, and the subjective horizons represented in consciousness. However, Levinas has distinguished his thought from the idea of the self having mastery over a project (*OB* 101, 184).

Like Purcell, Barnes reads an ethical-ontological perspective into Levinas. For example, in his conclusion to *Theology and the Dialogue of Religions,* Barnes speaks of theology of dialogue as a response in which the infinite horizon of the creature's being is equated with God:

> My subject has been the experience of relationality, the properly relational experience of Christian faith in the self-revealing God. "God is known," as Lash says, "by participating in that movement which he is. And it is this participation which constitutes the reality, the life and history, of everything that is." To that extent, all theology is a response to that dialogue which God initiates. But it is also properly heterological: a response to the otherness of God who alone can enable the other to speak. Understood in this way, an ethical meeting of persons and as much a moment of God's self-revelation as liturgy and prayer, dialogue opens the partners without limit towards that Infinite horizon of their being which is God.[35]

In this sense, Barnes's theology of dialogue emphasizes the importance of the personal experience of being altered or made other through the mystery of Christ's continuing presence. In regard to "the task for a Christian theology of dialogue," Barnes reflects, "the question is not, therefore, how Christians can find a way of including the other within a single story, still less a theological scheme, but whether they can discern in their own experience of being *altered*—made other—something of the mystery of Christ's death and Resurrection."[36] For Barnes, the idea of experience signifies a response to God's Otherness. In his emphasis on the self's transformation, Barnes makes clear that the "Christian *habitus*" is grounded in the personal, ethical experience of being altered: practical consciousness and its thematization in the goodness of Being. This suggests that Barnes's theological quest is first ethical and ontological because he grounds the Christian's being in the Being of God.

Again, we approach the difficulty or impossibility of using Levinas's philosophy outside ontotheology. Is a theology of alterity possible? In a nuanced reading, Levinas's ethical metaphysics does not ultimately reject Being. It thinks otherwise in order to return to Being with a sense of transcendence. Levinas is fearful of theology being contaminated by ontology. Theologians like Purcell, Ford, and Barnes play out this struggle between ontology and ethical metaphysics, discovering and discerning their own perspectives with which to do theology. The task of this study is not so different.

Consistently, though, Barnes makes good use of Levinasian categories. He provides a number of insightful reflections on how Levinas's ideas of for-the-other, passivity, prayer, and liturgy might be assimilated in a eucharistic theology. For example, in his recovery of the liturgical nature of theology, he employs the Levinasian notion of relationship — "for-the-other" — and singles out doxology as the concrete starting point for a Christian *habitus*. He argues that the eucharist, as liturgical practice, prevents any totalizing attempts on the part of theology to comprehend the Other. By reflecting "on a people's life and experience which begins with doxology," Barnes makes clear that he is aware of the Levinasian strictures against thematization and reducing the Other to the Same: "The Christian liturgy is never a neat and finished process, a mechanism for capturing the Word in a formula of words. As Levinas goes on warning us, every attempt to close the 'gap' between same and other risks betrayal, the act of Saying becoming encased in the Said." Nonetheless, Barnes admits, "it is impossible to speak of a relationship with what is other without dropping back into the language of totality."[37] And this caveat is telling. Perhaps a theology of alterity will always engage this risk. Purcell, Ford, and Barnes all evidence that a theology of alterity must have a relation to ontotheology; their contributions indicate that it is perhaps delusional to think that a pure or perfect theology of alterity is possible. However, Levinas's notions of alterity, ethical transcendence, and having a sense suggest that the ontology of Being can be redeemed and born anew in the environment and orb of ethical metaphysics. The vision is almost eschatological, evoking a messianic era of peace and justice. In Christian theological terms, we are led eschatologically to peace and justice through the sacramental encounter of "God revealed in Jesus' life, death and resurrection."[38]

Barnes fittingly describes the eschatological road to peace and justice as "the meeting of two freedoms—the freedom of God to command and of humanity to respond."[39] This formula comes to life in his article on Christian spirituality, "The Intimacy of Distance: Of Faith Learning from Faith." Here he brings together a triad of dialogue between Levinas's Judaism and philosophy, Masao Abe's Zen Buddhism, and his own long experience with Christian theology and spirituality. In this exploration Barnes hopes to find a way to approach Levinas's criticism of the Christian incarnation, "mystical atonement," and "infantile religious feeling" (*DF* 143, 145).[40] The article, understandably, takes on an apologetic tone. Levinas's critique of the sacred and spirituality almost seems to paint Barnes into a corner. He must take to heart the need for dialogue and proclaim that there is also "no soft option" for Christians; the Trinitarian experience of faith is equally commanding, demanding, and painful.[41]

A critical dimension emerges from the dialogue: the value of the affections for Christian spirituality (and theology): "Christian spirituality...exhibits both cognitive and affective dimensions. In this discussion Abe's proposals have forced us to consider the former while Levinas has warned us to be suspicious about possible excesses of the latter. In so doing they have, perhaps, highlighted an aspect of Christian faith which cannot be ignored without doing serious damage to the fabric of Christian practice and discipleship."[42]

Barnes is directing the course of dialogue with Levinas's Jewish and philosophical tradition. He aims to carefully highlight the significance of Levinas's caution in regard to affectivity and the sacred: the danger of falling into infantile emotionalism. Dialogue is not always easy. The Christian perception may cloud the Jewish one and vice versa. But there are times when it is necessary to take a risk to begin to enter the conversation. For Levinas, "religious feeling" without reason (cognition) produces "madness" because the believer sets out to have direct contact with God. The spiritual for Levinas is an intellectual relation of studying the Torah ("loving the Torah more than God"). The Law (Torah) invites the intimacy of a personal relation with God to the point of dying for God. Hence, even though God is for the most part absent or a trace, God's greatness reveals itself in the intellect and study of the Torah. The difficult adoration of God through Torah study underlines that the relation with God must be first ethical (*DF* 143–45). On the face of things, it would seem that Levinas rejects the affective experience of God; understandably there is the desire to caution Christians about the drunkenness of Christian mystical experience. This caution itself is set within the context of a greater polemic: "The ethical voice of God of the Covenant has been lost amid the self-serving metaphysical categories of Western philosophy."[43] The Levinasian metaphysical approach to God seems explicitly to advocate ethics and reason over affectivity.

From the stance of Christian theology and spirituality, Barnes is certainly within his rights to take issue with Levinas. Dialogue is not just about complimenting the Other but also being free to challenge and distinguish. For Barnes, it appears that Levinas has made a fundamental misinterpretation of the value of Christian tradition of mysticism and spirituality. Like the approach to the Torah, Christian spirituality and mysticism are deeply dependent upon the study of philosophy, theology, the Bible, and, in recent times, psychology and psychoanalysis. Like Purcell, Barnes needs to "leash" Levinas's critique and reduction of the incarnation to the presence of "infantile religious feeling" so that it may be brought into the conversation of a dialogue of religions. In a spirit of dialogue amid conflict, Barnes relates: "His [Levinas's] criticism appears to relegate Christianity to the status of—at best—a temporary stage for the religiously immature."[44]

Barnes's critique sets the stage for a Christian and (Zen Buddhist) theological deconstruction of Levinas's disparaging critique of Christian faith: "the link between God and man is not an emotional communion that takes place within the love of a God incarnate" (*DF* 144). Testifying to the value of the affections for Christian spirituality, Barnes suggests: "What Levinas slightingly refers to as an 'emotional communion' might be better formulated as the meeting of two freedoms—the freedom of God to command and of humanity to respond. To make that point with intellectual coherence and to keep it with a properly affective conviction is what Christian spirituality is all about—a response to Jesus' Christological question which is rooted in the practice of a faith that allows God to be God yet acknowledges God's free gift of Godself."[45]

Repositioning Levinas's "slight" in a positive way, Barnes elaborates: "Christians need to go on thinking about the coherence of faith while at the same time making sure that the intellectual framework both emerges from the more affective relationships of love and compassion which underpin the practice of Christian discipleship." Effectively, Barnes warns against thematizing the experience of the Other into "comforting analogies and comparisons."[46] Emotions are not to be nurtured in a naive fashion, but rather in developing a personal, kenotic relation to God. Yet in spite of Barnes's critical reflection of Levinas in regard to affectivity, Levinas implicitly employs ethical emotions such as bodiliness, melancholy, and vigilance. Loving the Torah more than God speaks of the ethical melancholy and vigilance of what it means "To be a Jew...to swim eternally against the filthy, criminal tide of man...I am happy to belong to the most unhappy people on earth, for whom the Torah represents all that is most lofty and beautiful in law and morality." The very bodiliness of suffering with the suffering of God—"having access to a personal God...for Whom one may die" (*DF* 144–45)—evokes a theological aesthetical horizon for an ethical "emotional communion" with God. In Christian theological terms, not only is this an eschatological vocation, but a eucharistic one of passion.

Toward a Trinitarian Praxis

Let us first attempt to view the Eucharist inspiring a Trinitarian praxis. We want to learn of Christ's paschal life, which teaches how to be human and how to relate to God. In the face of Christ, we hear the word of God. This is our eucharistic experience. To hear a message given in meditation and encountered in contemplation testifies to the ways God works in our innermost being. Learning from Christ, we are called to a Trinitarian praxis of surrendering our being to God.

It will not be easy to surrender our ego to God and for others; Christ's "eucharistic surrender" demonstrates an extreme passivity of openness to the Father's will (*GL* 1:572). Too often, in the melancholy of the moment, we can be tempted to leave Christ alone. Grieved and agitated to the point of death, Christ prays alone, "My Father, if it is possible, let this cup pass from me; yet not what I want but what you want" (Matt. 26:39). And he prays a second time, "My Father, if this cannot pass unless I drink it, your will be done" (Matt. 26:42). When the emotions of grief and agitation come together in a context of an impending fear of death, throbbing desires emerge. Christ's desire to remain alive with his disciples competes with the desire to follow the Father's will. A most terrible decision must be made. In the depths of his soul, the Spirit unveils an epiphany of a kenotic path to the Father. His disciples—John 15:15 calls them friends—are nearby. Jesus does not want to leave them, and a flood of ethical melancholy overwhelms his soul. Here, Christ demonstrates a Trinitarian praxis of moving from melancholy to a spontaneous ethical melancholy.

At the point where ethical transcendence and melancholy unite, the profundity of the Father's will unveils in its definite character. The depth of sadness and thought come together in the heartbreaking torment of having to make a decision. As the pull and temptation to remain and live long with his friends grieves and agitates his being, Jesus feels a sense of responsibility and love for his disciples. But like his plan for Lazarus, he must choose a path so that people will believe that he is the Messiah, the Son of God and "see the glory of God" (John 11:6, 27, 40). The choice underlines the terrible and heartbreaking decision to leave his disciples so that the world may see God's glory through his death and resurrection. This is a decisive and spontaneous moment of ethical melancholy in which we see divinity and humanity coming together in the trauma and sacrifice of dying for others.

Verging upon the emotion of ethical melancholy, Saint Paul relates the paradoxes of a paschal life. To accept God's grace, the servant of God must face up to life: "in honor and dishonor, in all repute and good repute. We are treated as impostors, and yet are true;

as unknown, and yet are well known; as dying, and see — we are alive; as punished, and yet not killed; as sorrowful, yet always rejoicing; as poor, yet making many rich; as having nothing, and yet possessing everything (2 Cor. 6:8–10).

Commenting on this passage, von Balthasar explains that the paradoxes have their root in the cross and resurrection. He concedes that there is no easy resolution, for they signify the breakthrough into the realm of God's glory, into that eschatological order on being made one in Christ (Gal. 3:28) (*GL* 7:494–95). The cost of discipleship signifies the Gethsemane of journeying through the paradoxes, dispossessing oneself of the self to possess the everything of the Father's will. Levinas identifies "one common destiny" evoked by a sense of alterity: "In the eyes of these crowds who do not take sacred history as their frame of reference, are we Jews and Christians anything but sects quarreling over the meaning of a few obscure texts? Through two billion eyes that watch us, History itself stares us down, shredding our subjective certainties, uniting us in one common destiny, inviting us to show ourselves able to measure up to that human wave, inviting us to bring it something other than distinctions and anathema" (*AT* 83).

For Levinas, there is the need to go "beyond dialogue," to have the "maturity and patience for insoluble problems" and "the idea of a possibility in which the impossible may be sleeping" (*AT* 87, 89).[47] This is the very difficult condition of alterity. To overlook the sense of ethical transcendence is to be left with the impression that existence is reduced to some form of personal experience or "subjective certainties." In the same way, Saint Paul's paradoxes of the Christian life evidence an ethical transcendence oriented by an ethical melancholy. We come close here to appreciating and imagining Trinitarian praxis in the "gifted passivity" of eschatological and eucharistic existence.

The paradox of being "as sorrowful yet always rejoicing," (2 Cor. 6:10) invites a state of ethical subjectivity to the point of having a paschal character. Assuming a paschal life is not only a calling, but the passivity of being chosen by God (Matt. 22:14). To be sorrowful yet rejoicing signifies the ethical transcendence of not allowing one's objectifying or everyday consciousness to judge on its own terms. This becomes possible where the emotion of ethical melancholy impels and heartens the ethical transcendence to take effect prior to consciousness. In the enigma of the moment, the nonphenomenal word of God bursts into an epiphany of the splintering of the cross throughout the world. Ethical transcendence interrupts its phenomenal world of self-interest through the diachrony of coming to a Christ-like Trinitarian praxis through time. The self has awoken to the word of God rattling an unheard-of and immemorial obligation. Humbled by the enigma of God's word, the self is forced into the condition of hostage to the Other's face wherein the face of Christ testifies to the "day of salvation" (2 Cor. 6:2). The alterity in which God comes to mind overwhelms consciousness, rupturing it with a new culture and climate of an Infinite and personal Triune God.

For Levinas, diachrony and other terms like fear, fission, trauma, anarchy, and persecution are modalities of passivity. The terms represent a language of alterity in which ethical transcendence and the word "God" might be heard (*GCM* 77–78; *DF* 225; *OB* 100–01). Moreover, they exemplify the difficult condition of passivity toward the Other; a context in which the logos, the very discourse of reason, might be articulated otherwise than through a theoretical consciousness. Taken together, the Levinasian terms build upon each other in ever-greater complexity to signify the nonphenomenal depths of solidarity with others or a horizon to imagine ethical transcendence as a form of Trinitarian praxis.

In a messianic era comprising grave responsibilities to end economic, social, and political sufferings, we need a passion to engage the heart and mind together and to bear forth hope and a maturity for doing what is seemingly impossible in an age of greed, war, and oppression: bring peace, mercy, and friendship to people's lives. Compassion begins where our own fears become a fear for the Other's death, suffering, loneliness, and forsakenness—when these experiences no longer have the character of being "mine" but are encounters that teach us an ethic of otherness. We can find the truth of our personal needs and fears when we invert them by taking responsibility for the Other's needs and fears. But in order to do this, we must be resolute to the point of hypervigilance and hypersensitivity to let ourselves be encountered by another's fear of suffering and death. This suggests a determination to let our hearts be wounded by the Other and so become an integral part of the passion of their lives. If empathy is getting into another's shoes, compassion is getting into another's skin—a disposition of vulnerability and of truly suffering with and for our neighbor.

The neighbor, by virtue of his or her face, calls and even orders us to be intimate and connected with him or her. What does, in effect, our neighbor truly desire? In a post-metaphysical sense, fission is demanded, whereby—to use a Levinasian deconstruction of Husserlian terms—the *noesis* (the act of consciousness itself, the *cogitatio*) has been freed from the *noema* (the objectifying act, the *cogitatum*). In this case, the *noesis* no longer is on the scale of its *noema*. But from a Levinasian point of view, a *noesis,* such as the thought of the mystery of God, even if it is ultimately beyond apprehension, can still be contaminated by the category of Being. Nevertheless, despite such a risk of falling into ontotheology, fission not only requires a rupture of the object of consciousness from the act itself, but also the possibility for an overwhelming of consciousness. And it is at this point we can begin to discern the makeup of prayer.

Prayer involves a fission in which the act of consciousness has been delivered to a space and time beyond the present—to the very eternity in which God's word comes to mind. We must no longer rely on our everyday sense faculties, but on a heightened sense of spirit that is passive enough to let itself be encountered by the inner word of God in the face of the other. Once our consciousness has been released from the pull of objectivity (and knowledge), we are in a position to permit the act of consciousness itself to coincide with a passivity of prayer. The effect of listening to God's word is overwhelming and transforming. Instead of desiring objective meaning and facts, we have an ethic of prayer taking the form of testimony, kerygma, confession, and humility (*BPW* 106; *OB* 149). These modalities of prayer map out the encounter of God's inward voice calling forth the self's responsibility for the Other. They also signify what it required in the messianic era: a spiritual-ethical life operating in the economic, political, and social spheres (*DF* 62).

Through fear and fission in the Levinasian sense, the face of the Other provokes a radical turnabout or conversion. This state signifies absolute surprise and trauma. The person is turned, we might say, inside out, moving from the self-enclosure of being in-oneself and for-oneself to enter into a relational-messianic state of prayer. This site of ethical transcendence or Trinitarian praxis discloses a surplus of meaning; it overwhelms and overflows consciousness eliciting an ethical melancholy and fear for the Other. We have here a place and time for the birth of the logos, the very discourse that effaces presence and signifies consciousness as passivity and moral conscience (*GCM* 175–76).

Conversion touches on the very possibility of rationally speaking of God through ethical behavior. But this has come at a cost; there has been a trauma in which one begins to feel the force of an overwhelming sense of obligation that, until now, has never come to mind. This obligation constitutes being inspired and ordered by God to repent. For the longest time, we have had a guilty conscience of forever doing too little and arriving too late for our neighbor. Repentance can no doubt be traumatic, but is a prayerful state of testifying our need for God by proclaiming the joy of the resurrection in confession and humility. We can begin to savor the future of world (cf. Isa. 64:4; 1 Cor. 2:9). Indeed, conversion becomes the path toward an encounter with mystery.

For Levinas, conversion touches on transcendence or a situation of "anarchy" (*BPW* 116). He explains that anarchy implies the bond between the subject and the good (*CPP* 136–37). It, rather than the analogy of Being, identifies the good beyond Being and constitutes ethical transcendence; thus, Levinas uses the idea of anarchy to emphasize that transcendence cannot be reduced to the event of Being and intentional consciousness but is signified through an immemorial past.

We can learn from this enigmatic Levinasian notion of anarchy that conversion is also an encounter with the mysterious time of God. Like the anarchy of the moment in which the disciples received the Spirit from the risen Christ, so conversion inspires us with a sense that since time immemorial we have been ordered and ordained to love our neighbor. For reasons of our salvific encounter of grace, our sense of time immemorial is, for the most part, veiled from us. However, the mystery of eternity—of a divine presence and trace—announces a future world that reserves blessings instead of curses and inverts the excess of evil into the waiting for the good. How might we be able to hope for such immemorial time to make itself seen and heard?

In Levinasian language, diachrony refers to a trace of an immemorial time: the way in which God or the Infinite come to mind. The diachrony at work here is related to the awakening to responsibility in a time beyond sense and everyday experience (*OB* 155). This time is the time of the Other who is suffering, dying, lonely, destitute, and/or abandoned. Could this be the "future world" and Trinitarian praxis of partaking of a "famous vintage" and an "ancient wine" that has been maturing since the days of creation? (*DF* 60, 66). This question touches upon a sense of the ethical transcendence in Being, suggesting that there is a way for Being to take on a just meaning without implying that alterity (otherness, beyond Being) is a function of Being.

If we truly desire to be in proximity of being-for-the-Other, our task may seem hyperbolic. Facing the immemorial command to be responsible, each moment can seem like an eternal encounter with the word of God in the face of the Other. Such a gift is a possibility because our consciousness has been transformed into one of uttermost passivity; yet it is an impossibility because, ultimately, God makes the donation of grace. Perhaps only in the kenotic space of responsibility can we imagine a space and time for the gift to take on the form of being given in and through the life of Christ.

When the enigmatic time of anarchy enters into our life (diachrony), an inversion of consciousness from intentionality to passivity occurs. Such anarchy produces an ethical state of persecution: it is "being called into question prior to questioning, responsibility over and beyond the logos of response. It is as though persecution by another were at the bottom of solidarity with another." To be called into question beyond the logos of response is to find that the self is stretched to the limits of responsibility. Levinas considers persecution obsessive in that, through an infinite passion of responsibility, the passivity of the self turns into expiation. In all this extreme language, Levinas is attempting to find words adequate to an ethics responsive to the good beyond Being. In short, persecution is the passivity of the self. Because the self is liberated from any project of mastery on the part of itself or others, it has an openness to what is otherwise than Being, namely, the possibility of sacrificing and suffering for the Other (*OB* 112–15).

We can name this a Trinitarian life in that the more we traverse beyond our self-interested lives, the more we can share in Christ's paschal life of suffering and expiation. In this space and time of otherness, a moment becomes a desire to imagine a future world: partaking of an ancient vintage of love to enlighten the truth of suffering, expiation, and death. Where is that world and how can we arrive there? To begin, we must learn how to laugh, cry, dance, and sing with our neighbor. We must pass through a number of formative events: the inversion of fear, conversion, having consciousness stretched by developing a sense of transcendence, and allowing the word of God to inspire daily life with kenosis and expiation. This sounds like both a litany and a liturgy of responsibility producing a difficult and grave freedom and adoration. Yet our future world is at stake. The sacrifice of our whole lives for the future world may well be worth it. From time immemorial, the ancient vintage of the future world is awaiting our communion, admiration, and interpretation.

We have pointed to ethical melancholy as an emotion associated with the state of ethical transcendence. The emotion can help to animate, modify, and deepen our behavior in relation to the Other. Ethical melancholy further uncovers a more hidden aspect of our everyday relations: by veiling and unveiling the gravity of agape, it assumes an ethical metaphysical character. In the state of ethical melancholy, the primordial call of responsibility invokes an utmost passivity, gifted by the glory and command of God's word in the inmost part of the self.

Associated with such terms as fear, fission, trauma, diachrony, and the primordial is a Levinasian melancholy. There is a sadness that lies deep in Levinas's thought. Humanity's unconscionable behavior to one another remains an open wound for Levinas. Not only does he respond pensively to his sadness, but also ethically, with a prophetic tone. We can intuit, for example, a degree of ethical melancholy in the following statement: "The unburied dead in wars and extermination camps make one believe the idea of a death without a morning after and render tragic-comic the concern of oneself and illusory the pretension of the rational animal to have a privileged place in the cosmos and the power to dominate and integrate the totality of being in a self-consciousness" (*CPP* 127). These words portray the heart of a prophet in an obscure and "disintegrating" world, so Levinas laments.

The emotion of melancholy is also beholden to eros. Von Balthasar helps us to see this, implying that where "the true infinity of *agape*" meets eros, there is a veiled melancholy. This is not surprising, given that agape disturbs eros into a paradox: the aesthetic in "mortal opposition" to the "ethical religious" (*GL* 5:265, 267). This insight helps uncover a veiled melancholy in Levinas's thought.

There is a spatial quality to melancholy that makes it different from just feeling sad. The sadness is touched by the nonphenomenal space of primordial otherness. The veil upon melancholy, it seems, is ethical transcendence; the emotion of an ethical melancholy is thus evident in Levinas's language of radical alterity. Accordingly, Levinas deepens and awakens hidden qualities of the common meaning of melancholy at the site of ethics, unearthing a primordial trace of ethics in melancholy as he reflects on how the neighbor's face confronts, disturbs, and approaches before all consciousness. He writes: "What is this original trace, this primordial desolation? It is the nakedness of a face that faces, expressing itself, interrupting order" (*CPP* 65). Levinas's language of alterity shapes a dramatic picture of the approach of the Other. Where the emotions of desolation and sadness are met responsibly by a reflective moral conscience, we can hopefully envisage a key moment in the drama of Levinasian ethics in which melancholy takes on an ethical character.

It is further helpful to see how Levinas awakens a primordial trace of ethics in melancholy. Not only may the self feel pensive and sad at the approach of the Other, but the desolation is deepened by the diachrony or responsibility, an ethical moment in which the face of the Other disturbs the innermost part of the self with a primordial word and call so vulnerable that it is easily effaced in explanations, interpretations, and experience. The passivity or the primordial nature of an ethical melancholy is demanding. The face of the Other and the word of God cannot easily by subsumed into the self's present experience. Something otherwise solicits the self's emotions under the veil of ethical transcendence. This something cannot be grasped by consciousness, but more through, in Christian theological terms, the eyes of faith. A key factor in Trinitarian praxis, therefore, is an eschatological existence. A new seeing and a new hearing come to mind where the self, in a state of ethical melancholy, is in touch with the paradoxes of life: "in honor and dishonor, in all repute and good repute. We are treated as impostors, and yet are true" (2 Cor. 6:8–10).

Von Balthasar singles out 2 Corinthians 5:11–6:10 for its eschatological bearing. He states, "The passage speaks...finally of the paradoxes—impossible to resolve in a tidy passage—of a radically Christian existence in the face of the Church and of the world (vv.8–10)." He goes on to say, "This is precisely what is to be expected from the union of Cross and Resurrection in the kerygma, and it is precisely this union which fills the human vessel" (*GL* 7:494). Von Balthasar cites this text to demonstrate the relationship between the ecclesial and the eschatological existence in a Christian existence that is aware of the presence of God in the Trinitarian-christological event. God, known as present and experienced as the human vessel, is filled with the one mystery of the cross and resurrection. At every stage, the correlation of objective and subjective experience is assumed. On one hand, there is the objective experience of having heard of, studied, and believed in the cross and resurrection.

On the other, there is the subjective experience of savoring and seeing its glory. This correlation is framed by the analogy of Being since the creature exists as a likeness and image of the Creator. But here von Balthasar is faced with the deepest problem of his theo-logic: he must situate his understanding of God's revelation within a Trinitarian and eschatological horizon (*TL* 1:9–10; *GL* 7:495).

By "having nothing" (2 Cor. 6:10), the self unveils a condition of extreme passivity to the Other's poverty and freedom. Inasmuch as the self possesses everything, the self is responsible for everything, even for the Other's faults, sufferings and death. The paradox of Trinitarian *praxis* is that the more the self returns to its identity of alterity, the more the self divests itself of its personal experiences. We see then a movement from personal experience to an ethical melancholy and fear that comes to the self from the Other's face. These emotions are not an intention or an act, but a passivity of being exposed to the Other. The passivity is so overwhelming that it causes a radicalization of conscience, which gives birth to the discourse of reason. What, then, might this conscience without intentions signify? Beyond the everyday emotions of being frightened and sad is the obligation to be responsible for the Other's death.[48] An ethical melancholy develops in reaction to sadness and desolation in a manner beyond being. Ethical melancholy, veiled in the self's eschatological sense of ethical transcendence, testifies to the capacity to learn from the word of God how to make a choice beyond self-interest.[49]

Feelings and emotions play a key role in fine-tuning an ethical response to the Other. To place a phenomenology of emotion in the site of alterity stands in opposition to fundamental ontology. A messianic or eschatological existence reveals that making a choice for the Other gives meaning and value. And this choice is not made without emotion. There is fear for the Other's death. We have a reversal of Heidegger's idea of death as mine (*jemeinigkeit*) into responsibility for the Other's death. And otherwise than Heidegger's idea of state-of-mind (*befindlichkeit*), the emotion of ethical melancholy can help to deepen our reflection on Levinas's sense of fear for the Other's death; it is not just an idea but reflects an ethical metaphysical fear, that is, another emotion. Such fear bears an eschatological character. And not far from this emotion is that of ethical melancholy, modifying and animating the expression of ethical transcendence.

In the process of forgiveness, for example, the emotions are instrumental to allow us to journey through change, trauma, and relations with the other. And to move from melancholy to a sense of ethical melancholy demonstrates a whole new momentum of responding to the word of God in the face of the Other. To hear God's call must affect us anarchically and diachronically to an immemorial responsibility building in momentum to make a crucial decision of being-for-the-Other. The cost for the self can be great as it breaks free from its self-interested existence. We can become so tempted and addicted by our desires and needs that they cloud the Other's face. But when the word of God jolts us into a state of transdescendence, the hope to encounter the glory of the Lord emerges from a simple benediction, "Hello."

Eschatologically, by facing up to the fear for the Other and nurturing ethical emotions, the self faces up to Christ's responsibility of dying for humanity. The passivity involved in this facing signifies that consciousness has been pushed beyond its limits. Consequently, the passivity of being faced by the Other in Christ is so overwhelming that the presence of self-interested emotions, specifically, fear for one's own death, is effaced. Divested of self and possessing nothing, the self, like Christ himself, is responsible for everyone. Behind the veil of this eschatological sense of ethical transcendence lies ethical melancholy at work in the inmost part of the soul. Fear for the Other becomes the trauma of a fission. The eschatological sense of fission as the self lies in its venturing to be united to the crucified and risen Christ. In this fission, Christ's inward voice is heard as the voice of the self, bearing testimony to Christ's eschatological existence.

The Pauline "having nothing" signifies that the self must divest itself of self-centered emotions and judgments before the Other. The self is commanded to leave behind these experiences since they do not lead to transcendence but to the immanence of knowledge and totality. God's reconciliation is everything insofar as the self lives for the Other beyond its powers, finitude, and emotions. This is to say that the Other, and not the self's experiences, is in Christ and in the Spirit. In the crucifixion and resurrection of Christ, God's reconciliation is encountered through Otherness. Hence, the sense of possessing everything is not that of experiencing self-interested senses and emotions, but of being obsessed with responsibility for the Other. Such a radical turnabout would signify being absolutely surprised, overtaken, by what has always been determined since time immemorial. Therefore, just as the Spirit had inspired in Christ a life of expiation, the Spirit, in the depths of the Other, also inspires the self to share in Christ's expiation. Being free of self-interested experience and emotions ("having nothing") is an eschatological existence of otherness ("possessing everything").

Levinas has pointed to the Other's face as the locus in which God's word is heard (*EN* 110). The Other's face provokes the signification and witness of God's word through the Other's Otherness or disturbing proximity (*OB* 89, 139). It follows, then, that the Other's face is the nonphenomenal locus in which to encounter Christ and his praxis of doing the Father's will in the Spirit. In other words, we are compelled to look at eschatological existence in the encounter of Christ's expiation for the Other. Like Christ and through Christ, the self has been ordered anarchically to expiate for another. In a Levinasian sense, the passion to take on the Other's persecution and to bear the Other's fault is the sign in which the very "donation of the sign" is made. In the Levinasian lexicon, "donation" or "giving" (*La Donation*) signifies what is beyond experience and explanations: the self is gifted since time immemorial with the passivity of sacrificing for another. In other words, we approach a space and time in which to imagine Trinitarian praxis as a "gifted passivity."

Gifted passivity is an unusual term. It signifies a sense of the diachronic and immemorial ways in which God's word is encountered through Trinitarian praxis. In the state of passivity, the self is ordered to expiate for the Other. The order is, however, a trauma overwhelming consciousness because the self's passivity has been gifted since time immemorial. This sense of anarchical being-affected arises out of being gifted through Christ and in the Spirit. In short, "passivity" refers to the overwhelming trauma of responsibility and "gifted" to being immemorially united with the Father's obedience through Christ and in the Spirit. Hence, the idea of being gifted with passivity identifies the diachrony of a past that cannot be represented in consciousness, a diachrony of God speaking in the self. God's word is already gifted since time immemorial and can only be signified in passivity.

In the eschatological drama of Trinitarian praxis, the state of gifted passivity testifies to a paschal character of ethical transcendence. Where the self encounters the Father's will in the Other's face and pronounces it in expiation for the Other, the self signifies that it has been gifted in the innermost depths of the self with a share in Christ's passivity in the Spirit. Beneath such gifted passivity exist key emotions such as ethical melancholy. The sense of gifted passivity can also help us to discover how the emotions can take on a messianic character, giving value to a future world of "What no eye has seen, nor ear heard" (1 Cor. 2:9). Such emotions too must amount to a gift, animating the condition of an utmost passivity toward God's word of salvation.

Ethical transcendence signifies Trinitarian praxis. Where the self solicits a liturgy of responsibility, it attests to a Trinitarian encounter. Beyond self-interest, in the giving of one's heart for another, the Spirit has uttered the Father's word in the inmost part of the soul. Outside of any concept or theme, a new sermon has been heard and implanted as gift: the person of Jesus the Christ. Through passivity to God's word, a biblical life or super-individuation takes shape. Ezekiel, perhaps prefiguring Levinas's ethics, seems to alert to this: "I will put my spirit within you, and make you follow my statutes and be careful to observe my ordinances" (Ezek. 36:27). It seems that the radical alterity of being-for-the-Other initiates a Trinitarian praxis of encountering Christ as the first word of responsibility: the one who sends us, the Spirit who ruptures the conscience into a new seeing and a new hearing, and the Father who has sent Christ to us (John 20:21–22). However, veiled behind ethical transcendence is the humility of ethical melancholy, disarming the ego and fears of the Other, opening up the possibility of a healing and heartfelt relationship. Such humility leads to an eschatological and eucharistic existence of utmost passivity and giftedness. The gifted passivity of Trinitarian praxis is consummately exemplified through the Eucharist and the eucharistic life. The Eucharist signifies a eschatological dimension in which transcendence develops ethically and the emotions like melancholy to take on, in Christian theological terms, a Trinitarian nature.

BUILDING JEWISH-CHRISTIAN FRIENDSHIP

Another eschatological dimension offering possibilities to develop the emotions ethically is Jewish-Christian friendship. For Christians, the quest toward friendship with Jews represents a practical challenge of ethical transcendence: to value both Jews and Judaism. In this way, Trinitarian praxis commands an awakening to the Jewish other as friend—the one for whose presence one may yearn and even die.

The love of friendship invites us to think about what is at the heart of human existence and reality. When people come together in search of friendship, they are evidencing a hunger and thirst for meaning and truth. Naturally, where we encounter and engage the face of a friend, we want to be understood, appreciated, and welcomed. Yet the face of the Other in our midst is overflowing with mystery and otherness. There is so much we do not understand. We may find ourselves helpless, lingering at the door of another's heart. Many of us lament at the loneliness of our Western culture and how difficult it is to be a friend or to find a friend. But it is here, in the melancholy of hemorrhaging cries of heartache and despair, that hope begins to emerge. We must allow ourselves to touch the terrible loneliness of our existence before we can begin to value the truth of friendship.

In many ways we live in an in-between (metaxic) world of loneliness and friendship. However, we should not see this as a void, but as an opportunity to encounter mystery. Mystery reminds us of the challenge to go beyond and transcend ourselves toward life-building possibilities. Further, mystery inspires us to acculturate to new cultures, learn different languages, meet new people, study different subjects, redefine our dreams, rehabituate our behaviors, and join together in what seems impossible. Mystery, perhaps unexpectedly, shares a deep affinity with the emotion of melancholy. Melancholy is forged in the coming together of eros (the personal love for self) with agape (the love for God and others). And stirring on the borders of hope, melancholy will cry out for mystery to the point of insomnia or vigilance. Where mystery meets melancholy, something wonderful, spontaneous, and beautiful emerges. This something is the human spirit made to resemble God. In a practical way, therefore, when we experience loneliness, a vigilant moment of melancholy may arise to remind us of the mystery of our human spirit within. Then, if we have the courage and confidence to befriend our own spirit, we may uncover the hope that the suffering of loneliness is not useless and for nothing.

The loneliness of our world today indicates our spiritual condition; thus, loneliness needs a spiritual response. Being open to the creative energies of melancholy and vigilance may help the self to move from loneliness to a state of solitude.[50] And pursuing the solitude of reflection and prayer to cope with the turbulence of our lives, two key forms of transcendence beckon to take place in the self: transfiguration and transformation. Transfiguration speaks of an instantaneous change, metamorphosis, or even a mutation. In terms of prayer and spirituality, we can think of transfiguration as a radical change from self-interest to a life of pursuing goodness and truth. The actual moment of meeting a friend could be a prayerful and spiritual experience of transfiguration; the face can radiate "like the sun" (Matt 17:2) over the joy of friendship. In contrast, transformation implies a gradual change. Carrying forward the experience of transfiguration, transformation can be articulated as an ethical condition of difficult responsibility. This is because it demands something so painful and so hard: a rehabituation of self toward a life of prayer and the love of friendship. In the context of friendship, transfiguration is the decision to be a friend while transformation is the process of journeying to make the decision.

Emerging, then, is the idea of friendship as an ethical-spiritual journey. It not only has an exterior quality, but also an interior one. Friendship invites one to be at home within oneself; in other words, for friendship with others to mature, the self must partake of solitude. In theological terms, meditation and contemplation are at the very center of the meaning of life. Solitude invites the challenge of learning simply to be, that is, to be at home within oneself nurturing hospitality and intimacy and discovering the creativity and power of melancholy and vigilance. Solitude is like a mode of transformation journeying toward transfiguration and enlightenment. Once we are settled in solitude, the gift of hospitality may soon begin to overflow spontaneously into our relations with others.

As it transforms into hospitality, solitude will begin to emanate its own heartfelt logic of welcome and find itself breaking out into a first transcendence, namely, the beatitude and blessing of "Hello!" This everyday greeting has the power to testify to transfiguration, transformation and solitude. For example, greeting 'Hello' to another may give hope to the transfiguration of opening to the vulnerabilities, sufferings and poverty of our lives, to the transformation of reflecting upon meaning in life, and to finding the solitude of prayer, meditation and contemplation. Something beautiful, true and good emerges in a heartfelt greeting of "Hello!" This first transcendence is at the very heart of friendship. This simple greeting, when said with a hunger for hospitality, intimacy, peace, healing, and prayer, is like a key to unlock some of the mystery or bodiliness of the Other.

In the act of smiling and saying "Hello!" we have the potential to transform our solitude into hospitality and intimacy. With this greeting, we could well find ourselves being invited into the time and world of the other. The everyday "Hello!" of the receiving of the Other invites an ethical, existential, and theological perspective on the mystery of time. Ethics, perhaps, begins with the time of the Other. Time then speaks of a loving, prayerful, and ethical relationship with "to-God" and "to-the-Other." Through the attention we show to receiving our neighbor as a friend, time awakens to a revelation of our common personhood, namely, "the priority of good in relation to evil."[51] Awake to ethical responsibility as both the immanent expectation of the good and the inspiration of hope, we may begin to reflect and enter into the gift of friendship.

The challenge to build friendship begins neither with cognition nor with objectivity. Cognition-without-personhood and objectivity-without-intersubjectivity are perhaps like a conversation between specters haunting one another with facts, self-interest, and the horror of anonymous and depersonalizing existence. Friendship depends upon the bodiliness (the transfiguration, transformation and solitude) of face-to-face relations. If we hope to resemble God's likeness, we must awaken to our identity of being an image of God. Being human, it is naturally a lifelong struggle to nurture love for self, others, and God. Nonetheless, there are everyday opportunities to be invited into the mystery of personhood and bodiliness. The suffering or loneliness of our neighbor presents one such opportunity. Suffering may take on infinite meaning whereby the Infinite One, God, is with us *in-the-finite*. Such being-with-us could also be called affectivity, transfiguration, transformation, solitude, and bodiliness. For example, in the bodiliness of suffering with the suffering of the Other, in the bodiliness of being wounded by the wounds of the Other, and in the bodiliness of enjoying the joy of the Other, we may journey toward a time of meaning and friendship: an epiphany of Trinitarian praxis.

The journey toward hospitality and intimacy is a path to friendship. Overflowing with emotion or affectivity, stirred by transfiguration, deepened by the gradual process of transformation, and centered through solitude, the heart of the journey is love. Friendship itself is a witness to the living reality of love. The truth of love demands that we allow love to be given and to be received; the passivity of love opens the invitation of intimacy and the gift of otherness; and the over-emphasis of love unveils a "super-obedience" (or transfiguration) of responsibility, care, sensitivity, and compassion. Pulling these senses of love then together, we can suggest that the love of friendship is a "super-craft" (or transformation) of personhood into bodiliness.[52]

The super-craft of spiritual friendship speaks of the metaphysical. The term "metaphysical," allows the ethical, spiritual, and theological imagination to conceive of possible metaphysical states for the super-craft of spiritual friendship, including ethical melancholy and ethical insomnia (or ethical vigilance). Each state underlines the sense of bodiliness found within the depths of transfiguration, transformation, solitude, and love. The two states further exemplify something that we cannot prove with the objectivity of facts: the representation of personal experience or even the thematization of ideas. Ethical melancholy and ethical insomnia are more than ideas; they resist being reduced to the worlds of objectivity, cognition, or self-interest. This is not to deny that melancholy and insomnia participate in the process of objectivity. In fact, for melancholy and insomnia to achieve objectivity, each state must journey beyond the ego's manipulation of reality and existence toward ethical transcendence. This is the realm of the Infinite God, that is, the unthematizable reign of God where peace, justice, mercy, and having a heart become divine words of melancholy and vigilance (*OB* 52, 162; *BPW* 64, 123). Once melancholy and insomnia have been transfigured and transformed, each state or emotion may then return to the world of Being, objectivity, and personal experience—to our everyday reality and existence—with a heightened sense of the good (solitude).

How might we find a way to relate the grace of Jewish and Christian friendship as a promise of hope? We may hesitate to respond, and it may be helpful to explore such hesitance. In the desire to relate grace and ethics together in Jewish-Christian friendship, we may hesitate because we have tasted a little of the bitter spice of melancholy in the search to create a recipe of compassion and responsibility. Indeed, compassion inspires a strange kind of ethical melancholy while provoking the hope of awakening the ethical dimension of friendship. In the hope of building Jewish-Christian friendship, perhaps we need to develop a taste for melancholy.

Since the end of World War II, Levinas eagerly took part to contribute to building up Jewish-Christian friendship. In recent decades, Christian theologians have sought to employ Levinas's thought to develop Christian theology. The sense of melancholy in the writings of Levinas may even nurture such affinity. In his essay "Jewish-

Christian Friendship" (1961), Levinas reflected with a little spice of melancholy on a previous encounter with the Catholic writer and philosopher, Jacques Madaule:

> What he said to me during the Colloquium is worth repeating to you here. For Madaule, the Jews who wait for the messianic age do not wait in vain, as so many Christians still believe, for an event that has been coming now for more than twenty centuries. The Jewish waiting for the Messiah makes complete sense to the Christian waiting for the return of his Savior, for Parousia. It is not, therefore, finished, even for a Christian. And Jews are necessary to the future of a humanity which, knowing it has been saved, has nothing more to wait for. The presence of the Jews reminds conformists of every kind that everything is not for the best in the best of all possible worlds. (*DF* 202)

Levinas's reflection here seems to swell toward an outpouring of melancholy. Both the inter-subjectivity of face-to-face relations and the bodiliness of enjoying the joy of Madaule speaking positively about Judaism invite Levinas into the affectivity of ethical melancholy and the hope for Jewish-Christian friendship. Levinas continues:

> Until this point, friendship between Jews and Christians seemed to be based on their both belonging to humanity, the modern world, the West. Of course, from the Jewish point of view, Christianity was justified: it brought monotheism to the Gentiles. But what, then, was Judaism in Christian eyes? A prophecy that outlived its fulfillment. The testimony incarnate of a failure. A blindfolded virgin. A residue. A remnant. An anachronism. A fossil. A relic. An exhibit. But now Madaule shows Christians that we are significant to the future and to life. This significance can transform the very meaning of Judaeo-Christian relations. (*DF* 202)

Having time to take a step back to reclaim the fertile gift of melancholy can be empowering; it creates new energies to jump deeper into creative possibilities such as the ones Levinas finds for Jewish-Christian friendship. In the drama of living, the intriguing and demanding quality of melancholy evokes the potential to announce the word of God. This evokes the sense of a theo-drama. Entering the theological drama, the rupture of an overwhelming surprise of something unheard-of arises in a new intimacy for transfiguration where the Jewish or Christian stranger becomes a friend. Rising beyond care for oneself, a little of the spice, beauty, and power of melancholy infuses otherness with the hope of friendship. In other words, where melancholy matures, the self may begin to hunger and thirst for friendship. Ethical melancholy is passivity, an openness inspiring a new curiosity and passion to journey toward friendship. We can also speak further of ethical melancholy as solitude, hospitality, the intimacy of a conscience, and a medium of love.

The power and beauty of Levinas's sense of melancholy demands from the Christian conscience the primacy of ethical relations. If friendship is going to be a possibility, not only must there by respect for Jews but also for Judaism itself. An outpouring of ethical melancholy gives rise to a revelation of responsibility toward the transcendence and transfiguration of a future world of Jewish-Christian friendship. Melancholy may inaugurate an "unforgettable" invitation of hospitality to the Christian to enter through the door of Jewish identity. Is this a revelation of a future world of partaking of an ancient vintage that has been maturing since the days of creation? Indeed, an eschatological seeing and believing (*Schauen und Glauben*) arises: the vision or transfiguration of Jews and Christians living "together in unity" (Ps. 133:1). This is what the emotion of ethical melancholy imagines. The hope "to see what can be accomplished" is a difficult challenge for it demands a state of freedom and responsibility (*TL* 2:287). Thus, the super-craft of Jewish-Christian friendship calls for ethical insomnia or ethical vigilance.

In Levinas's philosophical terms, ethical insomnia is a vigilance of responsibility for the Other. There is also something enigmatic and traumatic about its character. Insomnia speaks of "wakefulness" beyond everyday consciousness (*BPW* 133). The context of Levinas's philosophical idea is the memory of the Shoah and the evil of Hitlerism. Levinas has helped to show that evil divides the seeing and believing subject from the object of consciousness. In other words, where perpetrators of evil dehumanize victims, such evildoers have effectively lost their personhood, becoming "as anonymous as the night itself" and possessing their own state of insomnia—wakefulness or consciousness of "depersonalisation" (*EE* 65–66). Purcell writes: "There is *no thing* there, but this is not *nothing*. It is the fact that *there is*."[53] The self has been eaten up, expelling the 'I' through the presence of fear, threat, and vigilance to the dark horror of evil. Levinas gives a haunting portrait of an evildoer.

Responding to the excess of evil, we find an important context for Jewish-Christian friendship: an eschatological vocation to build up the good truth of friendship. Encountering the excess of evil invokes the hope of rupturing the impersonal and anonymous character of being-in-the-world. Levinas's philosophy therefore challenges us not to "extinguish" our neighbor through hostility, self-interest, and a dearth of empathy, compassion, sacrifice, and humility (*EE* 66). Where we encounter the Other's loneliness, destitution, and broken heart, there remains a difficult super-individuation toward the good and the true (*OB* 118). We can call such transformative process—in the hope of unveiling a time of friendship—a state of ethical insomnia and ethical vigilance.

Importantly, behind the good and the true is the beautiful. And bringing the duet of eros and agape together, the emotion of melancholy reminds us of the need to be aware of the beautiful. The more that the love of friendship "purifies the heart"[54] and transfigures the spirit, the more the work of ethical responsibility may create a space for intimacy and hospitality. Vigilance must be cultivated not only for "inner-worldly natural beauty" but also for the "transcendental beauty of revelation" (*GL* 1:41). Or in Levinas's terms, we need to keep our eyes open toward a "new hope" of partaking of the ancient vintage maturing since the days of Eden. Such a hope points toward the announcing of a new Logos or word of reason (a theo-logic) to articulate the "fecundity of time" and "the positive value of history" for both Jews and Christians to aspire together (*DF* 67–68). Indeed, Isaiah proclaims this very reality, "Peace, peace, to the far and the near, says the Lord; and I will heal them" (Isa. 57:19). The more that we allow the emotions of melancholy and vigilance to deepen our sense of the beautiful and the good, the more we may envision a future world of righteousness. Again, Isaiah reminds us, "From ages past no one has heard, no ear has perceived, no eye has seen any God besides you, who works for those who wait for him" (Isa. 64:4). Saint Paul too, paraphrasing from the Septuagint, shares this hope for "What no eye has seen, nor ear heard, nor the human heart conceived, what God has prepared for those who love him" (1 Cor. 2:9). As Isaiah and Paul remind us of the Holy Spirit's work through time and history, might we find a way to approach the "unforeseeable fecundity" of the "future moment" as the "hope" for building Jewish-Christian friendship (*DF* 67; *GL* 7:179)?

In conceiving the Jewish-Christian friendship as both an immanent future and an anticipation of hope, we reject the temptation to reduce Jewish-Christian friendship to only an anticipation of hope. If Jewish-Christian friendship is going to be a genuine possibility, there needs to be the confidence and courage to savor the fecundity of time not only as a qualitative anticipation of hope, but also as a "quantitative immanent expectation" (*GL* 7:179). In other words, both Jews and Christians need to be challenged to nurture the state of mind in which friendship is an immanent possibility. In spiritual and practical terms, this means: opening to the beauty, rapture, and radiance of being transfigured by friendship; beginning the journey of change and transformation; having time for the solitude of searching for meaning; being wounded by the encounter of love; and taking up the confidence and courage to make a decision to be friends. Such a defining stance toward hope, deepened by the bodiliness of the transcendent emotions of ethical melancholy and ethical insomnia, may well help to safeguard the positive value of history from contamination such as forgetting or denying the past.

Melancholy, insomnia, and hope may seem like a peculiar trio. However, examples of people living out a transfigured and transformed melancholy and vigilance exemplify the hope of building (and rebuilding) Jewish-Christian friendship. One such example is the life and work of Pope John Paul II. For example, in a March 2000 address at the Yad Vashem Holocaust Memorial in Jerusalem, Pope John Paul II begins with a lament from Psalm 31:

> I have become like a broken vessel.
> I hear the whispering of many — terror on every side! —

as they scheme together against me, as they plot to take my life.
But I trust in you, O Lord;
I say, "You are my God." (Ps. 31:12–15)[55]

Like Levinas—whom he admired, met, and engaged in fruitful dialogue—Pope John Paul II sets the solemn tone of his address at Yad Vashem by proclaiming the gravity of responsibility for the Other.[56] The Pope's words uncover a little of the drama of a soul giving fecundity to time and a sacred value to history. Speaking directly of the Shoah—the Pope continues: "In this place of memories, the mind and heart and soul feel an extreme need for silence. Silence in which to remember. Silence in which to make some sense of the memories that come flooding back. Silence because there are no words strong enough to deplore the terrible tragedy of the *Shoah*."[57]

For John Paul II, silence is a mode of remembering and hoping. The solitude of silence evokes an immanent expectation of remembering his experience of the Shoah and of anticipating the hope of building Jewish-Christian friendship. Bringing both together, he shares the meaning of his silence: "My own personal memories are of all that happened when the Nazis occupied Poland during the War. I remember my Jewish friends and neighbors. I have come to Yad Vashem to pay homage to the millions of Jewish people who, stripped of everything, especially of their human dignity, were murdered in the Holocaust. More than half a century has passed, but the memories remain."[58]

The Pope's words are almost a silent witness. Opening his heart to the silence, Pope John Paul II gives guidance on the importance of passion and emotion. He tastes silence with a spice of melancholy and an infusing of vigilance to remember the horror of evil. Wakeful to the eternity of outrage and the experience of countless murders, hope must turn into a decision to testify to truth. And it is in the insomnia of journeying through the inner logic (or theo-logic) of truth that it becomes possible to take a further step forward to establish hospitality, intimacy, trust, and even a time for friendship. By sharing his testimony and emotions, the Pope alerts us to his insomnia or psyche, which cannot escape or evade the word of God. For the In-finite word "traumatically commands" him to an "extreme urgency."[59]

In the silent listening, perhaps we can imagine the word of God (in hidden ways) encouraging the Pope to approach his talk in a spirit of humility. For Emmanuel Levinas, this would mean acknowledging, "I am first a servant of a neighbor, already late and guilty for being late" (*OB* 87). The interhuman responsibility to the Other is always primary. How then does the Pope respond to the memory of Auschwitz and other places "in which evil appears in its diabolical horror" (*EN* 97)? He must testify to his ethical insomnia and the shock, trauma, and stupor leading up to it. Finishing the first part of his address at Yad Vashem, he shares: "Here, as at Auschwitz and many other places in Europe, we are overcome by the echo of the heart-rending laments of so many. Men, women, and children cry out to us from the depths of the horror that they knew. How can we fail to heed their cry? No one can forget or ignore what happened. No one can diminish its scale."[60]

The Pope's address signifies a step of hope along the path toward Judeo-Christian friendship. Like God, we may indeed need to make a path straight with crooked lines and wounded memories. "The way is crooked."[61] For Christians, the temptation is to reduce relations with Jews to a theological-cognitive solution. This can never work because of the "disproportion between suffering and every theodicy," or theological attempts to explain suffering and why there is God. Auschwitz has shown the violence of falling into theological propositions "with a glaring, obvious clarity." So then if theology is going to help, then it must seek a path toward the interhuman (*EN* 97). In other words, theology needs to find a voice, place, and time to speak with humility, hospitality, hope, bodiliness, vulnerability, intimacy, and emotion. Entering the momentum of hope, the pope's words at Yad Vashem speak of the genuine prayer for a future world of friendship between Jews and Christians. In his final words, he witnesses: "The world must heed the warning that comes to us from the victims of the Holocaust and from the testimony of the survivors. Here at Yad Vashem the memory lives on, and burns itself onto our souls. It makes us cry out: 'I hear the whispering of many—terror on every side! — But I trust in you, O Lord'; I say, 'You are my God' (Ps. 31:13–15)."[62]

The pope alerts us to the intimacy and vulnerability of our bodiliness. To allow the memory of the Shoah to burn itself onto the soul signifies the decision for friendship. Not only is friendship guided by a qualitative inspiration of hope, but also through a quantitative hope of immediacy and immanency. Friendship needs the immediacy of the face-to-face relation. If friendship begins with the hospitality and benediction of the greeting, "Hello!," then the pope's address has alerted us to the next word, namely, a heartfelt bodiliness and immediacy deepened by ethical melancholy and ethical vigilance wherein contexts where emotions of melancholy and wakefulness have been ethically nurtured, we may discover faithfulness as yet another word and step toward the transformation and transfiguration of friendship.

In essence, the inner logic of friendship reveals a sacred truth that God is personal. Hence, building Jewish-Christian relations is as much prayerful as it is ethical. And the journey toward building Judeo-Christian friendship is a special and important entryway to partake of the good truth and beauty of God's love.[63] If indeed friendship is like an ancient wine maturing since the days of Eden, it reminds us of the perseverance of hope: "At the very moment where all has been lost, everything is possible" (*EE* 92).

The friendship between Jews and Christians signifies almost a prayer of "difficult adoration" in which theology and alterity may coincide. Taking up the opportunity to engage Jews and Christians (and Judaism and Christianity) in a more heartfelt way reminds theology of the need to have spiritual, ethical, and personal concerns. It remains always a challenge for theology to find a way to speak about God. Pope John Paul II's address at Yad Vashem is exemplary. His openness to the Jewish people is part of his personal, spiritual, and theological quest to encounter the person of Christ — a journey, among other things, of ethical melancholy and ethical transcendence. The pope's sense of the heart overflows with sacred feelings, inspiring ideas, and the logic of an eschatological faith. Accordingly, where there is the transdescendence of God in our hearts, we may encounter the ethical transcendence and Trinitarian praxis to serve and love the world, others, and God with all of our hearts, minds, souls, and strengths. Such praxis would necessarily take us beyond our everyday experience to the margins of life.

Today, we can communicate so swiftly that we no longer have to engage with each other face to face. Computers and the Internet objectify us as ghosts, lost in the presence of communication. We are like ghosts because even though we may express ourselves personally in an email, we have our faces hidden. We are lost because we do not know a way out of the impersonal ways of technology; its presence overwhelms us and turns us into specters of the night. While we haunt our neighbors with endless emails and Internet conversations, we forget about reserving a blessing for them. Can we see their face and hear their cry? We may experience their words but we will never really encounter them. We are left with objective and impersonal experiences that transform our consciousness into an apparition. Technology in all its wonder and celebration of human knowledge has made us more and more forgetful of each other and, above all, those who are truly on the margins of society.

The word of God in the face of the poor one on the margins of society has affected us like a past that is no longer present. Our inner self is called in a moment of connection with the other's sadness, to reflect inwardly about his or her presence. Allowing the self to be affected by the Other initiates a beginning for ethical melancholy to emerge. In the gift of passivity and hearing God's word in the Other's face, we can confess our guilt and invert it into an openness to those at the margins of society. Our eyes, ears, and hearts have to be opened. We will remain blind, deaf, and heartless to the extent that we seek our own possibilities for advancement, wealth, and good fortune. Even if we seek to develop our own talents for the good of society, we bury them in the self-interests of the ego.

Although the face of the Other—namely, the orphan, widow, and stranger—is beyond our intentional consciousness, it nonetheless affects us. We have learned that the Lord "executes justice for the orphan and the widow, and…loves the strangers, providing them food and clothing" (Deut. 10:18). But it remains a difficult freedom to execute justice for the orphan and the widow and to love the strangers by providing them with food and clothing. It is a difficult freedom to love those who hate us, even to the point of taking responsibility for their persecution of us and of others. Ethical subjectivity is an ethical transcendence.

The Other is not an object, a personal experience, or an interesting piece of knowledge. The face, disturbing us like a thief in the night, overwhelms our consciousness for it is never easy to touch upon the pain and suffering of another. To live at the margins of life signifies an ethical subjectivity of hemorrhaging for the Other. We bleed for the suffering Other when his or her hunger, oppression, and destitution come to mind. Such hemorrhaging draws us on to testify the sacred words, "Here I am!" In this sacred space and time of ethical transcendence we witness to the glory of the life of expiation and prayer for the Other. In such a way, we can begin to appreciate that discourse is otherwise than our self-interested lives and begins from and for the person.

Let us not then think of living at the margins of life as an idea, but as transcendence and *doing* theology. When we are therefore faced by the Other, we can set out to engage the language of theology with ethical transcendence animated by the ethical melancholy of having a heart. This will hopefully lead to a theology of alterity deriving from an encounter with Christ and with the Other in Christ. In this way of peace and justice, we can testify that the person of Christ is the very depths and glory of God in which the poor one might be fed, clothed, and loved.

If we are able to meet the challenge of doing theology at the margins of life, there is indeed hope that at the very moment where all is lost, everything is possible. Even though all might have been lost with past lives of ego-fulfillment and pleasure, everything is possible as God, in the face of the poor one, stirs our heart with the true life of commitment and expiation. Every sacred feeling and every wound are all openings to testify to the glory of God. Within our hearts we can desire such glory, savor its beauty, and come to a maturity of a Trinitarian praxis of doing theology in relation to the Other.

Notes

Notes to Chapter One

1. Kevin Hart, *The Trespass of the Sign: Deconstruction, Theology and Philosophy* (New York: Fordham University Press, 2000), 78.

2. Hart, *Trespass of the Sign*, 77–81, 254.

3. Michaël de Saint Cheron, *Conversations with Emmanuel Levinas, 1983–1994*, trans. Gary D. Mole (Pittsburgh: Duquesne University Press, 2010), 13–14.

4. Emmanuel Levinas, *Otherwise than Being or Beyond Essence*, trans. Alphonso Lingis (Pittsburgh: Duquesne University Press, 1999), 147; hereafter cited in the text as *OB*.

5. Psalm 133:1 reads, "How very good and pleasant it is when kindred live together in unity!" The Hebrew words *Hine ma tov uma nayim shevet achim gam yachad* become imprinted upon the Jewish heart and identity, especially as they are repeated via heartfelt song. In a way, taking Levinas's prophetic thinking to heart demands also beholding what is good and pleasant, when people join together in unity, responsibility, and love. On an anecdotal level, after presenting a paper at the conference on Levinas and Theology in Leuven in May 2008, I concluded with an impassioned utterance of the Hebrew words, "*Hine ma tov*," to which Levinas's daughter, Mme. Simone Levinas, wife of Professor George Hansel, seemed to respond with delight and joy.

6. Michael Purcell, *Mystery and Method: The Other in Rahner and Levinas* (Milwaukee: Marquette University Press, 1998); Graham Ward, *Barth, Derrida, and the Language of Theology* (Cambridge: Cambridge University Press, 1995); Michael Barnes, *Theology and the Dialogue of Religions* (Cambridge: Cambridge University Press, 2002); David F. Ford, *Self and Salvation: Being Transformed* (Cambridge: Cambridge University Press, 1999); Michele Saracino, *On Being Human: A Conversation with Lonergan and Levinas* (Milwaukee, Marquette University Press, 2003).

7. Robyn Horner, *Rethinking God as Gift: Marion, Derrida, and the Limits of Phenomenology* (New York: Fordham University Press, 2001), 56.

8. Emmanuel Levinas, *Basic Philosophical Writings*, ed. Adriaan T. Peperzak, Simon Critchley, and Robert Bernasconi (Bloomington: Indiana University Press, 1996), 98–100; hereafter cited in the text as *BPW*.

9. Unless otherwise stated, we will refer to transcendental in the sense of its relation with Being or as quality of Being. Robyn Horner also points to two other senses of transcendental: "the transcendental in Kant's sense is that which 'establishes, and draws consequences from, the possibility and limits of experience.' The transcendental in Derrida's sense (to which we should rightly

refer as the quasi-transcendental) is the condition of possibility and impossibility for meaning, which, without delaying further with the details here, is infinite interpretability." See Horner, *Rethinking God as Gift,* 71.

10. *BPW* 151; Levinas, *Collected Philosophical Papers,* trans. Alphonso Lingis (Pittsburgh: Duquesne University Press, 1998), 157; hereafter cited in the text as *CPP.*

11. *OB* 133–34; Horner, *Rethinking God as Gift,* 58.

12. Purcell, *Mystery and Method,* 297, 329.

13. See Ward, *Barth, Derrida,* 184–85.

14. See Barnes, *Theology,* 97.

15. See Ford, *Self and Salvation,* 32, 162.

16. The idea of ontotheology is complex. Peperzak gives two senses: Ontotheology refers to "the relations between beings and God," while ontotheology stresses "a theological conception on the being (*to einai, das Sein*) of all beings (*to on*)." Adriaan Peperzak, "Religion after Onto-theology," in *Religion After Metaphysics,* ed. Mark Wrathall (Cambridge: Cambridge University Press), 2003, 120. In regard to the notion of "b/Being," we will throughout the study refer to its ontological sense as "Being" (*Être*) and to its ontic sense as "being" (*étant*).

17. For a discussion of the various meanings of analogy, see Ward, *Barth, Derrida,* 71, 97–98, 152.

18. Cohen writes in italics: "*Heidegger's ontology permits Levinas to see beneath the representational character of Husserl's phenomenology, true, but the ethics and justice of Rosenzweig's 'Star' permit him to see through the ontological character of Heidegger's regrounding of phenomenology.*" See Richard A. Cohen, *Elevations: The Height of the Good in Rosenzweig and Levinas* (Chicago: The University of Chicago Press, 1994), 236–37.

19. See, for example, Plato's idea of the good and myth of Gyges, Descartes's idea of the Infinite, Shakespeare's *Macbeth,* Blanchot's idea of the neuter, Lévy-Bruhl's notion of participation, Dostoyevsky's *The Brothers Karamazov,* Grossman's *Life and Fate,* and Haim of Volozhin's *Nefesh ha'Haim.*

20. David Woodruff Smith, "Mind and Body," *The Cambridge Companion to Husserl,* ed. Barry Smith and David Woodruff Smith (Cambridge: Cambridge University Press, 1995), 328–29.

21. *BPW* 65–77; Levinas, *Entre Nous: On Thinking-of-the-Other,* trans. Michael B. Smith and Barbara Harshav (New York: Columbia University Press, 1998), 6–12; hereafter cited in the text as *EN.*

22. Emmanuel Levinas, *Discovering Existence with Husserl,* trans. Richard A. Cohen and Michael B. Smith (Evanston, IL: Northwestern University Press, 1998), 22–23.

23. Emmanuel Levinas, *The Theory of Intuition in Husserl's Phenomenology,* trans. André Orianne, 2nd ed. (Evanston, IL: Northwestern University Press, 1995), 44; Horner, *Rethinking God as Gift,* 49.

24. In reply to Philippe Nemo's question about *Sein und Zeit,* Levinas writes, "The work that I did then on 'the theory of intuition' in Husserl was

thus influenced by *Sein und Zeit*, to the extent that I sought to present Husserl as having perceived the ontological problem of being, the question of the status rather than the quiddity of beings.... In *Sein und Zeit*'s analyses of anxiety, care and being-toward-death, we witness a sovereign exercise of phenomenology." Emmanuel Levinas, *Ethics and Infinity: Conversations with Philippe Nemo*, trans. Richard A. Cohen (Pittsburgh: Duquesne University Press, 1999), 39; hereafter cited in the text as *EI*.

25. The other four works are Plato's *Phaedrus,* Kant's *Critique of Pure Reason,* Hegel's *Phenomenology of Spirit* and Bergson's *Time and Free Will* (*EI* 37–38). See Peperzak, *To the Other: An Introduction to the Philosophy of Levinas* (West Lafayette, IN: Purdue University Press, 1993), 4.

26. Simon Critchley refers to this as a "somewhat oedipal conflict" in "Introduction," in *The Cambridge Companion to Levinas,* ed. Simon Critchley and Robert Bernasconi (Cambridge: Cambridge University Press, 2002), 8. While his claim is understandable, one could perceive that Heidegger's involvement in Nazism would possibly destroy any affinity underlying a repressed oedipal relation in Levinas.

27. Sonia Sikka, "Questioning the Sacred: Heidegger and Levinas on the Locus of Divinity," *Modern Theology* 14, no. 3 (July 1998): 300.

28. Emmanuel Levinas, *Existence and Existents,* trans. A. Lingis (London: Kluwer Academic Publishers, 1995), 17; hereafter cited in the text as *EE*.

29. Critchley, "Introduction," *Cambridge Companion to Levinas,* 11.

30. Martin Heidegger, *Being and Time,* trans. John Macquarrie and Edward Robinson (Oxford: Blackwell, 1995), 223. See also Michael Inwood, *A Heidegger Dictionary.* The Blackwell Philosophical Dictionaries (Oxford: Blackwell Publishers, 2000), 219.

31. Critchley, "Introduction," *Cambridge Companion to Levinas,* 11.

32. Edith Wyschogrod, in *Emmanuel Levinas: The Problem of Ethical Metaphysics* (New York: Fordham University Press, 2000).

33. Emmanuel Levinas, *Is It Righteous to Be? Interviews with Emmanuel Levinas,* ed. Jill Robbins (Palo Alto: Stanford University Press, 2001), 94; hereafter cited in the text as *IR*.

34. John Caputo, *Demythologizing Heidegger* (Bloomington: Indiana University Press, 1993), 5.

35. *EE* 61. See also Levinas, "The Name of a Dog, or Natural Rights," in *Difficult Freedom: Essays on Judaism,* trans. Seán Hand (Baltimore: John Hopkins University Press, 1997), 151–53; hereafter cited in the text as *DF*. Levinas speaks of the experience of being stripped from one's human skin and of only having one's humanity recognized by "the last Kantian in Nazi Germany," a dog called Bobby.

36. Heidegger, *Being and Time,* 488, 278.

37. Emmanuel Levinas, *Time and the Other: And Additional Essays,* trans. Richard A. Cohen (Pittsburgh: Duquesne University Press, 1997), 119.

38. Critchley, "Introduction," *Cambridge Companion to Levinas,* 11.

39. Emmanuel Levinas, *God, Death, and Time,* trans. Bettina Bergo (Palo Alto: Stanford University Press, 2000), 43; hereafter cited as *GDT.*

40. Dallas Willard, "Knowledge," in Smith and Smith, *Cambridge Companion to Husserl,* 148.

41. John Macquarrie translates *Erfahrung* and *erfahren* as "experience" and *Erlebnis* as "Experience." See Heidegger, *Being and Time,* 72n1.

42. Inwood points out that *er-fahren* has an active sense: "In active experience, we 'go forth' (*er-fahren*) to look for something, whereas *Erfahrung* [defined by Heidegger as "any experience" (*Being and Time,* 72n1)] is at first passive: we come across something without going in search of it." See Inwood, *Heidegger Dictionary,* 62–64.

43. Heidegger states, "What oppresses is not this or that, nor is it the summation of everything present-at-hand; it is rather the *possibility* of the-ready-to-hand in general; that is to say, it is the world itself." *Being and Time,* 231.

44. Levinas, *Discovering Existence with Husserl,* 4.

45. *Da-sein* means, literally, Being-there or "the 'there' (*Da*) where being (*Sein*) shows itself." See Heidegger, *Being and Time,* 27; Robert Dostall, "Time and Phenomenology," in *The Cambridge Companion to Heidegger,* ed. Charles Guignon (Cambridge: Cambridge University Press, 1996), 152.

46. Heidegger, *Being and Time,* 334.

47. Inwood, *Heidegger Dictionary,* 230.

48. Levinas, *Of God Who Comes to Mind,* trans. Bettina Bergo (Palo Alto: Stanford University Press, 1998), 172–73; hereafter cited in the text as *GCM.*

49. Heidegger writes: "No matter how sharply we just *look* at the 'outward appearance' of Things in whatever form this takes, we cannot discover anything ready-to-hand. If we just look at things 'theoretically', we can get along without understanding readiness-to-hand." *Being and Time,* 98.

50. Inwood, *Heidegger Dictionary,* 218.

51. Heidegger, *Being and Time,* 223, 210–24, 321–22.

52. For a helpful discussion of Levinas, Husserl, and Heidegger, see Horner, *Rethinking God as Gift,* 43–60.

53. Michael L. Morgan, *Discovering Levinas* (Cambridge: Cambridge University Press, 2007), 94.

54. Morgan, *Discovering Levinas,* 94.

55. Emmanuel Levinas, "Foreword," in *System and Revelation: The Philosophy of Franz Rosenzweig,* by Stéphane Mosès, trans. Catherine Tihanyi (Detroit: Wayne State University Press, 1992), 15.

56. Franz Rosenzweig, *The Star of Redemption,* trans. William W. Hallo (Notre Dame: University of Notre Dame Press, 1985), 391.

57. Mosès, *System and Revelation,* 53.

58. See Emmanuel Levinas, *Outside the Subject,* translated by Michael B. Smith (Palo Alto: Stanford University Press, 1994), 61.

59. Cohen writes, "But Levinas's thought is also, from Rosenzweig's perspective, Christian, centrifugal as well as centripetal, a loving of others inspired

by being loved, a global mission as well as an eternal people. Indeed, for Levinas, who nowhere expresses Rosenzweig's exclusionary commitments, these two moments are inseparable. Irreplaceable election of the self and responsiveness to the incomparable alterity of the other person are two aspects of the same ethics." See Cohen, *Elevations,* 299.

60. Emmanuel Levinas, *Totality and Infinity: An Essay on Exteriority,* trans. Alphonso Lingis (Pittsburgh: Duquesne University Press, 1996), 28; hereafter cited as *TI.*

61. Heidegger, *Being and Time,* 488.

62. Emmanuel Levinas, "Foreword," in Stéphane Mosès, *System and Revelation: The Philosophy of Franz Rosenzweig,* trans. Catherine Tihanyi (Detroit: Wayne State University, 1992), 15.

63. Rosenzweig, *Star of Redemption,* 420, 394, 424.

64. Stephen Webb, "The Rhetoric of Ethics as Excess: A Christian Theological Response to Emmanuel Levinas," *Modern Theology* (January 1999): 9.

65. Levinas, *Outside the Subject,* 61–63.

66. See Glenn Morrison, "Jewish-Christian Relations and the Ethical Philosophy of Emmanuel Levinas: 'At the Very Moment Where All Is Lost, Everything Is Possible,'" *Journal of Ecumenical Studies* 38, no. 2–3 (Spring–Summer 2001): 316–29.

Notes to Chapter Two

1. Adriaan Peperzak, ed., *Ethics as First Philosophy: The Significance of Emmanuel Levinas for Philosophy, Literature and Religion* (New York: Routledge, 1995), 184.

2. Richard A. Cohen, "Difficulty and Mortality: Two Notes on Reading Levinas," *Philosophy in the Contemporary World* 7, no. 1 (Spring 2000), 59–61.

3. Morgan, *Discovering Levinas,* 94.

4. James F. Keenan, *A History of Catholic Moral Theology in the Twentieth Century: From Contesting Sins to Liberating Consciences* (New York: Continuum, 2010), 96.

5. Vatican Archive, "Pastoral Constitution on the Church in the Modern World, *Gaudium Et Spes.* Promulgated By His Holiness, Pope Paul VI, On December 7, 1965," www.vatican.va/archive/hist_councils/ii_vatican_council/documents/vat-ii_cons_19651207_gaudium-et-spes_en.html. See paragraph 16.

6. Karol Wojtyla (Pope John Paul II), *The Acting Person,* trans. Andrzej Potocki, Analecta Husserliana, The Yearbook of Phenomenological Research, vol. 10 (Dordrecht, Holland: D. Reidel, 1979), 173.87, 172–74.

7. Nigel Zimmermann, "Karol Wojtyla and Emmanuel Levinas on the Embodied Self: The Forming of the Other as Moral Self-Disclosure," *Heythrop Journal* 50, no. 6 (November 2009): 992.

8. Levinas, *Discovering Existence with Husserl,* 48, 17.

9. Jacques Derrida, *Writing and Difference,* trans. Alan Bass (London: Routledge, 2001), 103.

10. For references to Isaiah, see, for example, Levinas, "A Man-God?" in *EN* 57 and "Meaning and Sense" in *CPP* 97. In regard to Matt. 25, he states, "When I speak to a Christian, I always quote Matthew 25: the relation to God is presented there as a relation to another person. It is not a metaphor; in the other, there is a real presence of God. In my relation to the other, I hear the word of God" (*IR* 171).

11. Adriaan Peperzak, "The Significance of Levinas's Work for Christian Thought," in *The Face of the Other and the Trace of God: Essays on the Philosophy of Emmanuel Levinas,* ed. Jeffrey Bloechl, 184–85 (New York: Fordham University Press, 2000).

12. Ward, *Barth, Derrida,* 183–86; Purcell, *Mystery and Method,* 308.

13. Ward, *Barth, Derrida,* 131n9, 184.

14. Purcell, *Mystery and Method,* 308.

15. Ibid., 308.

16. Ford, *Self and Salvation,* 266–81; and Barnes, *Theology,* 97.

17. Ford, *Self and Salvation,* 266–71.

18. Ford follows a path by way of Jüngel's thought, resulting in an analogy of joyful obligation. Ibid., 74–79.

19. Barnes, *Theology,* 244.

20. Levinas reflects: "Horror is nowise an anxiety about death" (*EE* 61).

21. Willard Gaylin, *Feelings: Our Vital Signs* (London: Harper and Row, 1979), 215.

22. "Existence without existents" refers to the experience of existence before taking up any position in life.

23. Maurice Blanchot, *Thomas the Obscure,* new edition, trans. Robert Lamberton (New York: D. Lewis, 1973), 104.

24. Compare, particularly, Blanchot, *Thomas the Obscure,* 13–16.

25. In this analysis, I am indebted to John Caruana's critique of the sacred in Levinas's thought. See John Caruana, "Lévinas' Critique of the Sacred," *International Philosophical Quarterly* 42, no. 4 (December 2002), 519–34.

26. Caruana, "Lévinas' Critique," 525, 530.

27. Ibid., 525.

28. Caruana, "Lévinas' Critique," 520; David Tracy, "Response to Adriaan Peperzak on Transcendence," in Peperzak, *Ethics as First Philosophy,* 197.

29. St. John of the Cross, *The Collected Works of St. John the Cross,* trans. Kieran Kavanaugh, and Otilio Rodriguez (Washington, DC: Institute of Carmelite Studies Publications, 1979).

30. Alister McGrath, *Christian Spirituality* (Oxford: Blackwell, 2000), 6, 84.

31. Later, Levinas reflects: "I'm not saying that the other is God, but that in his or her Face I hear the Word of God" (*EN* 110).

32. Cohen, *Elevations,* 245–46.

33. O'Dowd points out: "In continuity with the rest of the wisdom literature, Qohelet expresses himself by engaging in creation theology. Most significant is his immediate appraisal of all things as 'obscure' (*hebel* [1:2]). Whilst most English translations collapse *hebel* to "vanity," an increasing number of commentators recognize the linguistic capacity of this word to point to a metaphorical "'ambiguity,' 'vapor,' or meaninglessness.'" Ryan O'Dowd, "A Chord of Three Strands: Epistemology in Job, Proverbs and Ecclesiastes," in *The Bible and Epistemology: Biblical Soundings on the Knowledge of God*, ed. Mary Healy and Robin Parry (Milton Keynes: Paternoster, 2007), 80.

34. David F. Ford, *The Modern Theologians,* 2nd ed. (Oxford: Blackwell, 1997), 214, 757.

35. Levinas, *Beyond the Verse: Talmudic Readings and Lectures,* trans. Gary D. Mole (Bloomington: Indiana University Press, 1994), 162; hereafter cited in the text as *BV*.

36. Levinas uses the word *vécu* for lived experience (*Erlebnis*) throughout his interviews and writings (*IR* 96; *OB* 31–34).

37. Further, Levinas states, "In an approach I am first servant of a neighbor, already late and guilty for being late" (*OB* 87).

38. Adriaan Peperzak, *Beyond: The Philosophy of Emmanuel Levinas* (Evanston, IL: Northwestern University Press, 1997), 62.

39. Lonergan writes, "moral conversion consists in opting for the truly good, even for value against satisfaction when value and satisfaction conflict." See Bernard Lonergan, *Method in Theology* (Toronto: University of Toronto Press, 1996), 240.

40. Levinas, "Ideology and Idealism," in *The Levinas Reader* (Oxford: Blackwell, 1999), 247.

41. Levinas, *Nine Talmudic Readings,* trans. Annette Aronowicz (Bloomington: Indiana University Press, 1994), 183; hereafter cited in the text as *NT*.

42. For a discussion of transascendence and transdescendence, see Roger Burggraeve, "Introduction: Awakened into Vigilance: In Conversation with a Recalcitrant Thinker" in *The Awakening of the Other: A Provocative Dialogue with Emmanuel Levinas*, ed. Roger Burggraeve (Leuven: Peeters, 2008), 2–3.

43. Heidegger, *Being and Time*, 336, 343.

44. Levinas states, "Recurrence is sincerity, effusion of the self, 'extradition' of the self to the neighbor. One might, at the limit, pronounce the word *prayer* here—testimony, kerygma, confession, humility" (*BPW* 106; cf. *OB* 149).

45. Emmanuel Levinas, *In the Time of the Nations,* trans. Michael B. Smith (Bloomington: Indiana University Press, 1994), 130; hereafter cited in the text as *ITN*. Levinas, *Alterity and Transcendence,* trans. Michael B. Smith (New York: Columbia University Press, 1999), 182; hereafter cited in the text as *AT*.

46. Horner points out that Levinas overcomes the difficulties of Husserl's idea of intentionality through developing the idea of "having a sense." See Horner, *Rethinking God*, 49.

47. See, for example, Lonergan, *Method in Theology,* 122–23. Lonergan writes, "Our love reveals to us values we had not appreciated, values of prayer and worship, or repentance and belief. But if we would know what is going on within us, if we would learn to integrate it with the rest of our living, we have to inquire, investigate, seek counsel. So it is that in religious matters love precedes knowledge and, as that love is God's gift, the very beginning of faith is due to God's grace."

48. Levinas, *Theory of Intuition,* 44–45.

49. Levinas writes, "The subject of saying does not give signs, it becomes a sign, turns into an allegiance" (*OB* 49).

50. Wyschogrod, *Emmanuel Levinas,* 108.

51. The Levinasian vocabulary, despite its daunting complexity, forges a language of alterity. Up to this stage of our rather complex and schematic analysis, we must recognize also a number of problematical dichotomies in Levinas's thought, each one of which deserves a book in itself. To give some examples, the problems inherent in relating subjectivity and objectivity, theodicy and useless suffering, the self and the Other, totality and infinity, Being and otherwise than Being, experience and encounter, and so on, are not small. Our efforts so far will lead no doubt to a considerable amount of theological vertigo. The theological task of employing this language of alterity is surely fraught with dangers, and the reader can be overwhelmed by a barrage of neologisms, historical associations and phases of development. But to see only the dangers and not to risk the opportunities for greater theological creativity latent in Levinas's thought, would be to evade a responsibility.

52. Christian notions in Levinasian writings include the Man-God (incarnation), transubstantiation, the Eucharist, and communion. See Levinas, "A Man-God?" in *EN* 53; Levinas, "Judaism and Christianity," in *ITN* 161–66. For Levinas's references to the New Testament such as Matt. 25; Phil. 2:6–8; 1 John 2:23 and 4:12, see *EN* 110; *ITN* 114; *DF* 49. Issues of interest to both Christianity and Judaism that appear in Levinas's work include prayer, the *imago Dei* relationship, and kenosis. In the case of kenosis, Levinas states, "I am pleased to accept the parallelism in the theory of kenosis, and in the idea of an omni-human universality and a 'for all men.' I have understood Christianity in its 'to live and die for all men'" (*ITN* 164).

53. Gillian Rose, "Angry Angels: Simone Weil and Emmanuel Levinas," in *Judaism and Modernity: Philosophical Essays* (Oxford: Blackwell, 1993), 221.

Notes to Chapter Three

1. Levinas, "Useless Suffering," in *EN* 91–101. For a moving account of the experience of "passion" in the Shoah, see Zvi Kolitz, *Yosl Rakover Talks to God,* trans. Carol Brown Janeway (New York: Vintage Books, 1999).

2. In referring to both of these "passions," Peperzak reflects, "How is it possible that we have not recognized the Passion in the persecuted of God's

people, and why is it so difficult for Jews to recognize the same passion in the man Jesus?" Peperzak, "The Significance of Levinas's Work," in *The Face of the Other*, ed. Jeffrey Bloechl, 193.

3. Gregory of Nyssa, *Life of Moses*, translated and with introduction and notes by Abraham J. Malherbe and Everett Ferguson (New York: Paulist Press, 1978), 137.

4. Gregory of Nyssa, *Life of Moses*, 135.

5. Abraham J. Malherbe and Everett Ferguson, "Introduction," in Gregory of Nyssa, *Life of Moses*, 11.

6. Malherbe and Ferguson, "Introduction," in Gregory of Nyssa, *Life of Moses*, 11.

7. Gregory of Nyssa, *Life of Moses*, 111.

8. Ibid., 110, 56.

9. See Peter Henrici, "Hans Urs von Balthasar: A Sketch of His Life," in *Pattern of Redemption: The Theology of Hans Urs von Balthasar* by Edward T. Oakes (New York: Continuum, 1994), 1.

10. John O'Donnell, *Hans Urs von Balthasar* (London: Geoffrey Chapman, 1992), 1–2.

11. Gregory of Nyssa, *Life of Moses*, 57.

12. Oakes, *Pattern of Redemption*, 2.

13. See Aidan Nichols, *The Word Has Been Abroad: A Guide through Balthasar's Aesthetics* (Edinburgh: T & T Clark, 1998), xiv.

14. Oakes, *Pattern of Redemption*, 3.

15. O'Donnell, *Hans Urs von Balthasar*, 4.

16. Nichols, *Word Has Been Abroad*, xiv.

17. Graham Ward, "Kenosis: Death, Discourse and Resurrection," *Balthasar at the End of Modernity* by Lucy Gardner, David Moss, Ben Quash, and Graham Ward (Edinburgh: T & T Clark, 1999), 67.

18. Ward, "Kenosis," in Gardner, *Balthasar at the End*, 67.

19. Gregory of Nyssa, *Life of Moses*, 114.

20. Hans Urs von Balthasar, *The Glory of the Lord. A Theological Aesthetics*. vol. 1, *Seeing the Form*, trans. Erasmo Leiva-Merikakis, (Edinburgh: T & T Clark, 1982), 643; hereafter all volumes cited in the text as *GL*.

21. Hans Urs von Balthasar, *Presence and Thought: Essay on the Religious Philosophy of Gregory of Nyssa*, trans. Mark Sebance (San Francisco: Ignatius Press, 1995), 168.

22. Anne Hunt, *The Trinity and the Paschal Mystery. A Development in Recent Catholic Theology*, New Theology Studies 5 (Collegeville, MN: The Liturgical Press, 1997), 57–59, 82–89, 142, 178.

23. Gregory of Nyssa, *Life of Moses*, 114.

24. Von Balthasar, *Presence and Thought*, 153.

25. Hans Urs von Balthasar, *Karl Barth, Darstellung und Deutung seiner Theologie* (Cologne: Olten, 1951); English translation: *The Theology of Karl Barth* (San Francisco: Ignatius Press, 1992).

26. O'Donnell, *Hans Urs von Balthasar*, 4–5; Nichols, *Word*, xvi.

27. Hans Urs von Balthasar, *Rechenschaft 1965* (Einsiedeln: Johannes-Verlag, 1965), 35, quoted in Medard Kehl and Werner Löser, *The von Balthasar Reader* (Edinburgh: T & T Clark, 1982), 42; hereafter cited in the text as *VBR*.

28. O'Donnell, *Hans Urs von Balthasar*, 5.

29. Oakes, *Pattern of Redemption*, 4; Nichols, *Word*, xvii–xviii. One of its first apostolates was to establish the publishing house *Johannes Verlag* in Einsiedeln (situated about halfway between Lucerne and Zürich).

30. In a statement to friends, von Balthasar writes: "I took this step, for both sides a very grave one, after a long testing of the certainty I had reached through prayer that I was being called by God to certain definite tasks in the Church. The Society felt it could not release me to give these tasks my undivided commitment.... So, for me, the step taken means an application of Christian obedience to God, who at any time has the right to call a man not only out of his physical home or his marriage, but also from his chosen spiritual home in a religious order, so that he can use him for his purposes within the Church. Any resulting advantages or disadvantages in the secular sphere were not under discussion and not taken into account." See Nichols, *Word*, xviii. According to Nichols, he is quoting from Peter Henrici, "The Philosophy of Hans Urs von Balthasar," in *Hans Urs von Balthasar: His Life and Work*, ed. David Schindler, (San Francisco: Ignatius Press, 1991), 21."

31. Oakes, *Pattern of Redemption*, 4–5.

32. John Riches and Ben Quash, "Hans Urs von Balthasar," in Ford, *Modern Theologians*, 135.

33. Nichols, *Word Has Been Abroad*, xix; Riches and Quash, "Hans Urs von Balthasar," in Ford, *Modern Theologians*, 135.

34. Nichols, *Word Has Been Abroad*, xix; Henrici, "Philosophy," in Schindler, *Hans Urs von Balthasar*, 152.

35. Gregory of Nyssa, *Life of Moses*, 136.

36. Ward, "Kenosis," in Gardner, *Balthasar at the End*, 43.

37. Jeffrey Bloechl, ed., *Religious Experience and the End of Metaphysics* (Indianapolis: Indiana University Press, 2003), viii.

38. Ward, "Kenosis," in Gardner, *Balthasar at the End*, 43.

39. Angelo Scola, *Hans Urs von Balthasar. A Theological Style* (Grand Rapids: William B. Eerdmans, 1995), 31, 54; Nichols, *Word*, 23; *GL* 1:118; O'Donnell, *Hans Urs von Balthasar*, 4–5.

40. Hart, *Trespass of the Sign*, 77.

41. Ibid., 77, 81.

42. Hans Urs von Balthasar, *Theo-Logic, Theological Logical Theory*, vol. 1, *The Truth of the World*, trans. Adrian J. Walker (San Francisco: Ignatius Press, 2000), 7; hereafter all volumes cited in the text as *TL*.

43. Hart, *Trespass of the Sign*, 259.

44. Bloechl, *Religious Experience*, viii; Hart, *Trespass of the Sign*, 76.

45. Angelo Campodonico, "Hans Urs von Balthasar's Interpretation of the Philosophy of Thomas Aquinas," *Nova et Vetera,* English Edition, 8, no. 1 (2010): 48–49; cf. *GL* 5:446.

46. O'Donnell, *Hans Urs von Balthasar,* 4.

47. Niels C. Nielsen Jr., "Przywara's Philosophy of the "Analogia Entis," *Review of Metaphysics* 5:4 (June 1952): 601.

48. Campodonico, "Hans Urs von Balthasar's Interpretation," 51–52.

49. Augustine Valkenburg, "Hans Urs von Balthasar: The Man and His Works," *Furrow* 40, no. 9 (September 1989): 534.

50. Campodonico, "Hans Urs von Balthasar's Interpretation," 34.

51. Adrian J. Walker, "Love Alone: Hans Urs von Balthasar as a Master of Theological Renewal," *Communio* 32 (Fall 2005): 523.

52. Nielsen, "Przywara's Philosophy," 601.

53. See Henrici, "Philosophy of Hans Urs von Balthasar," in Schindler, *Hans Urs von Balthasar,* 166.

54. Scola, *Hans Urs von Balthasar,* 31, 54; Nichols, *Word,* 23; *GL* 1:118; O'Donnell, *Hans Urs von Balthasar,* 4–5.

55. *GL* 1:18; von Balthasar, *My Work: In Retrospect* (San Francisco: Ignatius Press, 1993), 80; Scola, *Hans Urs von Balthasar,* 37.

56. Distinguishing between the German meaning of *erfahren* and *Erfahrung,* Inwood writes: "*erfahren* from *fahren,* 'to go, travel, etc.,' hence lit. 'to go forth,' has a more external quality. It can mean 'to learn, find out, hear of' but also 'to receive, undergo' something. An *Erfahrung* is an experience as, or of, an external, objective event, and the lessons one learns from such events." See Inwood, *Heidegger Dictionary,* 62.

57. For a discussion of von Balthasar's use of the German word for experience (*Erfahren*), see Aidan Nichols, *Say It Is Pentecost. A Guide through Balthasar's Logic* (Edinburgh: T & T Clark, 2001), 152; O'Donnell, *Hans Urs von Balthasar,* 24.

58. G. Koch, *Die Auferstehung Jesu Christi* (Tübingen: Mohr, 1965).

59. Hans Urs von Balthasar, *Mysterium Paschale: The Mystery of Easter* (Edinburgh: T & T Clark, 1990), 216; hereafter cited in the text as *MP.*

60. In another example emphasizing von Balthasar's phenomenology, Gardner and Moss give the example of his phenomenology of *diastasis.* See Lucy Gardner and David Moss, "Something like Time; Something like the Sexes," in Gardner et. al., *Balthasar at The End of Modernity,* 85–86.

61. O'Donnell, *Hans Urs von Balthasar,* 3.

62. Nielsen, "Przywara's Philosophy," 600.

63. For a discussion of Heidegger's influence on von Balthasar, see Nichols, *Word,* 173–74.

64. Nichols, *Word,* 173; *GL* 5:448.

65. Fergus Kerr, "Foreword: Assessing this 'Giddy Synethsis,' " in Gardner et. al., *Balthasar at the End of Modernity,* 13.

66. Hans Urs von Balthasar, *Der dreifache Kranz; Das Heil der Welt im Mariengebet,* 3rd ed. (Einsiedeln: Johannes-Verlag, 1978), 45, quoted in *VBR* 113.

67. Hans Urs von Balthasar, *Klarstellungen. Zur Prüfung der Geister* (Einsiedeln: Johannes-Verlag, 1978), 26, quoted in *VBR* 182.

68. Scola, *Hans Urs von Balthasar,* 63–64.

69. von Balthasar, *Der dreifache Kranz,* 65, quoted in *VBR* 149.

70. von Balthasar, *Pneuma und Institution* (Einsiedeln: Johannes-Verlag, 1974), 409, quoted in *VBR* 153.

71. Scola, *Hans Urs von Balthasar,* 54–57.

72. von Balthasar, *Pneuma und Institution,* 55, quoted in *VBR* 177.

73. von Balthasar, *My Work,* 80, cited in Scola, *Hans Urs von Balthasar,* 37.

74. Caputo, *Demythologizing Heidegger,* 166.

75. As a small sampling of works along these lines, see, for example: Adam Miller, *Badiou, Marion and St. Paul: Immanent Grace* (London: Continuum, 2008); Giorgio Agamben, *The Time that Remains: A Commentary on the Letter to the Romans,* trans. Patricia Dailey (Palo Alto: Stanford University Press, 2005); Alain Badiou, *St Paul: The Foundation of Universalism,* trans. Ray Brassier (Palo Alto: Stanford University Press), 2003; Jacques Derrida, *Memoirs of the Blind: The Self-Portrait and Other Ruins,* trans. Pascale-Anne Brault and Michael Naas (Chicago: University of Chicago Press, 1993); Theodore W. Jennings, *Reading Derrida/Thinking Paul* (Palo Alto: Stanford University Press, 2006); Anthony J. Kelly, *The Resurrection Effect: Transforming Christian Life and Thought* (Maryknoll, New York: Orbis Books, 2008).

76. Thomas Sheehan, "Heidegger's 'Introduction to the Phenomenology of Religion,' 1920–21," *Personalist* 60, no. 3 (July 1979): 315.

77. Eric Voegelin, *Order and History,* vol. 4: *The Ecumenic Age,* in *Collected Works,* ed. Franz, 303–39.

78. Kelly, *Resurrection Effect,* 80–82.

79. Ibid., 80, 100.

80. Sheehan, "Heidegger's 'Introduction,'" 312. A "privatdozent" is defined as "an unsalaried university lecturer or teacher in German-speaking countries remunerated directly by students' fees." Merriam-Webster's Online Dictionary. www.merriam-webster.com.

81. Sheehan, "Heidegger's 'Introduction,'" 319.

82. Ibid., 317–18.

83. Jim Vernon, "*Erfahren* and *Erleben:* Metaphysical Experience and its Overcoming in Heidegger's *Beiträge,*" *Symposium: Canadian Journal of Continental Philosophy* 12, no. 1 (Spring 2008): 111, 120–22.

84. Sheehan, "Heidegger's 'Introduction,'" 315.

85. Vernon, "*Erfahren* and *Erleben,*" 114.

86. Martin Heidegger, *The Phenomenology of Religious Life,* trans. Matthias Fritsch and Jennifer Anna Gosetti-Ferencei (Bloomington: Indiana University Press, 2010), 65. Sheehan translated *Gewordensein* as "'already having become' or 'already having been.'" See Sheehan, "Heidegger's 'Introduction,'" 320.

87. Sheehan, "Heidegger's 'Introduction,'" 320.

88. Heidegger, *Phenomenology,* 65–66.

89. Sheehan, "Heidegger's 'Introduction,'" 312–13.

90. See John Macquarrie, *Heidegger and Christianity: The Hensley Henson Lectures 1993–1994* (London: SCM Press, 1994), 6.

91. Sheehan, "Heidegger's 'Introduction,'" 313.

92. Macquarrie, *Heidegger and Christianity,* 6.

93. Macquarrie, *Heidegger and Christianity,* 6; Sheehan, "Heidegger's 'Introduction,'" 323.

94. Martin Heidegger, *Was heist Denken?* (Tübingen: *Niemeyer, 1954*), 96, quoted in Macquarrie, *Heidegger and Christianity,* 5.

95. Heidegger, *Phenomenology,* 66.

96. Sheehan, "Heidegger's 'Introduction,'" 322.

97. Heidegger, *Phenomenology,* 72.

98. Heidegger, *Phenomenology,* 73; Sheehan, "Heidegger's 'Introduction,'" 322. In many ways, Heidegger's phenomenology of religious life parallels some key themes in fundamental theology. It is not surprising, then, that Karl Rahner takes up Heidegger's philosophy in the development of his theological anthropology.

99. Kelly, *Resurrection Effect,* 79–100.

100. Henri J. M. Nouwen, *Reaching Out* (London: Fount, 1996), 84.

101. Voegelin, *Ecumenic Age,* 307.

102. Nouwen, *Reaching Out,* 75.

103. Sheehan, "Heidegger's 'Introduction,'" 322.

104. Michael Purcell, *Levinas and Theology* (Cambridge: Cambridge University Press, 2006), 89.

105. This is in contrast to the Heideggerian *Dasein:* "The essence of Dasein lies in its existence." Heidegger, *Being and Time,* 67.

106. Purcell, *Levinas and Theology,* 90.

107. Compare 1 Cor. 15:8: "Last of all, as to one untimely born, he appeared (*ôphthē*) also to me."

108. Purcell, *Levinas and Theology,* 88.

109. Voegelin, *Order and History,* 307.

110. Heidegger, *Phenomenology,* 70.

111. Sheehan, "Heidegger's 'Introduction,'" 320.

112. Compare 1 Thess. 5:2: "For you yourselves know very well that the day of the Lord will come like a thief in the night."

113. Heidegger, *Phenomenology,* 74.

114. Ibid., 72.

115. Ibid., 70.

116. *GCM* 58–59. Curkpatrick writes, "Emmanuel Levinas uses the metaphor 'insomnia' to describe the incision of infinity in the human subject, as an awakening to responsibility for the other to whom the subject is apprehended and made a hostage." Stephen Curkpatrick, "*Infinity, Insomnia,* and the (Im)possibility of Theology," *Pacifica* 17 (February 2004): 15.

117. Sikka, "Questioning the Sacred," 312.

118. Heidegger, *Phenomenology,* 71.

119. John Van Buren, *The Young Heidegger: Rumor of the Hidden King* (Bloomington: Indiana University Press, 1994), 191.

120. Van Buren, *Young Heidegger,* 192.

121. Sikka writes: "The 'pagan' elements in Heidegger's thought include his emphasis on human destiny as intertwined with place and landscape, his privileging of the revelatory power of art and poetry, and his elevation of non-human beings." Sikka, "Questioning the Sacred," 311.

Notes to Chapter Four

1. Hans Urs von Balthasar, *Theo-Drama, Theological Dramatic Theory,* vol. 3, *The Dramatis Personae: The Person in Christ,* trans. Graham Harrison (San Francisco: Ignatius Press, 1992), 505; hereafter all volumes cited in the text as *TD.*

2. Aidan Nichols, *No Bloodless Myth: A Guide through Balthasar's Dramatics* (Edinburgh: T. & T. Clark, 2000), 52, 104–05.

3. For a full account of the two triads, see *TD* vol. 1.

4. *TD* 3:532–33; Nichols, *No Bloodless Myth,* 29–32.

5. *TD* 3:533–35; Nichols, *No Bloodless Myth,* 32–34.

6. Nichols, *No Bloodless Myth,* 103.

7. For a discussion on the nominal sense of "being," see *OB* 52–53.

8. Nichols, *Word,* 173–74.

9. See Scola, *Hans Urs von Balthasar,* 59–64; *TD* 3:518.

10. Miroslav Volf, *Exclusion and Embrace: A Theological Exploration of Identity, Otherness and Reconciliation* (Nashville: Abingdon Press, 1996), 128.

11. Von Balthasar's account of Trinitarian inversion is found in *TD* 3:183–91, 521–23.

12. Levinas, "God and Philosophy," in *Collected Philosophical Papers,* 167.

13. For an analysis of the difference and connection between tragedy and comedy, see Nichols, *No Bloodless Myth,* 33, 37–38.

14. Quoted in Levinas, "God and Philosophy," in *CPP* 168.

15. One resource on the psychiatric understanding of trauma is Sidney Bloch and Bruce S. Singh, eds., *Foundations of Clinical Psychiatry,* 2nd ed. (Carlton South, Victoria: Melbourne University Press, 2001), 149.

16. Horner, *Rethinking God as Gift,* 232.

17. For further discussion, see Robert Bernasconi, "What Is the Question to which 'Substitution' Is the Answer?," in Critchley and Bernasconi, *Cambridge Companion to Levinas,* 242.

18. *TD* 3:340; Gardner and Moss, "Something Like Time; Something Like the Sexes," in *Balthasar at the End of Modernity,* 99.

19. *TD* 3:292; Gardner and Moss, "Something Like Time," in *Balthasar at the End of Modernity,* 98. Gardner and Moss point out that von Balthasar had frequently denied any implied inferiority in the character of the woman.

20. Gardner and Moss, "Something Like Time," in *Balthasar at the End of Modernity*, 134, 108, 137.

21. Ibid., 90.

22. Volf, *Exclusion and Embrace*, 190, 187.

23. Heidegger, *Being and Time*, 106, 123.

24. Nichols, *Say It Is Pentecost*, 9.

25. For a Levinasian-inspired discussion of the *as such* and its connection with alterity and the gaze of the Other, see Jean-Luc Marion, "The Intentionality of Love," in *Prolegomena to Charity*, trans. Stephen Lewis, Perspectives in Continental Philosophy (New York: Fordham University Press, 2002), 100–01.

26. Among other disciplines, there have been several attempts to enhance psychology through a Levinasian lens. Examples include, but are by no means limited to: C. Fred Alford, ed., *Levinas, the Frankfurt School and Psychoanalysis* (Middletown: Wesleyan University Press, 2002); Edwin E. Gantt and Richard N. Williams, eds., *Psychology for the Other: Levinas, Ethics, and the Practice of Psychology* (Pittsburgh: Duquesne University Press, 2002); Sarah Harasym, ed., *Levinas and Lacan: The Missed Encounter* (Albany: State University of New York Press, 1998); and George Kunz, *The Paradox of Power and Weakness: Levinas and an Alternative Paradigm for Psychology* (Albany: State University of New York Press, 1998). These studies indicate that there has not been a direct attempt to bring together Levinas's ethical metaphysics, Christian theology, and either psychology, psychiatry, psychoanalysis, or psychotherapy.

27. Wilfred Owens, "Mental Cases," *The Mentor Book of Major British Poets*, ed. Oscar Williams (Camberwell, Victoria: Penguin Group Australia, 1963), 486–87.

28. Hans Urs von Balthasar, *Love Alone Is Credible*, trans. D. C. Schindler (San Francisco: Ignatius, 2004), 62–63; hereafter cited in the text as *LA*.

29. For Levinas, such fear needs to go through an ethical inversion (or conversion) into fear for the Other's death.

30. Caruana, "Lévinas's Critique of the Sacred," 525, 530.

31. Ibid., 525.

32. Ibid., 525.

Notes to Chapter Five

1. Nichols, *Word*, 173.

2. Inwood, *Heidegger Dictionary*, 230; Heidegger, *Being and Time*, 176.

3. For an overview of the structure of *Theo-Logic* vols. 1–3, see Scola, *Hans Urs von Balthasar*, 42–44; John O'Donnell, "Truth as Love: the Understanding of Truth according to Hans Urs von Balthasar," *Pacifica* 1, vol. 2 (June 1988): 193–95.

4. See Scola, *Hans Urs von Balthasar*, 42.

5. Rosenzweig, *Star of Redemption*, 420, 417.

6. For a discussion on the analogy of Being, ontotheology, and representation, see Ward, *Barth, Derrida*, 102.

7. Ward, *Barth, Derrida,* 109.

8. For an example of Levinas's reflection on Isaiah 57:15, see Levinas, "A Man-God?," in *EN* 57.

9. Ward, *Barth, Derrida,* 183–86; Purcell, *Mystery and Method,* 308.

10. Ward, *Barth, Derrida,* 184. Here, Ward is referring to Jacques Derrida, *Psyché: Inventions de l'autre* (Paris: Editions Galilée, 1987), 564.

11. Ward, *Barth, Derrida,* 185–86.

12. Ibid., 184, 190.

13. Purcell, *Mystery and Method,* 329.

14. Ibid., 297.

15. Ibid., xiii.

16. Ibid., 343, 329.

17. Ibid., 168, 343.

18. Ibid., 297. A *tertium gaudens* is a happy (unforeseen) medium between two opposing positions.

19. Ibid., 297, 329.

20. Ibid., 329.

21. *GL* 7:242; von Balthasar, *My Work,* 80, cited in Scola, *Hans Urs von Balthasar,* 37.

22. Ivan Böszörményi-Nagy, "From Here to Eternity" [Interview], *Psychology Today* 26, no. 2 (March/April 1993): 12.

23. Ivan Böszörményi-Nagy, "Response to 'Are Trustworthiness and Fairness Enough?: Contextual Family Therapy and the Good Family,'" *Journal of Marital and Family Therapy* 23, no. 2 (1997): 172.

24. Böszörményi-Nagy, "Response," 172, 171.

25. Roger Burggraeve, "The Difficult but Possible Path towards Forgiveness and Reconciliation Between People," 1, unpublished English translation by the author from his article (in Dutch), "Stapstenen naar verzoening en vergeving tussen mensen," *Collationes. Vlaams Tijdschrijft voor Theologie en Pastoraal* 30, no. 3 (2000): 269–300, 1. Examples of the "steps" referred to in the text might be the experience of negative feelings; the realization of pain, harm, and wounds; naming the injustice; sharing the experience with others and giving meaning to it; approaching the aggressor with a reproach or accusation; and the many steps toward truth, justice, rectification, healing, and reconciliation.

26. Volf, *Exclusion and Embrace,* 119.

27. Stanley Hauerwas, "Why Truthfulness Requires Forgiveness: A Commencement Address for Graduates of a College of the Church of the Second Chance (1992)," in *The Hauerwas Reader,* ed. John Berkman and Michael Cartwright (Durham: Duke University Press, 2001), 307, 311.

28. Hauerwas, "Why Truthfulness Requires Forgiveness," 312.

29. Here and in the excerpts to follow, Levinas is working with *Tractate Yoma,* 85a–85b.

30. Morgan, *Discovering Levinas,* 35–38.

31. Dietrich Bonhoeffer, *The Cost of Discipleship* (London: SCM Press, 1971), 35.

32. Craig Detweiler, *Into the Dark: Seeing the Sacred in the Top Films of the 21st Century* (Grand Rapids: Baker Academic, 2008), 17.

33. Detweiler, *Into the Dark*, 38–41, 160–61.

34. David Henderson Slater, Laura May, and Dora Steel, "*Children of a Lesser God* at Oxford," Literature, Arts, and Medicine blog of the University of Oxford Division of Medical Sciences. http://medhum.med.nyu.edu/blog/?p=119.

35. James D. Whitehead and Evelyn Eaton Whitehead, *Shadows of the Heart: A Spirituality of the Painful Emotions* (New York: Crossroad, 1998), 168.

36. The Whiteheads reflect in regards to Lamentations 1:12, "Three thousand years ago our religious ancestors modelled a different method for dealing with depression. In a time of disaster or confusion they would lift up their voices in complaint. Refusing to collapse into private sadness, they gave public expression to their pain. The Book of Lamentations records their distress." Whitehead and Whitehead, *Shadows of the Heart*, 167.

37. Ibid., 170–71.

38. Ibid., 168.

39. St. Augustine, *Confessions* (Ringwood, Victoria: Penguin Books, 1974), 207.

Notes to Chapter Six

1. Hilary Putnam has written a very enlightening book applying the Jewish philosophy of Rosenzweig, Buber, Levinas, and Wittgenstein as a "guide to life." Hilary Putnam, *Jewish Philosophy as a Guide to Life* (Bloomington: Indiana University Press, 2008).

2. Michael Purcell, "Leashing God with Levinas: Tracing a Trinity with Levinas," *Heythrop Journal* 40 (July 1999): 301. The quote comes from Levinas, "Persons of Figures (On *Emmaüs* by Paul Claudel)," in *DF* 121.

3. Purcell, "Leashing God with Levinas," 301.

4. Purcell, *Mystery and Method*, 329.

5. Purcell, "Leashing God with Levinas," 303–04.

6. Ibid., 313–14.

7. Ibid., 314–15.

8. Ibid., 302, 315.

9. Ibid., 315.

10. Ibid., 315–16.

11. Ibid., 316.

12. Ibid., 316.

13. Ibid., 317.

14. Ibid., 317.

15. Purcell, *Levinas and Theology*, 155–56.

16. Ibid., 156.

17. Ibid., 158.

18. Ibid., 162, quoting Levinas, "A Man-God?," in *EN* 60.

19. Purcell, *Levinas and Theology,* 159.

20. Ford writes: "Salvation seen through the figure of feasting suggests an eschatology of selfhood." See Ford, *Self and Salvation,* 267. Also, for example, *GL* 1:572–75; 7:485–583.

21. Vatican II Council, "The General Instruction on the Roman Missal," para. 54–55, in *Vatican Council II, The Conciliar and Post Conciliar Documents,* Vatican Collection, vol. 1, rev. ed., ed. A. Flannery (Northport, NY: Costello Publishing, 1988), 175–76.

22. Ford, *Self and Salvation,* 146, 267–70.

23. Ibid., 82.

24. Ibid., 74.

25. Ford writes: "In *Totality and Infinity* a discussion of Descartes leads to one of Levinas's most eloquent affirmations of God in terms of personal relations with an other who is a 'Majesty approached as a face' and evokes 'admiration, adoration, and joy.' In *Otherwise than Being* the culminating statement about the exorbitant overflow of the caress of love plays a variation on the same theme, and both works have other hints of joy." Ibid., 74.

26. Ibid., 76, 82.

27. Paul Ricoeur, *Oneself as Another,* trans. Kathleen Blaney (Chicago: University of Chicago Press, 1992), 25.

28. Ford, *Self and Salvation,* 98, 162.

29. Ibid., 10, 140, 162.

30. Ibid., 164–65.

31. Ibid., 266–80.

32. Ibid., 275, 271.

33. Benedict XVI, *Deus Caritas Est* (Strathfield, NSW: St. Pauls, 2006), nos. 3, 5.

34. Barnes, *Theology and the Dialogue of Religions,* 95, 97.

35. Ibid., 254.

36. Ibid., 204.

37. Ibid., 196, 202, 204, 97.

38. Michael Barnes, "The Intimacy of Distance: On Faith Learning from Faith," *Spiritus* (Spring 2006): 61.

39. Barnes, "Intimacy of Distance," 60.

40. Ibid., 50–54.

41. Ibid., 61.

42. Ibid., 63.

43. Ibid., 52.

44. Ibid., 60.

45. Ibid., 60.

46. Ibid., 63.

47. See also Morrison, "Jewish–Christian Relations," 316–29.

48. For a discussion of this finding in relation to the Eucharist, see Glenn Morrison, "Emmanuel Levinas and Christian Theology," *Irish Theological Quarterly* 68, no. 1 (Spring 2003): 21–22.

49. William Gaylin states, "Feelings, therefore, particularly the complex and subtle range of feelings in human being, are testament to our capacity for choice and meaning." See Gaylin, *Feelings: Our Vital Signs*, 7.

50. Henri Nouwen, *Reaching Out* (London: Found, 1996), 43.

51. Nouwen, *Reaching Out*, 43.

52. For the terms "super-obedience" and "super-craft," see *TL* 2:353–54.

53. Purcell, *Levinas and Theology*, 89.

54. Christopher West, *Theology of the Body Explained: A Commentary on John Paul II's "Gospel of the Body"* (North Melbourne: Gracewing, 2003), 399.

55. Lawrence Boadt and Kevin di Camillo, eds., *John Paul II in the Holy Land: In His Own Words, with Christian and Jewish Perspectives by Yehezkel Landau and Michael McGarry, CSP* (New York: Paulist Press, 2005), 98–99.

56. Zimmermann, "Karol Wojtyla and Emmanuel Levinas," 982–83.

57. Boadt and di Camillo, *John Paul II*, 99.

58. Ibid., 99.

59. *OB* 87. Defining the notion of the "psyche," Wojtyla writes: " 'Psyche' refers to that which makes man an integral being, indeed, to that which determines the integrity of his components without itself being of a bodily or somatic nature. And yet, precisely for this reason, the notion of the 'psyche' is correlated with the notion of the 'soma.' " Karol Wojtyla (Pope John Paul II). *The Acting Person*, trans. from the Polise by Andrzej Potocki. In *Analecta Husserliana: The Yearbook of Phenomenological Research*, vol. 10 (Dordrecht, Holland: D. Reidel Publishing Company, 1979), 221.

60. Boadt and di Camillo, *John Paul II*, 99.

61. Levinas writes: "The way is crooked. Claudel chose as an epigraph for his Satin Slipper a Portuguese proverb that can be understood in a sense we have just put forth: 'God writes straight with crooked lines'" (*OB* 147).

62. Boadt and di Camillo, *John Paul II*, 101.

63. Von Balthasar writes, "God's truth is, indeed, great enough to allow an infinity of approaches and entryways" (*GL* 1:17).

BIBLIOGRAPHY

Agamben, Giorgio. *The Time that Remains: A Commentary on the Letter to the Romans.* Translated by Patricia Dailey. Palo Alto: Stanford University Press, 2005.

Alford, C. Fred, ed. *Levinas, the Frankfurt School, and Psychoanalysis.* Middletown: Wesleyan University Press, 2002.

Badiou, Alain. *Saint Paul: The Foundation of Universalism.* Translated by Ray Brassier. Palo Alto: Stanford University Press, 2003.

Barnes, Michael. "The Intimacy of Distance: On Faith Learning from Faith." *Spiritus* (Spring 2006): 48–67.

———. *Theology and the Dialogue of Religions.* Cambridge: Cambridge University Press, 2002.

Benedict XVI. *Deus Caritas Est.* Strathfield, NSW: St Pauls Publications, 2006.

Blanchot, Maurice. *Thomas the Obscure.* New edition. Translated by Robert Lamberton. New York: D. Lewis, 1973.

Bloch, Sidney, and Bruce S. Singh, eds. *Foundations of Clinical Psychiatry.* 2nd ed. Carlton South, Victoria: Melbourne University Press, 2001.

Bloechl, Jeffrey, ed. *The Face of the Other and the Trace of God: Essays on the Philosophy of Emmanuel Levinas.* New York: Fordham University Press, 2000.

———. *Religious Experience and the End of Metaphysics.* Bloomington: Indiana University Press, 2003.

Boadt, Lawrence, and Kevin di Camillo, eds. *John Paul II in the Holy Land: In His Own Words, with Christian and Jewish Perspectives by Yehezkel Landau and Michael McGarry, CSP.* New York: Paulist Press, 2005.

Bonhoeffer, Dietrich. *The Cost of Discipleship.* London: SCM Press, 1971.

Böszörményi-Nagy, Ivan. "From Here to Eternity." Interview. *Psychology Today* 26, no. 2 (March/April 1993): 12–13.

———. "Response to 'Are Trustworthiness and Fairness Enough? Contextual Family Therapy and the Good Family.'" *Journal of Marital and Family Therapy* 23, no. 2 (1997): 171–73.

Burggraeve, Roger. "The Difficult but Possible Path towards Forgiveness and Reconciliation between People," 1–15. Unpublished English translation by the author from his article (in Dutch), "Stapstenen naar verzoening en vergeving tussen mensen." *Collationes. Vlaams Tijdschrijft voor Theologie en Pastoraal* 30, no. 3 (2000): 269–300.

Burggraeve, Roger, ed. *The Awakening of the Other: A Provocative Dialogue with Emmanuel Levinas.* Leuven: Peeters, 2008.

Campodonico, Angelo. "Hans Urs von Balthasar's Interpretation of the Philosophy of Thomas Aquinas." *Nova et Vetera,* English edition, 8, no. 1 (2010): 33–53.

Caputo, John. *Demythologizing Heidegger.* Bloomington: Indiana University Press, 1993.

Caruana, John. "Lévinas's Critique of the Sacred." *International Philosophical Quarterly* 42, no. 4 (December 2002): 519–34.

Cohen, Richard A. "Difficulty and Morality: Two Notes on Reading Levinas." *Philosophy in the Contemporary World* 7, no. 1 (Spring 2000): 59–66.

Cohen, Richard A. *Elevations: The Height of the Good in Rosenzweig and Levinas.* Chicago: University of Chicago Press, 1994.

Critchley, Simon, and Robert Bernasconi, eds. *The Cambridge Companion to Levinas.* Cambridge: Cambridge University Press, 2002.

Curkpatrick, Stephen. "*Infinity, Insomnia,* and the (Im)possibility of Theology." *Pacifica* 17, no. 1 (February 2004): 15–33.

Derrida, Jacques. *Memoirs of the Blind: The Self-Portrait and Other Ruins.* Translated by Pascale-Anne Brault and Michael Naas. Chicago: University of Chicago Press, 1993.

———. *Psyché: Inventions de l'autre* (Paris: Editions Galilée, 1987).

———. *Writing and Difference.* Translated with an introduction and additional notes by Alan Bass. London: Routledge, 2001.

Detweiler, Craig. *Into the Dark: Seeing the Sacred in the Top Films of the 21st Century.* Grand Rapids: Baker Academic, 2008.

Ford, David F. *Self and Salvation: Being Transformed.* Cambridge Studies in Christian Doctrine. Cambridge: Cambridge University Press, 1999.

Ford, David F., ed. *The Modern Theologians.* 2nd ed. Oxford: Blackwell, 1997.

Gantt, Edwin E., and Richard N. Williams, eds. *Psychology for the Other: Levinas, Ethics and the Practice of Psychology.* Pittsburgh: Duquesne University Press, 2002.

Gardner, Lucy, David Moss, Ben Quash, and Graham Ward. *Balthasar at the End of Modernity.* Edinburgh: T. & T. Clark, 1999.

Gaylin, Willard. *Feelings: Our Vital Signs.* London: Harper and Row, 1979.

Gregory of Nyssa. *Life of Moses.* Translation, introduction, and notes by Abraham J. Malherbe and Everett Ferguson. New York: Paulist Press, 1978.

Guignon, Charles, ed. *The Cambridge Companion to Heidegger.* Melbourne: Cambridge University Press, 1996.

Hand, Seán. *Facing the Other: The Ethics of Emmanuel Levinas.* Richmond, Surrey: Curzon Press, 1996.

Harasym, Sarah, ed. *Levinas and Lacan: The Missed Encounter.* Albany: State University of New York Press, 1998.

Hart, Kevin. *The Trespass of the Sign: Deconstruction, Theology and Philosophy.* New York: Fordham University Press, 2000.

Hauerwas, Stanley. "Why Truthfulness Requires Forgiveness: A Commencement Address for Graduates of a College of the Church of the Second Chance." 1992. In *The Hauerwas Reader,* edited by John Berkman and Michael Cartwright. Durham: Duke University Press, 2001.

Healy, Mary, and Robin Parry, eds. *The Bible and Epistemology: Biblical Soundings on the Knowledge of God.* Milton Keynes: Paternoster, 2007.

Heidegger, Martin. *Being and Time.* Translated by John Macquarrie and Edward Robinson. Oxford: Blackwell, 1995.

———. *The Phenomenology of Religious Life.* Translated by Matthias Fritsch and Jennifer Anna Gosetti-Ferencei. Bloomington: Indiana University Press, 2010.

Horner, Robyn. "God and Philosophy." *Philosophy in the Contemporary World* 7, no. 1 (Spring 2000): 41–46.

———. *Rethinking God as Gift: Marion, Derrida, and the Limits of Phenomenology.* New York: Fordham University Press, 2001.

Hunt, Anne. *The Trinity and the Paschal Mystery. A Development in Recent Catholic Theology.* New Theology Series 5. Collegeville, MN: Liturgical Press, 1997.

Inwood, Michael. *A Heidegger Dictionary.* The Blackwell Philosophical Dictionaries. Oxford: Blackwell, 2000.

Jennings, Theodore W. *Reading Derrida/Thinking Paul.* Palo Alto: Stanford University Press, 2006.

Keenan, James F. *A History of Catholic Moral Theology in the Twentieth Century: From Contesting Sins to Liberating Consciences.* New York: Continuum, 2010.

Kelly, Anthony. *The Resurrection Effect: Transforming Christian Life and Thought.* Maryknoll, NY: Orbis Books, 2008.

Kolitz, Zvi. *Yosl Rakover Talks to God.* Translated by Carol Brown Janeway with afterwords by Emmanuel Levinas and Leon Wieseltier. New York: Vintage Books, 1999.

Kunz, George. *The Paradox of Power and Weakness: Levinas and an Alternative Paradigm for Psychology.* Albany: State University of New York Press, 1998.

Levinas, Emmanuel. *Alterity and Transcendence.* Translated by Michael B. Smith. New York: Columbia University Press, 1999.

———. *Basic Philosophical Writings.* Edited by Adriaan T. Peperzak, Simon Critchley, and Robert Bernasconi. Bloomington: Indiana University Press, 1996.

———. *Beyond the Verse: Talmudic Readings and Lectures.* Translated by Gary D. Mole. Bloomington: Indiana University Press, 1994.

———. *Collected Philosophical Papers.* Translated by Alphonso Lingis. Pittsburgh: Duquesne University Press, 1998.

———. *Difficult Freedom: Essays on Judaism.* Translated by Seán Hand. Baltimore: John Hopkins University Press, 1997.

———. *Discovering Existence with Husserl.* Translated by Richard A. Cohen and Michael B. Smith. Evanston: Northwestern University Press, 1998.

———. *Entre Nous: On Thinking-of-the-Other.* Translated by Michael B. Smith and Barbara Harshav. New York: Columbia University Press, 1998.

———. *Ethics and Infinity: Conversations with Philippe Nemo.* Translated by Richard A. Cohen. Pittsburgh: Duquesne University Press, 1999.

————. *Existence and Existents.* Translated by A. Lingis. London: Kluwer Academic, 1995.

————. *God, Death, and Time.* Translated by Bettina Bergo. Palo Alto: Stanford University Press, 2000.

————. *In the Time of the Nations.* Translated by Michael B. Smith. Bloomington: Indiana University Press, 1994.

————. *Is It Righteous to Be? Interviews with Emmanuel Levinas.* Edited by Jill Robbins. Palo Alto: Stanford University Press, 2001.

————. *The Levinas Reader.* Edited by Hand. Oxford: Blackwell, 1999.

————. *Nine Talmudic Readings.* Translated and with an introduction by Annette Aronowicz. Bloomington: Indiana University Press, 1994.

————. *Of God Who Comes to Mind.* Translated by Bettina Bergo. Palo Alto: Stanford University Press, 1998.

————. *Otherwise than Being or Beyond Essence.* Translated by Alphonso Lingis. Pittsburgh: Duquesne University Press, 1998.

————. *Outside the Subject.* Translated by Michael B. Smith. Palo Alto: Stanford University Press, 1994.

————. *The Theory of Intuition in Husserl's Phenomenology.* Translated by André Orianne. 2nd ed. Evanston: Northwestern University Press, 1995.

————. *Time and the Other: And Additional Essays.* Translated by Richard A. Cohen. Pittsburgh: Duquesne University Press, 1997.

————. *Totality and Infinity: An Essay on Exteriority.* Translated by Alphonso Lingis. Pittsburgh: Duquesne University Press, 1969.

Lonergan, Bernard. *Method in Theology.* Toronto: University of Toronto Press, 1996.

Macquarrie, John. *Heidegger and Christianity: The Hensley Henson Lectures 1993–1994.* London: SCM Press, 1994.

Marion, Jean-Luc. *God without Being.* Translated by Thomas A. Carlson with a foreword by David Tracy. Chicago: University of Chicago Press, 1995.

————. *Prolegomena to Charity.* Translated by Stephen Lewis. Perspectives in Continental Philosophy. New York: Fordham University Press, 2002.

McGrath, Alister. *Christian Spirituality.* Oxford: Blackwell, 2000.

Medoff, Mark. *Children of a Lesser God.* New York: Dramatists Play Service Inc., 1980.

Miller, Adam. *Badiou, Marion and St. Paul: Immanent Grace.* London: Continuum, 2008.

Morgan, Michael. *Discovering Levinas.* Cambridge: Cambridge University Press, 2007.

Morrison, Glenn. "Building Jewish–Christian Friendship." Paper presented at the Council of Christian and Jews Western Australia, Claremont, Perth, September 20, 2011.

———. "Children of a Lesser God: Truth as Bodiliness and Forgiveness." *Australian eJournal of Theology* (August 2011): 175–88.

———. "Emmanuel Levinas and Christian Theology." *Irish Theological Quarterly* 68, no. 1 (Spring 2003): 3–24.

———. "The (Im)possibilities of Levinas for Christian Theology: The Search for a Language of Alterity." In *Festschrift Roger Burggraeve: Responsibility, God and Society, Theological Ethics in Dialogue,* edited by J. De Tavernier, J. A. Selling, J. Verstraeten, and P. Schotsmans, 103–22. Leuven: Peeters, 2008.

———. "Jewish-Christian Relations and the Ethical Philosophy of Emmanuel Levinas: 'At the Very Moment Where All is Lost, Everything is Possible.'" *Journal of Ecumenical Studies* 38, no. 2–3 (Spring–Summer 2001): 316–29.

———. "Living at the Margins of Life: Encountering the Other and *Doing* Theology." *Australian eJournal of Theology* (February 2006): 1–7.

———. "Phenomenology, Theology, and Psychosis: Towards Compassion." *Heythrop Journal* (July 2007): 561–76.

———. "Renewing Christian Theology with Levinas: Towards a Trinitarian *Praxis.*" *The Awakening of Meaning: A Provocative Dialogue with Levinas,* edited by Roger Burggraeve, 137–60. Leuven: Peeters, 2008.

———. "A Review of Michael Purcell's Theological Development of Levinas' Philosophy." *Heythrop Journal* 44 (April 2003): 147–66.

———. "Understanding Levinas's Origins: Husserl, Heidegger and Rosenzweig." *Heythrop Journal* 46 (January 2005): 41–59.

Mosès, Stéphane. *System and Revelation. The Philosophy of Franz Rosenzweig.* Foreword by Emmanuel Levinas. Translated by Catherine Tihanyi. Detroit: Wayne State University Press, 1992.

Nichols, Aidan. *No Bloodless Myth: A Guide through Balthasar's Dramatics.* Edinburgh: T. & T. Clark, 2000.

———. *Say It Is Pentecost: A Guide through Balthasar's Logic.* Edinburgh: T & T Clark, 2001.

———. *The Word Has Been Abroad: A Guide Through Balthasar's Aesthetics.* Edinburgh: T & T Clark, 1998.

Nielsen, Niels C., Jr. "Przywara's Philosophy of the 'Analogia Entis.'" *Review of Metaphysics* 5, no. 4 (June 1952): 599–620.

Nouwen, Henri. *Reaching Out.* London: Found, 1996.

O'Donnell, John. *Hans Urs von Balthasar.* London: Geoffrey Chapman, 1992.

———. *The Mystery of the Triune God.* London: Sheed and Ward, 1988.

———. "Truth as Love: The Understanding of Truth according to Hans Urs von Balthasar." *Pacifica* 1, vol. 2 (June 1988): 189–211.

Oakes, Edward. *Pattern of Redemption: The Theology of Hans Urs von Balthasar.* New York: Continuum, 1994.

Peperzak, Adriaan. *Beyond: The Philosophy of Emmanuel Levinas.* Evanston: Northwestern University Press, 1997.

———. *To the Other: An Introduction to the Philosophy of Levinas.* West Lafayette: Purdue University Press, 1993.

Peperzak, Adriaan, ed. *Ethics as First Philosophy: The Significance of Emmanuel Levinas for Philosophy, Literature and Religion.* New York: Routledge, 1995.

Purcell, Michael. "Leashing God with Levinas: Tracing a Trinity with Levinas." *Heythrop Journal* 40 (July 1999): 301–18.

———. *Levinas and Theology.* Cambridge: Cambridge University Press, 2006.

———. *Mystery and Method: The Other in Rahner and Levinas.* Milwaukee: Marquette University Press, 1998.

Putnam, Hilary. *Jewish Philosophy as a Guide to Life.* Bloomington: Indiana University Press, 2008.

Ricoeur, Paul. *Oneself as Another.* Translated by Kathleen Blaney. Chicago: University of Chicago Press, 1992.

Rose, Gillian. *Judaism and Modernity: Philosophical Essays.* Oxford: Blackwell, 1993.

Rosenzweig, Franz. *The Star of Redemption*. Translated (from 2nd ed. of 1930) by William W. Hallo. Notre Dame: University of Notre Dame Press, 1985.

Saint Cheron, Michaël de. *Conversations with Emmanuel Levinas, 1983–1994*. Translated by Gary D. Mole. Pittsburgh: Duquesne University Press, 2010.

Saracino, Michele. *On Being Human: A Conversation with Lonergan and Levinas*. Milwaukee: Marquette University Press, 2003.

———. *Openness as Gift: Subject and Other in Postmodern Context. A Study of Lonergan and Levinas*. Dissertation. Marquette University. January 1, 2000.

Schindler, David L., ed. *Hans Urs von Balthasar: His Life and Work*. San Francisco: Ignatius Press, 1991.

Schrag, Calvin O. *The Self after Postmodernity*. New Haven: Yale University Press, 1997.

Scola, Angelo. *Hans Urs von Balthasar: A Theological Style*. Grand Rapids: William B. Eerdmans, 1995.

Sheehan, Thomas. "Heidegger's 'Introduction to the Phenomenology of Religion,' 1920–21." *Personalist* 60, no. 3 (July 1979): 312–24.

Sikka, Sonia. "Questioning the Sacred: Heidegger and Levinas on the Locus of Divinity." *Modern Theology* 14, no. 3 (July 1998): 299–323.

Smith, Barry, and David Woodruff Smith, eds. *The Cambridge Companion to Husserl*. Cambridge: Cambridge University Press, 1999.

St. Augustine, *Confessions*. Ringwood, Victoria: Penguin, 1974.

St. John of the Cross. *The Collected Works of St. John the Cross*. Translated by Kieran Kavanaugh and Otilio Rodriguez. Washington, DC: Institute of Carmelite Studies Publications, 1979.

Valkenburg, Augustine. "Hans Urs von Balthasar: The Man and His Works." *Furrow* 40, no. 9 (September 1989): 532–36.

Van Buren, John. *The Young Heidegger: Rumor of the Hidden King*. Bloomington: Indiana University Press, 1994.

Vatican Archive. "Pastoral Constitution on the Church in the Modern World, *Gaudium Et Spes*. Promulgated By His Holiness, Pope Paul VI, On December 7, 1965." http://www.vatican.va/archive/hist_councils/ii_vatican_council/documents/vat-ii_cons_19651207_gaudium-et-spes_en.html.

Vatican Council II, The Conciliar and Post Conciliar Documents, edited by A. Flannery. Vatican Collection, Vol. 1. Rev. ed. Northport, NY: Costello, 1988.

Vernon, Jim. "*Erfahren* and *Erleben*: Metaphysical Experience and Its Overcoming in Heidegger's *Beiträge.*" *Symposium: Canadian Journal of Continental Philosophy* 12, no. 1 (Spring 2008): 108–25.

Voegelin, Eric. *Order and History.* In *Collected Work of Eric Voegelin,* Vol. 4: *The Ecumenic Age.* Edited by Michael Franz. Columbia, MO: University of Missouri Press, 2000.

Volf, Miroslav. *Exclusion and Embrace: A Theological Exploration of Identity, Otherness and Reconciliation.* Nashville: Abingdon Press, 1996.

von Balthasar, Hans Urs. *Der dreifache Kranz. Das Heil der Welt im Mariengebet.* 3rd ed. Einsiedeln: Johannes-Verlag, 1978.

———. *Engagement with God.* Translated by John Halliburton. London: SPCK, 1975.

———. *The Glory of the Lord: A Theological Aesthetics.* Vol. 1, *Seeing the Form.* Translated by Erasmo Leiva-Merikakis. Edinburgh: T. & T. Clark, 1982.

———. *The Glory of the Lord: A Theological Aesthetics.* Vol. 4, *The Realm of Metaphysics in Antiquity.* Translated by Brian McNeil, Andrew Louth, John Saward, Rowen Williams and Oliver Davies. San Francisco: Ignatius Press, 1989.

———. *The Glory of the Lord: A Theological Aesthetics.* Vol. 5, *The Realm of Metaphysics in the Modern Age.* Translated by Oliver Davies, Andrew Louth, Brian McNeil, John Saward and Rowen Williams. Edinburgh: T & T Clark, 1991.

———. *The Glory of the Lord: A Theological Aesthetics.* Vol. 7, *Theology: The New Covenant.* Translated by Brian McNeil. Edinburgh: T. & T. Clark, 1982.

———. *The God Question and Modern Man.* New York: Seabury Press, 1958.

———. *Karl Barth, Darstellung und Deutung seiner Theologie.* Cologne: Olten, 1951. English translation: *The Theology of Karl Barth.* San Francisco: Ignatius Press, 1992.

———. *Klarstellungen. Zur Prüfung der Geister.* Einsiedeln: Johannes-Verlag, 1978.

———. *Love Alone Is Credible*. Translated by D. C. Schindler. San Francisco: Ignatius Press, 2004.

———. *Love Alone: The Way of Revelation: A Theological Perspective*. Edited by Alexander Dru. London: Burns & Oates, 1968.

———. *My Work: In Retrospect*. San Francisco: Ignatius Press, 1993.

———. *Mysterium Paschale. The Mystery of Easter*. Translated with an introduction by Aidan Nichols. Edinburgh: T & T Clark, 1990.

———. *Pneuma und Institution*. Einsiedeln: Johannes-Verlag, 1974.

———. *Presence and Thought: Essay on the Religious Philosophy of Gregory of Nyssa*. Translated by Mark Sebance. San Francisco: Ignatius Press, 1995.

———. *Rechenschaft 1965*. Einsiedeln: Johannes-Verlag, 1965.

———. *Theo-Drama: Theological Dramatic Theory*. Vol. 1, *Prolegomena*. Translated by Graham Harrison. San Francisco: Ignatius Press, 1988.

———. *Theo-Drama: Theological Dramatic Theory*. Vol. 2, *The Dramatis Personae: Man In God*. Translated by Graham Harrison. San Francisco: Ignatius Press, 1990.

———. *Theo-Drama: Theological Dramatic Theory*. Vol. 3, *The Dramatis Personae: The Person in Christ*. Translated by Graham Harrison. San Francisco: Ignatius Press, 1992.

———. *Theo-Drama, Theological Dramatic Theory*. Vol. 4, *The Action*. Translated by Graham Harrison. San Francisco: Ignatius Press, 1994.

———. *Theo-Logic: Theological Logical Theory*. Vol. 1, *The Truth of the World*. Translated by Adrian J. Walker. San Francisco: Ignatius Press, 20.

———. *Theo-Logic: Theological Logical Theory*. Vol. 2, *Truth of God*. Translated by Adrian J. Walker. San Francisco: Ignatius Press, 2004.

———. *Theo-Logic: Theological Logical Theory*. Vol. 3, *The Spirit of Truth*. Translated by Graham Harrison. San Francisco: Ignatius Press, 2005.

———. *The von Balthasar Reader*. Edited by Medard Kehl and Werner Löser. Edinburgh: T & T Clark, 1982.

Walker, Adrian J. "Love Alone: Hans Urs von Balthasar as a Master of Theological Renewal." *Communio* 32 (Fall 2005): 517–39.

Ward, Graham. *Barth, Derrida and the Language of Theology*. Cambridge: Cambridge University Press, 1995.

Ward, Graham, ed. *The Postmodern God: A Theological Reader*. Oxford: Blackwell, 2000.

Webb, Stephen. "The Rhetoric of Ethics as Excess: A Christian Theological Response to Emmanuel Levinas." *Modern Theology* (January 1999): 1–16.

West, Christopher. *Theology of the Body Explained: A Commentary on John Paul II's "Gospel of the Body."* North Melbourne, Victoria: Gracewing, 2003.

Whitehead, James D., and Evelyn Eaton Whitehead. *Shadows of the Heart: A Spirituality of the Painful Emotions.* New York: Crossroad, 1998.

Wiesel, Elie. *All the Rivers Run to the Sea: Memoirs.* New York: Alfred A. Knopf, 1996.

Williams, Oscar, ed. *The Mentor Book of Major British Poets.* Camberwell, Victoria: Penguin Group Australia, 1963.

Wojtyla, Karol (Pope John Paul II). *The Acting Person.* Translated from the Polish by Andrzej Potocki. In *Analecta Husserliana: The Yearbook of Phenomenological Research,* vol. 10. Dordrecht, Holland: D. Reidel, 1979.

Wrathall, Mark A., ed. *Religion After Metaphysics.* Cambridge: Cambridge University Press, 2003.

Wyschogrod, Edith. *An Ethics of Remembering: History, Heterology, and the Nameless Others.* Chicago: University of Chicago Press, 1998.

———. *Emmanuel Levinas: The Problem of Ethical Metaphysics.* New York: Fordham University Press, 2000.

Zimmermann, Nigel. "Karol Wojtyla and Emmanuel Levinas on the Embodied Self: The Forming of the Other as Moral Self-Disclosure." *Heythrop Journal* 50, no. 6 (November 2009): 982–95.

Žižek, Slavoj. *Welcome to the Desert of the Real.* London: Verso, 2002.

INDEX

absolution, 214–15
agape, 220–21, 234
aletheia, 164
analogia entis, 83
analogy, 9–10, 34–35, 94, 179–80
anarchy, 57–58, 229, 231–33
anhedonia, 38
aporia, 135–36
appresentation, analogy of, 180
approach, encounter and, 50
Aquinas, Thomas, 82–84
"as such," 144–45, 147, 176–77
Augustine, Saint, 206

Barnes, Michael, 13, 35–36, 221–26
Barth, Karl, 79–80
beauty and beautiful, 84–85, 99, 192, 208–09, 247–48
Being: good beyond, 55–56, 179–84, 189; Heidegger's notion of, 3; *illeity* and, 66; knowledge and, 67, 114–15; language of alterity and, 12–13; in Levinas's philosophy, 36–37; as love, 164–65, 167; meaning of, 4, 20–22; philosophical origins of Levinas and, 17–18; reason and, 165–66; *there is* and, 37–39; truth and, 22; in von Balthasar's theology, 78–79, 82–84, 99, 126–28
Benedict XVI (pope), 221
Blanchot, Maurice, 39
bodiliness: in *Children of a Lesser God*, 203–08; of Christ, 100, 111; forgiveness and, 115–16, 119; friendship and, 243–44, 251; hope and, 118; of Paul, 107; truth and, 69–70, 192–201

Bonhoeffer, Dietrich, 199
Böszörményi-Nagy, Iván, 193–94
Burggraeve, Roger, 10, 58

Caputo, John, 19
Caruana, John, 40, 41, 153, 156
Catholic Church, 31–32, 76–77, 108
Children of a Lesser God, 201–09
Christian theology, 6–8, 33–34, 58, 71–72, 76–77. *See also* Jewish-Christian friendship
Claudel, Paul, 212
Cohen, Richard, 29, 258–59n59
communication, 252
compassion, 160–61, 229–30
confession, 199
confrontation, 197
conscience, 29–32, 59, 120–21
consciousness: ethical transcendence and, 70; fear and, 152–53; finite and infinite, 168; "having a sense" and, 64–66; loneliness of Other's face and, 48; philosophical origins of Levinas and, 15–16, 23–24; relationality and, 194–95; and responsibility for Other, 135; suffering and, 120
conversion, 231–32
Creation, 94–95, 124, 174, 175–76
Curkpatrick, Stephen, 267n116

Dasein, 21–22, 24, 59, 106, 117–19
dead, Christ's descent to, 89–98, 125
death: fear and, 151–52, 160–61; idol and, 157–58; meaning of, 63; of Other, 51, 236–37

287